CANNABIS

Reaktion's Botanical series is the first of its kind, integrating
horticultural and botanical writing with a broader account
of the cultural and social impact of trees, plants and flowers.

Published

Apple Marcia Reiss
Bamboo Susanne Lucas
Cannabis Chris Duvall
Geranium Kasia Boddy
Grasses Stephen A. Harris
Lily Marcia Reiss
Oak Peter Young
Pine Laura Mason
Willow Alison Syme
Yew Fred Hageneder

CANNABIS

Chris Duvall

REAKTION BOOKS

Published by
REAKTION BOOKS LTD
33 Great Sutton Street
London EC1V 0DX, UK

www.reaktionbooks.co.uk

First published 2015
Copyright © Chris Duvall 2015

Printed and bound in China by 1010 Printing International Ltd

A catalogue record for this book is available from the British Library

ISBN 978 1 78023 341 3

Contents

Preface 7

one What is *Cannabis?* 9

two Ancient *Cannabis* 27

three Hemp Travels the World 59

four The Drug Goes Global 89

five Things to Make With and For *Cannabis* 119

six Symbolism Starring *Cannabis* 146

seven How Do You Know *Cannabis?* 179

Timeline 194
References 199
Further Reading 251
Associations and Websites 252
Acknowledgements 255
Photo Acknowledgements 256
Index 257

Plate XV.

Preface

Cannabis grows on all inhabited landmasses to about 60 degrees latitude, a distribution broader than any other crop. This book is my attempt at understanding how *Cannabis* gained its cosmopolitan status.

Cannabis has been a fellow traveller of human migrations from Palaeolithic Central Asia to the present. The human–*Cannabis* relationship is complicated, and challenging to present in a historical narrative. To outline this relationship I have employed a geographically broad-scale analysis of a multidisciplinary range of sources. This book, like any world history of *Cannabis*, must omit many aspects of the plant's past. One notable focus is the important, but generally overlooked, roles Africans and African-descent peoples have had in *Cannabis* history. Additionally, I find the United States significant for understanding current events, because it is a global centre of efforts to sustain *Cannabis* prohibition, and efforts to end it. Beyond these justifications is the reality that I live in the U.S., and my professional experience is in the field of African Studies. All *Cannabis* histories bear particular perspectives.

There are many world histories of *Cannabis*. In this book I am regularly critical of these works, which I believe are too generally founded on opinions, explicit or implicit, about whether the plant is good or bad. Instead, my starting point is that *Cannabis* has shared

Cannabis sativa, from Edward Hamilton, *Flora Homeopathica* (1852).

pleasant to unpleasant interactions with very many people, and that we must recognize the diversity of these interactions before judging it (if such judgement is necessary). My hope is that this book will move beyond the good–bad polarity, and enable more informed management of the world's most widespread crop.

one

What is *Cannabis*?

The title of this chapter is a deceptively simple question. At first glance, perhaps, the book's cover provides the answer – it shows a plant leaf that many people immediately identify as marijuana, a widely used drug. Few plants have such an iconic leaf. The *Cannabis* leaf is effective visual shorthand, whether scrawled as graffiti or illustrating the cover of the *Wall Street Journal* (as on 20 April 2012). Many who see the leaf in this book will know they are reading about marijuana.

Yet *Cannabis* is not just marijuana. It is a plant that furnishes numerous products, not just drugs. The variety of its uses has for centuries fascinated many people, who have generated a massive literature on the plant. The book you are reading holds few of the millions of pages, paper and digital, published on *Cannabis*. Yet the immensity of this literature is misleading. As others have recognized, the literature has been unsatisfying for decades, littered with errors, received wisdom and narrow-minded judgements. It is vital to ask 'What is *Cannabis*?' to make sense of the jumbled portrayal of the plant in current global society.

To understand *Cannabis* means working through layers of complication, beginning with language. *Cannabis* terminology is confused and confusing. In English, 'cannabis', '*Cannabis*', 'hemp' and 'marijuana' are sometimes synonyms, but at other times differentiate botanical species, legal and illegal substances, good and bad uses of the plant, or even

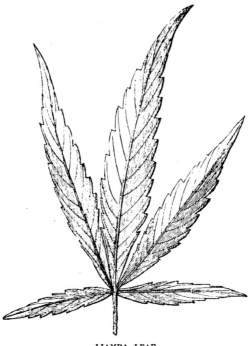

LIAMBA LEAF.

Hasheesh and the *Cannabis Indica* are so well known that it is not necessary to say any thing about them here.

Paul du Chaillu, *Explorations and Adventures in Equatorial Africa* (1861).
He overstated what was known about the plant.

specific parts of the plant. These four terms also intermingle with esoteric vocabulary, whether English slang, standard and slang terms from other languages, formal scientific binomials or antiquated forms of any of these. Furthermore, meanings of *Cannabis* terms have varied over time and space. Equivalent terms in other languages are similarly confusing. Poor translations have compounded miscommunication for millennia.

The terms '*Cannabis*' and 'cannabis' are fairly easy to define. When capitalized and italicized, *Cannabis* refers to a plant genus in the formal language of scientific taxonomy. In this scientific sense, the term has a history that predates the current, standard system of botanical nomenclature.¹ The Swedish botanist Carolus Linnaeus formally described *Cannabis* in 1753.² Subsequent taxonomists saw affinity between *Cannabis* and the genus *Humulus*, which includes the common hop (*Humulus lupulus*). There are obvious differences between *Cannabis* and *Humulus* – the former has compound leaves and an upright habit, while the hop is a straggling vine with simple leaves – but the genera share many anatomical characteristics. Indeed, in 1772 an Italian botanist considered the common hop a type of *Cannabis*, renaming it 'Cannabis lupulus'.³ Later taxonomists rejected the idea. *Cannabis* and *Humulus* share basic floral structure, and both have achenes (a distinct type of fruit) and laticifers (structures that exude resin).⁴ *Cannabis* achenes are famous as hempseeds, which can provide food, oil, medicine and feed. *Cannabis* laticifers produce sticky resin that famously transports psychoactive phytochemicals.

Cannabis is now considered prototypical of a distinct botanical family, the Cannabaceae. This family was first proposed in 1820 by a Russian botanist,⁵ but *Cannabis* (and *Humulus*) has been assigned periodically to other botanical groups. During the nineteenth century,

Marijuana inflorescence with resin.

botanists usually placed *Cannabis* in the nettle family (Urticaceae), although by 1900 some assigned it to the mulberry family (Moraceae). Neither arrangement satisfied everyone. In 1925 a British taxonomist, ignorant of the earlier Russian proposal, placed *Cannabis* and *Humulus* together in a new family, 'Cannabinaceae'.[6] Most botanists ultimately accepted this arrangement, but the prior name Cannabaceae was adopted in 1969.[7] Nonetheless, older taxonomies persist. The State of Oregon still legally defines *Cannabis* as belonging to the mulberry family.[8]

Cannabis is more closely related to hackberries (*Celtis* species) than mulberries.[9] Hackberries are the largest component of Cannabaceae, with hundreds of species compared to three species of *Humulus* and one (or two or three) species of *Cannabis*. Many *Celtis* species are valuable, multi-use plants. Hackberries were important food in the prehistoric Old World. The North African hackberry *Celtis australis* possibly provided the apathy-inducing 'lotus fruit' that Ulysses encountered in Homer's *Odyssey*.[10] Hops have been preservatives in European beer for more than a millennium.[11]

Tiny anatomical characteristics are important in scientific taxonomy, but for most people chemistry distinguishes *Cannabis*. All individuals in this genus produce phytochemicals called cannabinoids. The most famous is the psychoactive compound $\Delta 9$-tetrahydrocannabinol (THC), but there are at least 60 others, many of which have known, non-psychoactive pharmacological effects.[12] Cannabinoid production varies between plants, owing partly to environmental conditions but primarily to genetic differences between *Cannabis* lineages.[13]

How does '*Cannabis*' differ from 'cannabis'? When uncapitalized and unitalicized, 'cannabis' refers to a plant genus understood informally outside scientific taxonomy. All cultures classify and name plants according to subjective naming rules and concepts of what makes different plants different, and base decisions about plant use on these so-called folk taxonomies.[14] When 'culture' is mentioned, people often think of linguistically distinct human groups, whether 'the Xhosa' or 'the Han Chinese'. This is one form of culture, which means any set of socially transmitted ideas and behaviours. Academic disciplines are 'knowledge cultures' that transmit ideas about specific conceptual domains such as biological systematics, the purview of scientific taxonomy. Other knowledge cultures include the know-how of non-scientists – farmers, midwives, herbalists, cooks and others – which is often as accurate and experiment-based as formal sciences.[15] Scientific taxonomy is important because global society has broadly agreed that laws and policies regulating plants should reflect formal taxonomic concepts. This is certainly the case for *Cannabis*, whose controlling laws are embedded in the current, formal taxonomy of the genus.[16]

Nonetheless, scientific taxonomy is one of many knowledge cultures relevant for understanding human–*Cannabis* relationships. *Cannabis* has been mostly prohibited worldwide since the 1930s, which has stunted formal, scholarly research on the plant, including scientific taxonomy.[17] European scholars started paying attention to drug *Cannabis* only about a century before prohibition, and stopped paying much attention afterwards. Although there are a few formally trained *Cannabis* experts, in current global society most experts are informally trained, whether marijuana aficionados, hemp activists or anti-drug crusaders. Outsiders might find the expertise of another group insightful or nonsensical, because knowledge has relevance only within specific sociocultural contexts.

The leaf in law enforcement: insignia for the Office Central pour la Répression du Trafic Illicite des Stupéfiants, France, c. 1990s.

Historically, many knowledge cultures have maintained bodies of *Cannabis* expertise, and nearly all have understood cannabis as a distinct folk genus. Formal *Cannabis* must be distinguished from informal cannabis concepts because each circumscription reflects culturally specific ways of interacting with the plant. For instance, the cannabis concept of marijuana aficionados may entirely overlook non-psychoactive *Cannabis* bred for fibre.[18] Recognizing cultural differences is necessary in order to understand human–*Cannabis* interactions.

The words we use for *Cannabis* encapsulate the plant's historical geography. Begin with 'marijuana', the most important use in current global society. For etymologists, 'marijuana' has been mysterious, appearing seemingly from nowhere. The word was first published in Mexico in the 1840s, but before this the word's origin is considered unknown.[19] People from western Central Africa were by far the most numerous group to bring knowledge of drug *Cannabis* to the New World, yet etymologists have barely considered possible African etymologies. Drug *Cannabis* came initially to the New World from

The leaf in advertising: matchbooks for an American drinking lounge, 1970s.

14

Africa, and its primary New World names reflect this geography. The italicized word *marihuana* is Central American Spanish, but originally a mispronunciation of *mariamba*, which is the plural of *riamba*, meaning 'cannabis' in several Central African languages.[20] *Riamba* derives, firstly, from Old Arabic *bang*, meaning 'psychoactive cannabis'; secondly, from Hindi *bhang*, one of three primary terms for 'cannabis' in that language; and, ultimately, from Sanskrit *bhaṅgā*, meaning 'psychoactive cannabis'. *Riamba* comes from truncation of the Arabic term and addition of a euphonic prefix.[21]

In the late Neolithic, people from temperate Central Asia who knew *Cannabis* as a food and fibre plant discovered another *Cannabis* species that additionally provided a psychoactive drug. The two plants gained two different names. The provider of hempseed and fibre was called *śāṇa* in Proto-Indo-European languages, while *bhaṅgā* signified various psychoactive plants, including *Cannabis indica*. Each of these basal terms changed over time; *śāṇa* eventually became a word like *kannab*.[22] Languages westward from Mongolia adopted forms of *kannab* to name *Cannabis sativa*, which is indigenous to temperate Eurasia. In northern Europe, *kannab* became something like *hannap*, which evolved into the hemp-type terms of northern Europe, including German *Hanf* and Dutch *hennep*.

The English word 'cannabis' encapsulates a series of historically situated experiences that people have had with the plant. The English word is a Latin form of the Greek *kánnabis*, first documented in the *Histories* of Herodotus (fifth century BCE). Classical Greek knowledge of *kánnabis* originated across the Black Sea, through interaction with people who used non-psychoactive *Cannabis* for hempseeds and fibre. Ancient Greeks knew little about psychoactive *Cannabis*. They did know of psychoactive plants, and possibly called drug *Cannabis* something other than *kánnabis*.

To Greek physicians like Dioscorides and Galen (both first century CE), *kánnabis* for human consumption was a minor seed crop used as food and medicine.[23] Importantly, *Cannabis* seeds are not psychoactive, and its green parts become psychoactive only after heating (optimally

Cannabis in a 6th-century CE copy of Dioscorides' *De Materia Medicae.*

to 104°C/220°F).[24] In documented Greek preparations, the plant material was hempseeds, oil, or green parts processed without explicit heating.[25] The sole Greek mention of psychoactive *kánnabis* came from Galen. Somewhere in the Levant he encountered psychoactive sweetmeats similar to hash-based ones known historically. His description, though, projects Greek knowledge, because he presumed the sweetmeats must be concocted of hempseeds, which he considered 'unwholesome' food. For Galen, the unfamiliar observed use made the unobserved parent plants undoubtedly different. He began his section on 'cannabis seed' with the disclaimer 'Not like our cannabis plant'. In a sixteenth-century Latin translation, Galen's Other cannabis could 'strike the head', which amusingly suggests the atavistic meaning of 'stoned'.[26] Greek medicine remained current in Europe for fifteen centuries or more. However, Galen's Other cannabis faded from memory. Instead, the non-psychoactive Greek prescriptions defined the pharmacological potential of *Cannabis* in European thought.

Ancient Greek scholarship was also fundamental to medicine of the Islamic Golden Age (800s–1200s CE). Arabic-speaking scholars rarely wrote of psychoactive *Cannabis*, partly because they repeated the Greeks. Islamic physicians prescribed the plant they called *qinnab* in manners that mostly would not have been psychoactive, and only vaguely suggest that they might have been referring to the psychoactive *Cannabis* species.[27] In the tenth-century *Canon of Medicine*, for instance, Avicenna prescribed hempseeds and oil, and poultices of green material; perhaps he suggests drug *Cannabis* — which can affect sensations of hunger — by recommending macerated green material for stomach ailments.[28] Frustratingly, though, few of the original Arabic texts are easily available, and translations are often suspect. For example, a translation of 1966 of the ninth-century *Book of Poisons* glosses an unknown Arabic term as 'Indian hemp', which the translator defined as 'hashish' although the text describes a plant, not a preparation.[29] 'Indian hemp' was coined in 1689 in London.[30]

When the Arabic-writing physicians wrote *qinnab*, they referred primarily to *Cannabis* used for medicinal seeds. People in Islamic Golden Age societies used drug *Cannabis*, but this use was unfamiliar to upper-class scholars, who showed little knowledge of psychoactive *Cannabis* until the twelfth century. In Old Arabic, psychoactive *Cannabis* was sometimes called *bang*, something separate and distinct from *qinnab*.[31] The recipes including *bang* yielded poisons as often as medicines, because *bang* referred generically to psychoactive plants, including *Cannabis indica* and the more toxic datura (*Datura metel*), belladonna (*Atropa belladonna*) and henbane (*Hyoscyamus niger*). In modern Arabic *beng* simply means 'intoxicant'. In the 1100s some Arabic-speaking scholars began to mention *qinnab hindi* ('Hindi cannabis') to name a different folk species, the psychoactive one they associated with India.[32] Another psychoactive folk species was called 'Anatolian cannabis' in the fifteenth century.[33] European languages did not adopt these terms, even though Islamic medicine became fundamental to Western medicine during the Renaissance.

In many European languages, 'cannabis' became a generic name because European scholars transferred the linguistic privilege of *qinnab* and *kánnabis* to Latin *cannabis*. These Mediterranean words were socially more appropriate for European scholars than northerly terms like *hampa*, from Linnaeus's Swedish. Outside formal botany, early uses of 'cannabis' required explanation, including the earliest English use, from 1548 ('Canabis [*sic*] is called in Englishe hemp').[34] As scientific botany began in the 1500s, a new, scholarly term entered European languages, although a new folk species did not. *Cannabis* and hemp became synonyms.

In European languages, terminological confusion about 'hemp' arose after 1492 when travellers encountered many non-European fibre plants. *Cannabis* provided outstanding cordage and textile fibre but its processing was labour-intensive, which made the best products quite expensive. The economic importance of ropes and sailcloth during the Age of Sail made substitutes for *Cannabis* fibre a high priority. *Cannabis* was the gold standard, though, and 'hemp' became a generic term for any plant fibre. There are, for instance, 'African hemp' (either *Sansevieria guineensis*, a monocot, or *Sparrmannia africana*, a dicot), 'Manila hemp' (a type of banana, *Musa textilis*), 'New Zealand hemp' (monocot *Phormium tenax*), 'Sisal hemp' (monocot *Agave rigida*) and 'Sunn hemp' (the *Corchorus* species now known as jute).[35] There was also 'Indian hemp' (*Cannabis indica*), which the British in India tried for cordage decades before exploring its pharmacological applications.[36] Yet in eighteenth- and nineteenth-century North America, 'Indian hemp' meant dogbane (*Apocynum cannabinum*), because Native Americans used it for fibre. 'India hemp' also referred sometimes to jute. Rope-makers decried 'careless'

The letterhead of a hempen rope manufacturer, Italy, 1908.

use of the term 'hemp' and tried to clarify things by calling *Cannabis sativa* 'true hemp',[37] but the adjective didn't resolve the semantics. 'Hemp' designates plant uses, and not *Cannabis* itself.[38]

Comprehending the genus is easier than sorting through confusion about *Cannabis* species, which has persisted from antiquity to the present. What is a botanical species? Fundamentally, species represent ideas about what types exist in a general category, and about how these types are different. All knowledge cultures that have interacted significantly with *Cannabis* have recognized it as a distinct folk genus having one or more folk species. Millennia-old semantic confusion about the plant exists because there is no objective, visible marker of difference between *Cannabis* species. *Cannabis* comprises a pair of cryptic species, which are physically indistinguishable but chemically unmistakable. Illustrations that represent *Cannabis* species as physically distinct represent idealized types, not portraits. 'Variation within the genus *Cannabis* is continuous for all [physical] characters . . . that have been investigated in any detail', wrote the botanists who published the current one-species taxonomy. The plant is 'a single highly variable species' whose plasticity distracts people from seeing the overarching sameness of all *Cannabis* individuals.[39] This represents one way of thinking about *Cannabis*. Scholars who adopt multi-species concepts might agree that physical characteristics do not reliably differentiate *Cannabis* species, but instead focus on invisible chemical characters, whether cannabinoids or DNA.[40]

In this book, I adopt the geneticist Karl Hillig's two-species concept of *Cannabis*.[41] When italicized, the terms *sativa* and *indica* refer to

Le chanvre, from Jean-Jacques Rousseau, *Recueil de plantes coloriées* (1789).

genetic species. Hillig's concept reflects formal genetic analysis, and differs from the current, formal taxonomy of *Cannabis* as well as from folk taxonomies. Formally, all *Cannabis* individuals represent the single species *Cannabis sativa* L.[42] Many scholars, however, have supported two- or three-species concepts.[43] Hillig's research shows that there was more than one genetic type before humans domesticated two different *Cannabis* species, and it seems likely that the formal taxonomy will change in coming years. Or at least it would seem likely for other plants – genetic analyses have transformed taxonomy in recent decades – but *Cannabis* taxonomy has important legal ramifications.

Humans have always relied on subjective criteria to differentiate species. For *Cannabis*, human use has been an important criterion across cultures. It is easier to see what people are doing with *Cannabis* than to see differences between plants. Until the discovery of THC in 1964, drug use was the sole means of certainly distinguishing *sativa* and *indica*. In 1968 the first modern biomedical study of drug *Cannabis* evaluated drug strength in part by asking 'chronic users [to] sample and rate marijuana' before it was given to test subjects.[44] Chemical assays were costly and widely unavailable into the 1980s. In many societies, the plant's mysterious psychoactive potential has contrasted with its provision of mundane products like cordage and cloth. A good-versus-bad characterization of *Cannabis* uses is old, even if re-emphasized under prohibition. Value judgements imprint *Cannabis* nomenclature in many ways, some subtle and others obvious. It is clear, for instance, that the current one-species concept arose from moralistic and legalistic debates about *Cannabis* uses, couched in scientific taxonomy.[45]

This book is in the tradition of Western scholarship, in which the knowledge culture of scientific taxonomy has strongly shaped species concepts. Yet many other influences persist too. For one, Western ideas about *Cannabis* predate scientific taxonomy and reflect ancient, cross-cultural pollinations that have been generally forgotten. Renaissance European botanists inherited from ancient scholars a two-species concept for cannabis, distinguishing a wild type and a cultivated type. This concept extends at least to Herodotus, who wrote that '[*kánnabis*] grows both wild and cultivated'.[46] Botanists adopted the Latin *cannabis* as generic, and needed additional names to differentiate the types. The descriptive name '*sativa*' – meaning 'cultivated' in Latin – was first used in a 1516 translation of Dioscorides' ancient pharmacopoeia.[47] The term persists, of course, in the binomial *Cannabis sativa*. In the current, official taxonomy, '*sativa*' also designates the subspecies and domesticated variety bred for fibre and seed production.[48]

In Latin, '*sativa*' contrasts with '*sylvestris*' (which means 'living in the forest'), an early name for the putative, vaguely known wild *Cannabis*. The question remains if any truly wild populations survive, or if wild types simply escaped long ago from cultivation. '*Cannabis sylvestris*' first appeared in print in the tenth century, but may have referred then or subsequently to a mallow (*Althaea cannabina*).[49] By the mid-1500s, botanists had mostly abandoned the idea of wild-type *Cannabis*, at least in European environments. The idea that wild *Cannabis* exists has come and gone, leaving behind putative species like '*erratica*', '*vulgaris*' and '*spontanea*'.[50] The idea gained greater acceptance in the 1960s once Soviet botanists began publishing in English their studies of *Cannabis* in Central Asia.[51] Few scholars have seen these populations. In 1924 a Soviet botanist designated the wild type '*ruderalis*', which connotes 'weedy' in botanical Latin. There is insufficient genetic data to accept this possible species.[52]

European scholars began to conceptualize a third kind of *Cannabis* during the 1700s. The Latin name *indica* has been associated with psychoactive *Cannabis* since 1747, although the British polymath Robert Hooke earlier proposed 'Indian hemp'.[53] The locative term *indica* links this plant with India, which European scholars considered its 'natural' habitat. The name persists because in 1783 a French naturalist chose '*indica*' to name a new species, which he considered 'very distinct' from European hemp. The 'principal virtue' of *Cannabis indica* was 'to derange the brain . . . and give a sort of gaiety'.[54] 'Cannabis indica' became a pharmacological term in the nineteenth century, and current taxonomy preserves '*indica*' as the formal name of the psychoactive subspecies and domesticated variety.[55]

Cannabis mas, from Elizabeth Blackwell, *Herbarium Blackwellianum* (1757).

In this book, 'hemp' means *Cannabis,* regardless of species, used for fibre, food, feed or oilseed. In East Asia, *Cannabis* cultivars bred for fibre and hempseed represent the species *indica.* In South Asia, *indica* has also been grown for these uses. I contrast hemp with 'drug *Cannabis*', meaning *Cannabis,* regardless of species, used for its psychoactive potential, even if this is low. Usually, drug *Cannabis* is *indica,* but *sativa* has supplied potentially mind-altering but generally unsatisfying drugs.[56] In North America, for instance, 'ditchweed' comes from feral plants originally bred for fibre, not drugs.[57] Ditchweed gives headaches, not highs.

The names 'indica' and 'sativa' also persist in the language of marijuana aficionados, who adopted Latin names from early 1970s

Cannabis foemina. { 1–3 Frücht
4.5 Saame } Hanf
Hanf-Weiblein.

Cannabis foemina, from Blackwell, *Herbarium Blackwellianum*.

scientific taxonomy. When printed without italics, 'sativa' and 'indica' refer to the folk species of marijuana aficionados, which differ from the formally defined species. Physically, the ideal types of these folk species correspond with the 'wide-leaflet' and 'narrow-leaflet' drug varieties recognized by botanists.[58] However, aficionados identify the folk species based on subjective effects, not physical form.[59] The folk species indica has sedative-like effects, while sativa is stimulant-like.[60] The folk species sativa and indica differ chemically and genetically,[61] although their contrasts are different from those between the scientific species *sativa* and *indica*.

Does semantic muddiness matter? According to one botanist, for whom *Cannabis* is one single species, debating the precise meanings of *Cannabis* nomenclature comes from 'lawyers [seeking] to deceive laymen', who should instead use 'common sense and regard for context' to know what is meant when *Cannabis* is discussed.[62] This advice may suffice in jurisprudence, but glossing over semantics overlooks millennia of confusion. Furthermore, confusion seems inescapable when dealing with cryptic species whose differences we can directly sense only by testing a plant's psychoactive potential. Taxonomists have privileged the name *sativa* because it was Linnaeus's name for the single-species *Cannabis* concept he developed, based on his historically situated experience in northern Europe. Taxonomists have always privileged visible characters, even though this visuality has been unsatisfactory to *Cannabis* observers who find invisible differences more meaningful.

Paying attention to semantics is crucial because what people mean by any *Cannabis* term is conditioned by their experience with the plant. Linnaeus knew almost nothing about psychoactive *Cannabis*, while non-psychoactive *Cannabis* was prominent in eighteenth-century northern Europe. It made sense for Linnaeus to conceptualize *Cannabis* as a singular, cultivated species, with perhaps some variation at the distant edges of its distribution. The one-species concept made sense for taxonomists of the 1970s, who mostly focused on visible characters. One reasonable interpretation of the limited data of the 1970s was to consider *Cannabis* a highly variable species distorted through millennia of farming, even if some disagreed with this interpretation. Now that robust genetic studies are available it makes sense to view *Cannabis* as two cryptic species, because global society increasingly accepts that invisible chemistry differentiates related organisms more meaningfully than visible characters. A U.S. court concluded as much in 2004, ruling that non-psychoactive 'industrial hemp' is not a controlled substance, despite the one-species *Cannabis* concept embedded in drug laws.[63]

The semantic shades of the *Cannabis* vocabulary reflect the diversity of experiences people have had with the plant. To ignore these shades of meaning is to ignore many facets of the human–*Cannabis* relationship, which has unfolded through vast sweeps of space and time.

two

Ancient *Cannabis*

annabis history began long before humans. The most closely
related family, nettles (Urticaceae), originated about 55 million
years ago.[1] The *Cannabis* cousin *Humulus* (hops) was genetically
distinct 6.5 million years ago.[2] *Cannabis* originated some time in the
intervening aeons.

Spatial patterns of genetic diversity suggest that *Cannabis indica*
originated in the southwestern Himalayas, while *sativa* was from temperate Central Asia.[3] Knowledge of Asian landscape evolution suggests
how *Cannabis* became two genetically distinct species. During the
Eocene geological epoch (56–34 million years ago) *Cannabis* ancestors
probably occupied the highlands of south-central Laurasia, the ancient
continent that existed before the Indian tectonic plate converged with
Asian plates. Climate in these mid-elevation highlands was moist and
temperate. The aboriginal *Cannabis* population probably varied from
south to north in tolerance for the climate and day-length conditions
of different latitudes. Change in day-length is the primary stimulus for
flowering in *Cannabis*.[4]

The collision of India into Asia 50 million years ago caused
geological uplift that produced the Himalayas and connecting mountain ranges. Uplift and latitude together produced variation in THC
production. THC serves as sunscreen for the plant to prevent cellular
damage from ultraviolet-B radiation.[5] Exposure to solar radiation
increases at lower latitudes and higher elevations. Geological uplift

Cannabis sativa, from F. E. Köhler, *Medizinal-Pflanzen* (1887).

was greatest at low latitudes in the aboriginal *Cannabis* area, creating natural selection for plants that could provide themselves with sunscreen, perhaps most importantly to protect female inflorescences. Although THC also deters herbivorous insects and prevents plant infections,[6] its ecological role does not explain how *sativa* and *indica* became different.

India and Asia converged completely eleven million years ago, which initiated regional climate changes during the remaining Miocene epoch (which ended two million years ago). Tectonic plate convergence produced mountains and the most landlocked region on earth, interior Central Asia. As this area became isolated from maritime influences its summertime climate became hotter and drier, which helped to initiate the South Asian monsoon. Increased aridity in Central Asia divided the *Cannabis* area in two. The proto-*sativa* population survived in temperate, moist areas along the mountains extending northeast of the Tien Shan range into Siberia. The earliest physical evidence of *Cannabis* is fossil pollen from 130,000-year-old sediments from Lake Baikal.[7] (Technically, scientists identify 'Cannabis-type' pollen, because *Cannabis* and *Humulus* produce nearly identical grains.) South of the dry zone, proto-*indica* plants survived in mid-elevation forests in the Hindu Kush range, between alpine highlands and drier lowlands.

The northern and southern *Cannabis* sub-populations experienced different natural selection pressures. Geological uplift remained strong in the south, where plants encountered increasing exposure to ultraviolet radiation. The Hindu Kush rose 2,700 m (8,800 ft) during the Pleistocene epoch (the last two million years).[8] The northern population did not experience the same conditions; Central Asian ranges rose less and later than mountains further south. The northern population also occupied lower elevations, because alpine conditions extend further downslope in mid-latitude zones.

During the Pleistocene, earth experienced cyclical change between glacial and interglacial climate, which impacted ecosystems worldwide.

Cannabis, from C. F. Millspaugh, *Medicinal Plants* (1892).

Cannabis indica and *sativa* experienced these changes differently because the shape of the land surface affects how ecosystems interact with climate. For *sativa*, during cold periods the plant's preferred climate zone shifted significant distances into the rolling plains of Central Asia. During interglacial periods the plains were drier, and forests gave way to grassy steppes. *Cannabis sativa* found suitable conditions near streams in the steppes, and moved mainly westwards, probably following hoofed animals. By 16,000 years ago, *Cannabis*-type pollen entered sediments in the Black Sea; by 10,000 years ago, pollen was present in Bulgaria and Italy.[9]

For *indica*, rapid uplift in the Hindu Kush produced steep slopes, so that ecological zones moved slightly uphill or downhill as climate warmed or cooled. The mid-elevation zone hosted a stable ecosystem relatively unaffected by cyclical changes.[10] *Cannabis indica* probably favoured sunny patches in mountain valleys. Apparently wild *Cannabis* remains common in northern Pakistan's mid-elevation forests.[11]

About 30,000 years ago, modern humans first shared landscapes with *Cannabis indica*. The generally eastward human migration from Africa to East Asia followed the mid-elevation forest band along the southern Himalayas and extending into China's Pacific shoreline. A broad cultural region developed in lakeside, riparian and coastal environments within this band.[12] These people were mobile hunter-gatherers who interacted with *indica* sufficiently for it to reach temperate East Asia by the start of the Holocene period (12,000 years ago). The earliest evidence of *Cannabis* in East Asia is 11,000-year-old pollen from central China, and 10,000-year-old hempseeds from central Japan.[13]

Palaeolithic *Cannabis* cultures are unknown. Most likely, *Cannabis* seeds provided food. Humans must consume food containing essential fatty acids, which are available in fish, shellfish and grass-fed antelopes,[14] but relatively few plants. Hempseed is a noteworthy source that also supplies proteins.[15] Ancient people probably used stems to fasten objects, too, although direct evidence of *Cannabis* cordage is relatively recent at just several thousand years old. Earlier evidence, such as twine

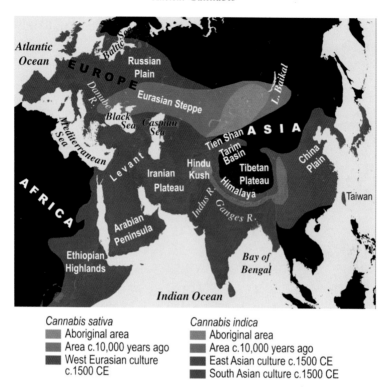

Cannabis sativa
- Aboriginal area
- Area c.10,000 years ago
- West Eurasian culture
  c.1500 CE

Cannabis indica
- Aboriginal area
- Area c.10,000 years ago
- East Asian culture c.1500 CE
- South Asian culture c.1500 CE

Ancient *Cannabis* zone in Eurasia.

impressions preserved in potsherds, cannot be certainly identified even though *Cannabis* became a primary cordage-fibre source across Eurasia.[16]

If *Cannabis* attracted humans, humans also attracted the plant. *Cannabis* thrives in recently disturbed, fertile soil, and the plant was probably first 'farmed' as volunteer plants around settlements.[17] Into the 1920s, *sativa* remained primarily a weed at seasonal livestock camps in central Siberia. *Cannabis* can colonize distant sites without human assistance, because birds disperse hempseeds and wind carries pollen. The plant's dispersal capabilities mean that Moroccan marijuana production can be monitored from pollen in Spanish air,[18] and *Cannabis* remains a common weed in North America despite decades of eradication efforts. It is impossible to specify how *Cannabis* colonized locations from Japan to Italy during the Pleistocene, but its dispersal capabilities meant that ancient humans encountered it widely. Ultimately, human–*Cannabis* interaction produced three domestication episodes, in East Asia, South Asia and Central Asia.

East Asian Domestication

Cannabis entered agriculture earliest in East Asia, probably in the Chinese Plain. *Cannabis* grew in open vegetation there by 4000 BCE, associated with mobile hunter-gatherers who were beginning to domesticate several plants.[19] This cultural ecology extended into the Korean Peninsula. The earliest evidence of *Cannabis*-based industry is South Korean fabric from 3000 BCE.[20] The earliest unequivocal Chinese evidence is 1,000 years younger.[21] Earlier, suggestive evidence of cultivated *Cannabis* – preserved cordage made of unidentified fibres, cord and textile impressions in pottery, and spindles – is known from both countries as well as Japan. The Jōmon culture of sedentary hunter-gatherers in Japan initiated *Cannabis* domestication in the early Holocene.[22] The Jōmon declined when rice agriculture arrived, in about 300 BCE, part of a cultural package with roots in China. The Japanese word *taima* ('cannabis') is from the Chinese plant name *ta mà*.

In northern East Asia, *Cannabis* was the earliest known textile fibre, for which the first weaving and spinning technologies were invented.[23] Worldwide, spinning and weaving transformed cultures that had previously lacked textiles and rope.[24] *Cannabis* hemp cloth retains honoured status in Korea and Japan, but hemp has had lower status in China. In southern China, ramie (*Boehmeria nivea*) provided fibre as early as *Cannabis*, and people preferred ramie textiles across China in ancient times.[25] Hemp cloth was coarser, but *má* ('cannabis') provided good ropes and food too. During the Shang Dynasty (1600–1100 BCE), *má* was considered one of six staple crops.[26] Hempseed provided food in ancient Korea and Japan too.[27] East Asian *Cannabis* represents *indica*, although psychoactive use in the region has always been limited. Chinese documents suggest psychoactivity as early as 1500 BCE, but clear and consistent evidence dates from the Han Dynasty (200 BCE– 200 CE).[28]

*Immortal Màgu with
Deer and Peach Tree,*
silk tapestry, China,
Ming or Qing
Dynasty, c. 1575–1725.
The mythical Magu
('Hemp Goddess')
first represented
beauty, longevity
and tantalization
in China during
the Han Dynasty
(200 BCE–200 CE).

Chinese *Cannabis* culture is the best known in ancient East Asia.
Farmers developed intensive and sustainable *Cannabis* agricultures to
produce hempseed and fibre.[29] Male plants were harvested for fine
fibre soon after releasing pollen. Female plants were harvested in autumn
for hempseeds and rough fibre. Fibre processing entailed many steps
over several months: sorting the stalks, followed by boiling, drying, soak-
ing in water, drying again, peeling the fibre from the stalks, cleaning the
fibre, smoothing it, then spinning it into threads before manufacturing
finished products. Fibre industries also probably provided fodder, in

Workers harvesting plants apparently grown for hempseed, probably China, c. 1910.

the form of leaves trimmed from stems.[30] People ate hempseed and produced hempseed oil, although the seeds were most important as next year's fibre crop.

The peak importance of hempseed food came during the early Chou Dynasty (1100–200 BCE). Although ancient Chinese writers called hempseed a staple, it was never prominent. Hempseed declined as rice (*Oryza sativa*), foxtail millet (*Setaria italica*), broomcorn millet (*Panicum miliaceum*) and other cereals gained favour.[31] By the Han period, hempseed was a secondary food, increasingly important during famine. People collected seeds from feral stands that survived when crops succumbed to drought.[32]

Thousands of years after *Cannabis* first came to East Asia, it again travelled east from the South Asian centre of domestication. Before the Silk Road trade network arose, people brought *indica* over the western Himalayas into historic East Turkistan, now western China's Xinjiang region.[33] The Chinese anciently called this region *Xiyu*, or 'western lands', where Indo-European groups farmed and kept livestock in the arid Tarim Basin.[34]

We know the Tarim Basin culture from grave goods, exquisitely preserved in the region's dry, alkaline soil. In the 1990s archaeologists recovered nearly a kilogram of female *Cannabis* inflorescences in a 2,500-year-old tomb, alongside other remains of a *Cannabis* culture centred on drug use in spiritual contexts.[35] The ancient stash was both psychoactive and genetically different from eastern Chinese plants.[36] The Tarim Basin people wore clothing made from wool and flax (*Linum usitatissimum*), not *Cannabis*, and had shoes, ropes and baskets made of leather.[37] The official history of the Han Dynasty (written in the 440s CE) indicates that 'hemp' grew in the *Xíyu* region alongside grapes by 150 BCE, when Han China sustained contact with Indo-European Central Asians via Silk Road trade.[38] The Tarim Basin *Cannabis* remains pre-date by several centuries the earliest unequivocal accounts of psychoactive use in eastern China, a dissemination pattern shared with other western Eurasian crops during the Han period, including grape (*Vitis vinifera*).[39] *Cannabis* histories often cite the herbal *Pên-tsao Ching* as the earliest record of psychoactive use. This compilation dates from about 100 CE, despite its attribution to a legendary emperor who died 2,000 years before.[40]

Psychoactive use became a minor but persistent element of Chinese *Cannabis* culture. This use began in the subculture of *wu* shamanism, which arose from indigenous and imported ideas about spirituality, magic and medicine.[41] Practitioners were expert herbalists. This historic subculture is known incompletely because it was secretive and syncretic, bearing influences from Mongolia, Siberia and the Tarim Basin.[42] *Wu* shamanism declined as Taoism became dominant in the Han period. Drug *Cannabis* gradually entered Chinese medicine, appearing among thousands of other plants in herbals written between 500 and 1500 CE.[43] Drug *Cannabis* was important conceptually in Chinese pharmacognosy; written characters for 'narcotic' and several specific drugs derive from the character *má*.

Linguistic evidence also suggests ancient Western influence. Psychoactive *Cannabis* has recently been called *húo má*, or 'fire cannabis'.[44] This name is probably a corruption of *hu má*, which provides biogeographic information.[45] In the Han Period, *hu má* would have meant 'cannabis of the western foreigners'. During the first millennium CE, Chinese writers named multiple types of *má*, many of which were not *Cannabis*. About 500 CE, a history of the Han period (which ended 300 years earlier) attributed the introduction of *hu má* to a Han ambassador to *Dàyuān* – the Ferghana Valley, over the mountains west of the Tarim Basin. A later history, from 1100 CE, distinguished *hu má* from *ta má* ('great cannabis'), which was described as 'the Chinese species'. However, common names are imprecise. In modern Chinese, *hu má* means 'foreign cannabis', and refers usually to sesame (*Sesamum indicum*), which is sometimes called *yu má* ('oil cannabis'). Both names have also referred to flax, another introduction from western Eurasia.[46]

In any case, East Asian *Cannabis* culture has always centred on fibre uses. By 1500 BCE, *Cannabis* cordage was fashioned into ropes, shoes and other items, practices that have been maintained with modifications

Hempen goods shop displaying processed fibres, China, *c.* 1933–46. The central character on the sign is *má*.

Hmong looms in highland Southeast Asia descend from ancient Chinese technology.

to the present. In China, *Cannabis* hemp fabric was less expensive than silk, ramie and cotton (*Gossypium arboreum*), which arrived from South Asia after 100 BCE.[47] Paper was first made about 100 BCE from waste fibre – rags and old rope – from several plants including *Cannabis*. Paper-makers relied on *Cannabis* because it made good paper and was readily available. Military officers kept maps and received orders on paper just after its invention. Commercial and governmental accounting was paper-based soon afterwards. By 1000 CE paper had become money, books, toilet tissue, hats, slippers, screens, tents and raincoats. Hemp papermaking declined and effectively disappeared during the Tang Dynasty (600–900 CE) as other fibres – particularly bamboo – gained favour.[48] Paper-making spread to Korea around 300 CE and to Japan about 300 years later.[49] Hemp paper was also used in Tibet,[50] although the plant probably did not grow on the dry, high-elevation plateau. Chinese *Cannabis* culture arrived in Southeast Asia some time during the first millennium CE.[51]

Chinese *Cannabis* culture did not spread to western Eurasia, where other plants already satisfactorily provided the same products. For instance, paper-making slowly travelled west along the Silk Road, arriving in Central Asia by 400 CE and in Baghdad by 800 CE. From this cultural centre, paper-making spread through the Islamic world to Spain by 1100 CE. *Cannabis indica* did not also disperse westward because other suitable plant fibres were already available along paper's pathway, including flax, cotton, *Cannabis sativa* and various tree barks. Early European travellers to China, including Marco Polo, reported aspects of Chinese hemp culture, but *Cannabis* had long before been domesticated for similar uses in Central and South Asia. This human–plant geography discouraged biological and cultural dissemination of East Asian *indica*.

South Asian Domestication

Cannabis indica diffused eastwards with early human migrations from the southwestern Himalayas. As East Asian *Cannabis* culture developed, so did a different set of human–*Cannabis* interactions in South Asia. The early history of South Asian *Cannabis* is vaguely known, encapsulated in cryptic legends of plant use recorded in extinct languages.

In South Asia, four different *Cannabis* cultures developed at uncertain dates. The first cultural divergence happened by perhaps 3000 BCE, suggested faintly in linguistic patterns. Simplistically, this division distinguished *Cannabis* as either a multi-use plant, or primarily a drug. After 1000 BCE, the drug-orientated culture split into three traditions. The four South Asian cultures have distinct histories, although these overlap with one another, and with *Cannabis sativa* and East Asian *indica*.

The earliest South Asian texts – written in Sanskrit, an early Indo-European language – give two different plant names translated as 'cannabis'. First, *śāṇa* named a plant used to make cordage, textiles and food.[52] Second, *bhaṅgā* named a plant drug, most famously described in the sacred *Atharva Veda* hymn of Hinduism as one of the 'five kingdoms of plants having Soma as their chief'.[53] Understanding these words in ancient texts is anything but straightforward,[54] and *Cannabis* histories include many erroneous quotations supposedly from early Sanskrit sources.

Of these terms, *śāṇa* was probably the one that initially meant 'cannabis'. In early texts, *śāṇa* is a plant that has identified parts with different uses.[55] *Śāṇa* fibre was used for textiles, *śāṇa* seeds were food, and the *Mahābhārata* epic (perhaps 400 BCE) counsels that people seeking prosperity should avoid eating *śāṇa* leaves,[56] a suggestion of psychoactivity. By the first centuries CE, derived forms of *śāṇa* became generic for 'plant fibre' in South Asian languages. In contrast, the original meaning of *bhaṅgā* was probably something like 'psychoactive drug plant'. Ancient uses of *bhaṅgā* mainly suggest a use, not necessarily any specific plant.[57]

The *śāṇa*–*bhaṅgā* distinction probably arose in the southwestern Himalayas. Neolithic farmers first entered the mid-elevation Hindu Kush 5,000 years ago.[58] These farmers probably spoke Proto-Indo-European, the precursor to modern languages from western Europe to Bangladesh. Proto-Indo-European originated in the steppes northwest of the Caspian Sea, and *śāṇa* probably originated there to name *Cannabis sativa*. When Proto-Indo-European speakers moved into the southwestern Himalayas, the people recognized *indica* and found that it could be used in the same ways as *sativa* – hempseeds collected for food and stems for fibre. The name *śāṇa* was transferred to *indica*.

Feral *Cannabis*, Pakistan.

These farmers also encountered previously unknown drug plants, including datura, belladonna, henbane and *Cannabis indica*. The farmers eventually came to value *indica* uniquely, but initially numerous drug plants were called *bhaṅgā*.[59]

Around 3000 BCE, a pioneering trade network encompassed much of southern Asia, from the Indus Valley to Mesopotamia and north into the Caspian Sea basin.[60] Ideas, goods and peoples travelled widely. *Cannabis* went as far west as Egypt. Slim physical evidence – sparse pollen in scattered sites, a few fibres from one tomb – suggests that the plant had a minimal presence in Pharaonic Egypt at 3000 BCE.[61] Ancient Egyptian *Cannabis* culture did not persist, except possibly as faint echoes in Greek and Arabic medicine.[62] By 2000 BCE, trading extended north of the Hindu Kush to central Siberia, along the western front of the Tibetan Plateau.[63] Its weediness enabled *Cannabis* to disperse with trade in this vast commercial network, even if people did not carry it on purpose.

Like many sets of related plants, *sativa* and *indica* can interbreed. Farmers at oases in Central Asia likely acquired both *indica*, from the south, and *sativa*, from the north, probably producing genetically mixed *Cannabis* populations in the Caspian basin. However, research collections lack genetic samples from this area.[64] *Cannabis sativa* may have anciently entered China, but there is no genetic evidence.[65]

Around the Hindu Kush, people began to consume heated *indica* green material orally. Heating is necessary to activate its psychoactive potential, because very little THC occurs in a pharmacologically active form within plants. We don't know how Neolithic farmers used

Man making *bhang* tea, Turkmenistan, *c.* 1871, from K. P. Von Kaufman, *Turkestansk al'bom* (1871–2).

drug *Cannabis*. Psychoactive use seems to have been uncommon, occult, compartmentalized within societies, or all three, contibuting to the vague meaning of *bhaṅgā* in early sources.[66]

Bhaṅgā can be linked to the earliest Indo-Iranian cultures that arose around the Hindu Kush, and which remain poorly understood.[67] The Harappan civilization flourished in the Indus Valley from 2600 to 1900 BCE. The ancient civilization northwest of the Hindu Kush – modern Turkmenistan – has received the inelegant name Bactria-Margiana Archaeological Complex (BMAC). The BMAC civilization existed between about 2300 and 1700 BCE. The Hindu Kush was peripheral to both civilizations. By 2000 BCE, Harappans had established a trade outpost north of the mountains, where they interacted with BMAC farmers who had arrived earlier from the west. Finally, an Indo-European civilization flourished in the Tarim Basin between 2500 and 500 BCE, leaving vast, well-preserved graveyards. The origins of this culture are uncertain, but seemingly somewhere around the Hindu Kush.[68]

Circumstantial evidence suggests that *indica* was an ingredient in sacramental beverages in these civilizations, which broadly shared a drinking culture. Harappan sites have yielded hempseeds from 2000 BCE, which archaeologists have interpreted as crop introduction from China.[69] More parsimoniously, they indicate adoption of *indica* from the Hindu Kush. Ritualized drinking was important in Harappan cities, al though we do not know what was drunk. Many disposable clay cups have been unearthed, and an important icon is the so-called sacred filter that shows liquid flowing from a sieve into a bowl.[70] Harappan ruins have yielded many clay sieves, sometimes within large pots, and similar artefacts come from BMAC sites.[71] The sieves and pots were apparently for brewing a non-alcoholic beverage.[72] Putative *Cannabis* remains – perhaps hempseeds, but possibly just millet – were found in 4,000-year-old BMAC pots, alongside putative remains of opium poppy (*Papaver somnifera*) and *Ephedra*, whose species contain the stimulant ephedrine.[73] The sieve-and-pot set is comparable to the cylindrical leather basket and perforated wooden bowl that accompanied drug *Cannabis* buried in the Tarim Basin, where people did not make pottery because suitable clay was not available locally.[74]

The beverage suggested by these remains was probably the legendary sacrament called *soma* in Hinduism (centred in India) or *haoma* in Zoroastrianism (centred in Iran). The *soma/haoma* beverage was named after a plant, probably *Ephedra*. Nonetheless, other plants were also ingredients.[75] As we have seen, the *Atharva Veda* (perhaps 1000 BCE) lists *bhaṅgā* as one of five 'kingdoms of plants' under chief *soma*. Tarim Basin grave goods include *Ephedra*, drug *Cannabis* and capers (*Capparis spinosa*).[76] *Cannabis* entered Tibet probably in religious contexts before Buddhism arrived about 700 CE. In the Tibetan language, drug *Cannabis* is called *so-ma-ra-tsa*.[77] In the *Rig Veda* (perhaps 1500 BCE), *soma-rasa* referred specifically to the prepared beverage rather than to any plant. Tibet's pre-Buddhist religion seems related to Zoroastrianism; its origin story tells of a land west of Tibet.[78] The Zoroastrian text *Dēnkard* (perhaps 1000 CE), described magical–medicinal drinks mixed from various plants, including *Cannabis*.[79]

South Asian ephedras remain confined to dry highlands from Bhutan to Iran, and north into China. *Cannabis*, however, adapted to the subtropical lowlands of India, where it grew by 1600 BCE.[80] It was thus available when Hinduism and Buddhism arose in the lowlands around 500 BCE.[81] In Old Hindu, drug *Cannabis* was called *bhaṅgā*, which later became the name of a milk-based sacramental beverage distinct from the legendary *soma*.

The primary division in South Asian *Cannabis* culture – *śāṇa* versus *bhaṅgā* – lost significance as drug uses became dominant and as other plants gained preference as sources of fibre and oilseeds. Eventually, three different cultures of drug *Cannabis* developed in South Asia. The basal drug culture is *bhang*; the other two cultures, *ganja* and *charas*, represent concentrated drugs.

Bhang developed differently in the Indian subcontinent versus the Iranian Plateau and areas westward, where drug *Cannabis* anciently gained no obvious importance. Midwifery was possibly where the plant found greatest use. The Zoroastrian text *Zend Avesta* (perhaps 700 BCE),

2. Hanf.
Cannabis sativa L.

The Hindu god Shiva with *bhang*. India, *c.* 1940s.

written in the ancient Avestan language, listed *banghem* among four abortifacients, all prohibited.[82] (In modern Morocco, *Cannabis* is mixed with datura, henbane and other plants to induce abortion.[83]) Near Jerusalem about 350 BCE, drug *Cannabis* was burnt in the burial of a fourteen-year-old girl who died giving birth.[84] In Old Arabic works from the Islamic Golden Age (800s–1200s CE), *banj* referred generically to any psychoactive plant and was associated in stories with crime, dark magic and poisoning.[85]

Hanf (hemp), from Friedrich Losch, *Kraüterbuch: Unsere Heilpflanzen in Wort und Bild* (1905).

45

In contrast, *bhang* became prominent in the Indo-Gangetic tradition of northern India, which extended southward along the subcontinent's coasts. Its use seems to have been relatively common, although written accounts of *bhang* do not certainly refer to *Cannabis* until about 1200 CE. *Bhang* sometimes meant other plants, and other common names could mean *Cannabis* or various unrelated species. Documents before 1500 CE describe *bhang* as a recreational drug, as a medicinal plant with numerous applications and as a sacrament, especially among devotees of Shiva.[86] *Bhang* was mostly prepared as a beverage, although sometimes made into topical medicines or included in incense. Maritime trade carried the plant from western India to the Arabian Peninsula and East Africa, arriving in Kenya by 700 CE.[87] In Yemeni Arabic, marijuana is *bango*; in Swahili, *bangi*.

In sub-Saharan Africa, the *bhang* culture was significantly transformed. The plant came into contact with pipe-smoking. The independent, pre-Columbian invention of smoking in Africa is unequivocal. The oldest smoking pipes are from Central Africa from 400 CE,[88] centuries before *indica* arrived in East Africa. Before *Cannabis*, *Datura metel* was smoked. Resurgence in pipe use in eastern African sites after 1000 CE tenuously suggests *Cannabis* diffusion. *Cannabis* residue has been found in Ethiopian pipe bowls from 1350 CE.[89] Smoking profoundly changes *Cannabis* as a drug because its pharmacological effects are felt almost immediately upon inhalation (THC is slowly and inefficiently absorbed through the digestive tract). African smoking-pipe technology allowed precise control of dosage, but pipes did not diffuse beyond the continent until the fifteenth century.

Layered over these iterations of *bhang* were the two other drug cultures. THC is most abundant in female inflorescences, and specifically in resin from glandular hairs that are densest on the flowers. People learned anciently to concentrate the drug, by collecting either only female flowers or only resin. The standard terms in the *Cannabis* literature for these forms are *ganja* (the Hindi term for female flowers) and *charas* (the Persian name for masses of *Cannabis* resin). In English, *Cannabis* resin is called hashish, an Arabic loanword.

Plant genetics provides the best evidence of the antiquity of *charas* and *ganja*. The two drug-production techniques entailed different approaches to agricultural selection. *Ganja* farmers selected seeds based on the psychoactive characteristics of individual plants. *Charas* farmers saved seeds from particular fields based on the phytochemistry of the entire crop.[90] The ancient application of these selection practices produced two genetically distinct varieties of *indica*,[91] the folk species indica and sativa of marijuana aficionados. Hashish cultivars — initially only the indica folk species — were bred to be short, so that people could collect resin by rubbing bodies against plants. In contrast, *ganja* and *bhang* cultivars — the sativa folk species — generally grow tall. Height was unimportant for farmers who harvested plants at ground level, yet for plants tallness enables an individual to surpass its neighbours and catch more sunlight. Importantly, the arrival of hashish production in the Levant by 1200 CE did not bring with it the indica folk species, which remained endemic to the Hindu Kush area into the twentieth century.[92] Instead, farmers in the Levant selected *bhang* and *ganja* cultivars to make *charas*.

The histories of *ganja* and *charas* are vaguely known before 1500 CE. The Tarim Basin *Cannabis* from 500 BCE consisted of only female flowers,[93] but the next-oldest suggestion of *ganja* is 1,700 years younger. During the 1300s and 1400s CE, books from the eastern and western Ganges Valley listed 'gañjá' as a synonym for *bhang*.[94] Some of these works also called the drug *Indrasana* – Indra's *śāṇa* or, more idiomatically, 'Indra's food' – referring to a Hindu deity. *Ganja* was primarily roasted, then chewed before the introduction of smoking, but both *bhang* and *ganja* were occasionally administered via smoke inhalation before 1500.[95] The association with Indra suggests tenuously that *ganja* appeared in the *Atharva Veda* as 'jañgída', an 'all-healing' tree to which 'the formidable Indra imparted . . . formidableness'.[96] *Ganja* strains are adapted to hot subtropical and tropical growing conditions, as in the Ganges Valley.[97] *Ganja* voyaged towards Southeast Asia via maritime trade, but seemingly after 1500. By that year *bhang* was probably known as far east as modern Myanmar, where Burmese speakers say *bhén*.[98]

Sergei Mikhailovich Prokudin-Gorskii, *Cannabis* field, Russia, 1902.

In contrast, the original *charas* strain – the indica folk species – prefers cool, moist conditions, such as are found in the mid-elevation Hindu Kush and neighbouring ranges.[99] *Charas* probably arose as a by-product of harvesting *Cannabis* for other uses. *Cannabis* is a sticky, resinous plant, and the most basic technique of hashish production is to collect resin accumulated on the skin. A more developed technique is to dry harvested plants, sift the resinous hairs from the other material and press the sifted dust into lumps of hashish.[100] A Sanskrit grammar from about 600 BCE uses a term glossed as '*bhaṅgā* dust', possibly meaning *charas*.[101] In the Levant around 100 BCE, Galen encountered psycho-active sweetmeats similar to hash-based ones known historically, but Galen's may have been made of *bhang* or *ganja* instead.

The *charas* culture experienced its greatest development from Central Asia to the Levant.[102] Hashish distinctly appeared in Old Arabic literature beginning in the 1200s, when the term *ḥashīsh* was used from modern Iran to Egypt.[103] *Ḥashīsh* initially meant, generically, 'grass', 'weed' or 'medicinal herb', but became an endearing nickname for drug *Cannabis* – '*the* herb' – and, eventually, the name of the preparation now called hashish. Islamic societies debated the morality of drug *Cannabis*, which the Qu'ran does not mention, and efforts to suppress its use began in the thirteenth century.[104] These efforts were unsuccessful.

Domestication of *Cannabis sativa*

During the Pleistocene epoch, *Cannabis sativa* dispersed from its centre of origin. From its initial habitat in the temperate, mid-latitude forests of southern Siberia, the plant adapted to steppe environments, probably accompanying native hoofed animals like the horse. Palaeolithic mammoth-hunters occupied western Siberia during the Pleistocene, and *Cannabis* possibly interacted with them, but we do not know.

The plant was mobile during prehistory well before it was farmed. Based on fossil pollen, *Cannabis* grew from Bulgaria to Sweden by 5000 BCE,[105] and in many other northern European locations from subsequent millennia. Hempseeds dating from about 5500 BCE have been excavated in Germany and Ukraine, and slightly younger, putative *Cannabis* fibres have been found in southern France.[106] The plant spread with Neolithic agriculture including bread wheat (*Triticum aestivum*), but for millennia *sativa* was not clearly farmed, even if humans practised selection on self-seeded plants.

In ancient western Eurasia, *sativa* was not particularly prominent, even if useful. Earlier, the most widely important fibre plants were flax and nettle (*Urtica dioica*), while rushes (*Juncus* spp.), weaver's broom (*Spartium junceum*), esparto (*Stipa tenacissima*) and various tree barks were locally important.[107] Despite this diversity, fantastic stories have been told about ancient *Cannabis*. For instance, an archaeologist concluded that a German Neolithic culture made psychoactive *Cannabis* drinks, solely because they decorated their drinking cups with cord impressions.[108] Inferring psychoactive *Cannabis* is bio-geographically incorrect and unnecessary. Alcoholic drinks, sometimes mixed with opium poppy, transformed prehistoric European cultures; poppy entered central Europe from the Mediterranean by 4000 BCE.[109] Furthermore, the invention of netting, cordage and textiles supplied motifs that carried meaning without drug enhancement.

Later immigrants overwhelmed Europe's earliest *Cannabis* users.
Following the domestication of the horse (about 4000 BCE), Proto-
Indo-European speakers rode east, west and south from the Central
Asian steppes. Linguistic patterns suggest that *Cannabis* was salient to
these people. They probably called *sativa* something like *śāṇa*, a term
that transformed into the widespread root words *kannab* and *hannap*
across temperate Eurasia. Speakers of Indo-European languages entered
Europe from about 2000 BCE, and carried derived forms of *śāṇa* as far
as the plant travelled. Nonetheless, *Cannabis* was not particularly important to these people, and *Cannabis* farming did not become clearly
evident until just before the Current Era.

The European documentary record of *Cannabis* begins with Herodotus
(400s BCE), who described *Cannabis* cloth from Thrace (west of the

Hempseeds still on the plant, Austria, 2008.

Black Sea), and ceremonial burning of hempseeds in Scythia (north of the sea).[110] The Scythian example is prominent in *Cannabis* histories. Herodotus described a chieftain's funeral, where some attendees showed emotion after visiting a tent fumigated with smoke from *kánnabis* seeds. Archaeologists have found braziers with charred hempseeds at roughly contemporaneous burial sites in central Siberia and modern Romania,[111] but no green material, the only psychoactive parts of any *Cannabis* plant.

Scythian funerals, broadly characteristic of steppe cultures, were undoubtedly emotional events that included ritualized waste of valuables. Elite tombs were filled with grave goods, sacrificed horses and sometimes sacrificed humans. With few exceptions,[112] *Cannabis* histories have read Herodotus' Scythian story as early drug *Cannabis* in western Eurasia. Again, inferring psychoactivity is incorrect and unnecessary, and an example of the historian's fallacy of presentism, or anachronistically applying modern ideas to past events. The presumption is that any smoking *kánnabis* must be psychoactive, because marijuana smoking is nowadays common. This presumption traces to 1870,[113] and permeates *Cannabis* literature. A 1938 book concluded that Herodotus 'strongly suggest[s . . .] the use of hemp narcotics, since no other drug fits [his] description'. A key archaeological report stated, 'without a doubt . . . hashish was used as a narcotic' by the Scythians; a 2005 history averred, 'it is believed the Scythians were actually [burn]ing cannabis flowers.'[114] Scythians burned hempseeds for unknown reasons.[115] Hempseeds carry no psychoactive compounds, although smoke from the chemically complex hempseed may carry unrecognized effects.

Herodotus embellished his histories,[116] and his purpose in the Scythian passage was to portray non-Greek foreigners as barbarian Others. He luridly attributed behaviour – 'the skulls [of their enemies they fashion into] drinking-cup[s]' – and emphasized their alterity – the 'Scythians . . . avoid foreign customs at all costs, especially those of the Hellenes [Greeks]'.[117] Herodotus did not fabricate Central Asian hempseed burning, but his ethnocentric portrayal unfortunately resonates with recent discourse of drug-induced delirium and violence.

Hemp processing tools, France, 1854.

Furthermore, a comparison of modern editions of his writing shows that translators have often amplified this resonance.

Herodotus' Thracian story is more important.[118] During Herodotus' century, Athens depended upon grain imported from the Black Sea.[119] Trade enriched the Scythians and Thracians, and exposed the Greeks to new ideas, technology and practices. Thracian use of *Cannabis* to make cloth was noteworthy to Herodotus because this practice was previously unknown in the Mediterranean.[120]

Thracian *Cannabis* fabric represented a sophisticated industry that originated in association with flax. In Central Asia, ancient fabrics were primarily felted wool or high-status imports like Chinese silks. Woven woollens were important from modern Iran to Britain. Mediterranean weavers relied on flax. Technically sophisticated flax processing was developed in Neolithic Switzerland by 1600 BCE. These practices diffused in all directions. Eventually, in the lower Danube Valley – modern Bulgaria, Romania and Moldova – someone discovered that the flax methods also work with *Cannabis*.[121] Herodotus credited Thrace, and *sativa* hemp production emerged widely across the Mediterranean after 400 BCE, including present-day Turkey, France, Greece and Italy.[122] In Greece, state monopolies controlled hemp production from 259 BCE.[123] *Cannabis* was clearly agricultural in this diffusion, which was led ultimately by Rome. Spanish *cañamo*, Portuguese *cânhamo* and French *chanvre* derive from Old Latin *cannabis*.

Roman expansion transformed European agriculture. No longer just a weed, *Cannabis* demanded attention from farmers for whom the plant became preferred for cordage and valued for cloth. Roman farm writers described agriculture in the Roman Empire (27 BCE–476 CE). 'Do not buy anything . . . which can be grown on the farm', counselled Varro in the first century BCE, including 'articles made of hemp'. 'Have a place where you can sow hemp, flax, rush [or esparto-grass], from which to weave shoes for the oxen, twine, cord and rope.'[124]

Cannabis demanded fertile soil, and considerable labour to process into finished goods. Flax and wool widely remained the preferred clothing fibres, but *Cannabis* gained favour for heavy fabrics and strong ropes; other plants, and leather, supplied cordage too.[125] Hempen ropes became important to maritime, military, agricultural and industrial endeavours. Regional variation in *Cannabis* culture developed under the Romans. Several important industries within the empire pre-dated the Romans – rope manufacturing in Britannia (modern Britain), textiles in Gaul (modern France) – but *Cannabis* industries in northern Europe mostly arose after Roman expansion.[126] Roman *Cannabis* did not flourish in the Iberian Peninsula and failed in North Africa, if it was tried there.

Cannabis continued its expansion during the medieval period, after the fall of Rome. The English word 'canvas' is first documented from

1260; it came ultimately from Old Latin *cannabaceus* ('hempen').[127] Hempen sailcloth began replacing woollen sails in Norway by 1000.[128] The Norse brought *sativa* to Iceland by 1240.[129] The plant advanced slowly into the Iberian Peninsula; the Spanish word *cañamo* is first documented from 1202, Portuguese *cânhamo* from 1441.[130] In this region, esparto ropes had been preferred for maritime applications since Roman times, while hempen ropes were favoured ashore.[131] Physical evidence of hemp processing in Spain dates from about 1300.[132] Medieval Spanish *Cannabis* made household fabrics and various minor products; sailcloth was made from flax or cotton, following Mediterranean traditions established by Roman times.[133] There is no evidence of significant hemp production in Portugal.

Cannabis contributed to the dramatic transformation of the landscape of Iron Age Europe, when land cover shifted from forests to fields. *Cannabis* brought several landscape changes via farming and processing. The processing step called retting particularly had environmental impact. Retting is a living process: harvested stalks are wetted

Bondeno – Grammolatura della Canape nel Bondesano

Hemp from Italy's Emilia-Romagna region supplied Rome and Venice, and still retains commercial value. Postcard, *c.* 1910.

British promotional cigarette cards representing hemp, 1902 and 1917.

and allowed to moulder for a week or two, so that bacteria rot away tissues around the stem fibres, making them easier to process further. Retting ceases upon drying; over-retting discolours or damages the fibres. Initially, farmers relied on dew retting, leaving harvested stalks in fields to collect morning moisture. Over time, pond retting became dominant; stalks were thrown into ponds or streams, allowed to decay, then removed and dried. Massive increases in *Cannabis* pollen in underwater sediment indicate the diffusion of pond retting in the first millennium CE. Pond retting could be noxious, as described in an English rhyme of 1580:

> Now pluck up thy hemp, and go beat out the seed,
> And afterward water it, as ye see need;
> But not in the river, where cattle should drink,
> For poisoning them, and the people with stink.[134]

In some areas, putrid, microorganism-filled water was preferred, because the process was faster.[135] If large quantities of hemp are treated in a water body, retting causes eutrophication, a smelly die-off in aquatic ecosystems polluted with too many nutrients. Lake sediments across Europe preserve evidence of eutrophication caused by medieval retting.[136]

Cannabis sativa had several minor uses, but mostly documented only after 1500. Hempseed foods have been at best insignificant in western Eurasia. Hempseed soup was eaten to remember the dead on Christmas Eve in Poland and Lithuania, one of several faint echoes suggesting Scythian funereal use of hempseeds.[137] In the early 1500s, Polish works described this soup as nearly inedible; more palatable hempseed foods later had minimal use.[138] Numerous folk medicines were concocted from *sativa*, although before the 1700s medicinal uses of *Cannabis* in Europe were mostly centuries-old repetitions of the recommendations of Greek and Islamic physicians. Dioscorides' prescription of hempseed oil as an analgesic eardrop was particularly repeated in European herbals. Modern research has found that hempseed oil is useful in treating ear, nose and throat injuries.[139]

Fibre has always been the dominant aspect of western Eurasian *Cannabis* culture. Hemp rope and fabric became important commercial products in medieval Europe. Hemp-breaking mills in France were powered by animals before 1000 CE, and by water 200 years later; irrigated fields were sown in Italy by 1295.[140] Ponds were ceded to *Cannabis* retting to ensure fibre supplies. Increasing demand stimulated new political and economic configurations, such as the Hanseatic League. This trade confederation, centred in modern Germany and Poland, encompassed the Baltic Sea and flourished from the 1300s to the 1600s. Hemp had flourished for millennia in the eastern Baltic, and the Hanseatic League sold hemp fibre to countries where production did not meet demand – most notably Britain, Spain and Portugal. For, despite the plant's colonization of Europe, human societies were widely unable to produce as much hemp as they needed.

The economic importance of *Cannabis sativa* made it a plant of power. European elites increasingly sought to control hemp to accumulate wealth. Merchant networks for hemp developed across France by the tenth century.[141] In the thirteenth century, Parisian *chanevaciers* ('cannabis cloth merchants') enriched themselves by controlling the trade in finished products (which were lightly taxed) to the exclusion of outsiders, who could sell only in bulk (more heavily taxed). The system was an early example of separate wholesale and retail trades.[142] In 1303 the city-state of Venice began closely controlling hemp production to ensure supplies for its maritime empire.[143]

As Europe entered the Age of Sail with an advantageous location beside the Atlantic, *sativa* became crucial to the global expansion of European mercantile and colonial empires.

Hemp was classified as a 'naval store' across Europe, a category
of raw materials considered vital for national defence.

three
Hemp Travels the World

C annabis sativa began the post-Columbian era primed for globalization. Hempen products became vital for European authorities during the Age of Sail, enabling industrial development and colonial expansion. Although people used hemp across temperate Eurasia, its global dispersion resulted from European political and economic expansion.

The historic importance of hemp to European authorities has strongly flavoured *Cannabis* histories, especially those promoting hemp. These histories posit that the past importance of *sativa* indicates its inherent excellence, and argue that hemp was unfairly suppressed to allow the prohibition of drug *Cannabis*. Conspiracy theories abound, of conniving industrialists and politicians who defeated hemp in the 1930s to favour competing industries, particularly petroleum and logging.

Such tales neglect much economic history. Hemp *Cannabis* was indubitably important, but its historical success generally arose from the imposition of political and economic authority within highly stratified societies. Ancient adoption of hemp across Europe reflected the plant's excellence as a fibre source with secondary uses. After 1500, farmers willingly produced enough *sativa* to meet household needs. However, as European authorities became increasingly reliant on hemp, farmers found *Cannabis* unprofitable at the levels of production needed to supply maritime empires.

Patriotic discourse has often encouraged hemp production, although the words more clearly motivated poets and politicians than producers. Hemp work is gruelling and heavy, but also requires considerable technical skill to make high-quality finished goods. This combination of capabilities – physical strength and technical knowledge – is poorly suited to most labour systems, from free to slave.[1] European authorities struggled for centuries to find sustainable labour for hemp production. A long-term problem was that governments and manufacturers constantly worked to push prices down for naval stores – including ropes and sailcloth – which decreased income for workers. Authorities widely encouraged, coerced and required hemp production, although usually with little success because labourers avoided the poorly paid, onerous work.

Hemp history comprises two interwoven perspectives. The needs and desires of European imperial authorities determined where, when and why *sativa* was transported worldwide. Nonetheless, farmers and processors directly decided whether or not to produce hemp. *Cannabis* was often difficult to place within agricultural systems because it demanded soil fertility, did not provide desirable food and required considerable labour for processing.[2] The powerful and the poor together steered the global diffusion of *sativa*.

The plant was not passive. Humans might decide where to sow hempseeds, but *Cannabis* determines where and how it will grow. Sunlight is a key variable. *Cannabis sativa* is a successful fibre crop only between about 30 and 60 degrees latitude; at higher latitudes the growing season is too short, and at lower latitudes day-length conditions prevent the plant from producing usable fibre.[3] At mid-latitudes, *sativa* grows tall during the long days of early summer, and begins flowering as day-length decreases after the summer solstice. In tropical latitudes, days are always about twelve hours long, which causes *sativa* to flower too quickly to grow tall, fibrous stems. In contrast, East Asian *indica* hemp cultivars can succeed at tropical latitudes.[4] Stunted, individual *sativa* plants survive at low latitudes, but provide insufficient fibre to justify further farming. *Cannabis sativa* was introduced to

European colonies globally, but failed everywhere except in some mid-latitude areas.

Cannabis sativa is a good example of the Columbian Exchange, the European-led transfer of plants, animals and diseases across the Atlantic after 1492.[5] Europeans have been central to the global dissemination of *sativa* and many other plants. However, *sativa* is distinct from *indica*, whose globalization was led by people from southern Asia and sub-Saharan Africa.

The global experience of *Cannabis sativa* was foreshadowed in the medieval rise of Venice. The Italian city-state created a merchant empire across the Mediterranean that persisted from the 1200s to 1797. The powerful Venetian navy enabled mercantile trade and political expansion, primarily in the eastern Mediterranean. Patriotic hemp discourse is earliest known from Venice, where senators in the early 1400s pinned the 'security of our galleys and ships and . . . our sailors and capital' on hemp. In northeastern Italy, robust hemp industries developed to supply Venice. The Venetian state assured its supply of naval stores by directly controlling the manufacture of cordage and fibre, and indirectly controlling *Cannabis* cultivation and marketing. Beginning in 1303, Venetian authorities assigned a monopoly to the state-owned textile and cordage factory, where managers developed commodity grading of unfinished hemp to standardize product quality. Over subsequent centuries, the skilled labourers who made rope and textiles were subject to increasing controls imposed by the state to assure quality. Workers resisted control through slowdowns and by cheating the factory financially.[6]

Despite its manufacturing capabilities, Venice depended upon imports of unfinished hemp. Initially, Bologna (to the south) was its main source, but by the mid-1400s Venice began looking elsewhere. Soon after 1500, Venetian envoys, aided by a Bolognese defector, helped to establish the industrial cultivation of hemp in another city-state to the west. Venice demanded lower prices from Bologna once the new supply was established. Throughout the sixteenth century, Venice self-servingly manipulated regional prices to influence hemp production.

Price-fixing did not benefit farmers, who increasingly planted wheat as hemp became unprofitable. Small-scale, local production persisted, but northern Italian hemp industries did not recover until the mid-1700s.[7]

Venice's main rival, the Ottoman Empire, found hemp all around the Black Sea, but especially in Asia Minor (present-day Turkey), where farmers have grown *sativa* for more than 2,000 years.[8] However, Turkey's hemp cultivars are absent from research collections.[9] By 1340, the Italian city-state of Genoa imported Turkish hemp.[10] As the Ottoman navy gained strength after 1400, the need for rigging grew and exports declined. The Ottoman state increasingly controlled the hemp industry to assure its own supplies,[11] with unanticipated consequences. In the 1700s, the state imposed heavy, in-kind taxes on hemp producers and traders to prevent profiteering and to keep prices low. The policy instead stunted Turkish industrial development during the 1800s and made the empire dependent upon imports from Greece, northern Italy and probably Russia.[12]

Imperial desire for naval stores shaped *Cannabis* history from the top, but labourers exerted influence from the bottom. Hemp

Hemp in action: Venice versus the Ottomans. *The Battle of Zonchio,* c. 1499, by an unknown Italian artist.

processing across Eurasia comprised a series of tedious, heavy tasks, and eventually represented suffering in Italy and China.[13] Harvesting entailed either uprooting individual plants or cutting them near the ground – both back-breaking tasks. Harvesting was often done twice, for male and female plants. In western Eurasia, harvested hemp was dried, stored to age and then retted. Fine fabrics and maritime-quality rope require water retting, while dew retting produces inexpensive cordage and coarse cloth. After retting, the stalks were dried and aged again. Next, the stalks were broken to separate fibres ('lint') from the pith ('hurd'). Breaking relied on a simple hand-operated vice – a hemp break – to crush the stalks. In some areas people manually peeled fibres from stalks instead of breaking. The fibres were then scutched (scraped with a dull knife or pounded with a mallet) to remove the remaining hurd, then heckled (passed through a comb) to straighten them and remove impurities. The fibres were further straightened and cleaned to make unfinished 'tow', which was spun into either threads for weaving, or yarns for rope-making. Each type and grade of finished product entailed different manufacturing tasks. Few steps were mechanized until the mid-1800s, although mechanical processing remained uncommon into the 1900s. Processing hempseeds and extracting oil were different endeavours.

The Western technique of fibre processing originated with flax, the doppelgänger of hemp. However, flax is small and slender. Taller, thicker *Cannabis* stems made hemp processing more difficult. In Venice, *Cannabis* was euphemistically '[the plant] of a hundred operations [processing steps]'.[14] The poem *Il Canapajo* ('the hemp field'), annotated with agricultural instructions in 1741, records Bolognese ambivalence. *Cannabis* was 'so noble a sapling', but hemp work was not necessarily ennobling:

[Go] Far [away, he] who has dainty nostrils,
Far from here: this is [the] Song [of retting.]
Stench and filth turn the stomach, and severe[ly] . . .
But here, . . . here in this stench,

Taking a rest during the hemp harvest, Italy, c. 1910.

[There is the] Transformation of nature . . .
The bark begins to be thread . . .
[As you toil] You will see the results of your hard work:
Here [your labour should] behove the sailor who is seeking port.[15]

Contemporaneous French farmers considered retting-water poison-ous.[16] Hemp-fibre processing is also risky; dust inhalation caused high rates of lung disease among labourers.[17] Fieldworkers also complained of light-headedness while harvesting.[18] *Cannabis* pollen is a chemically complex allergen that carries flavonoid glycosides, a class of chemical that includes central nervous system depressants.[19] Hemp labour was often unpleasant.

Venetian dominance increased the importance of hemp beyond Italy. Commercial production in the Balkans began in the 1400s, and Venetian authorities required Croatians to grow hemp or flax in the early 1700s.[20] However, northern Italian *canapa* cultivars and agri-cultural practices did not travel far until the 1900s. Venetians and Ottomans alike probably traded only fibre, with hempseeds removed, and neither empire embarked colonies whose members might have planted hemp. Italian *Cannabis* culture travelled across the Adriatic sea in the 1700s, to Serbia, when the Austro-Hungarian Empire imported Italian settlers and hempseeds to improve local production.[21] Hemp remained important in Serbia into the 1900s.

Venice and the Ottoman Empire exhibited hemp's importance to European maritime empires. European global expansion began with Portugal and Spain, where *sativa* was initially little used in shipping. Esparto was anciently preferred for maritime rope, while Iberian sail-cloth was cotton or flax, as elsewhere around the Mediterranean. In France, for instance, in the sixteenth century Mediterranean ports supplied cotton sails but Atlantic ports used hemp.[22] Hemp rope and fabric production increased in The Netherlands, France, Britain and Italy before 1500, but not in Spain or Portugal. The lack of domestic production forced these countries to import hempen sailcloth and rope from northern France and Belgium by 1500.[23] The Iberian nations relied on imports throughout the Age of Sail.

Large-scale *Cannabis* farming began in southern Spain about 1515.[24] A southern town was renamed Santa Cruz de los Cañamos in the

The location of this significant work in the Serbian naive tradition is unknown: Zuzana Chalupova, *Konoplje*, Italian postcard of retting in a stream, *c.* 1970.

1600s.[25] Hemp had strategic value, and the Spanish tried hempseeds in soils claimed throughout the Americas. In 1530 a conquistador from southern Spain gained royal licence to farm *cañamo* in New Spain (modern Mexico).[26] This introduction failed. The Spanish king ordered viceroys to plant fibre crops in all the colonies in 1545, but the order had little effect on *Cannabis* because colonists lacked seeds, expertise and interest. Throughout the 1600s, Spain constantly struggled to supply maritime rope and sailcloth, and became reliant on Russian hemp.[27] Spanish efforts redoubled in the 1700s, when import reliance became a liability. Domestic production increased.[28] Political authorities repeatedly tried to encourage hemp in the American colonies, but hempseeds were unavailable locally and not normally trafficked from Europe.[29]

In the 1700s, Spanish colonial farming trials likely also failed because locally produced hempseed came from *indica* cultivars bred for drugs, not fibre. *Cannabis indica* separately crossed the Atlantic as early as the 1500s. The first documents suggesting the psychoactive species are from mid-eighteenth-century Brazil and Mexico. *Cannabis indica* arrived in Mexico overland from the south, but the authorities did not connect marijuana with *Cannabis* until the mid-1800s. Mexican farmers were capable agriculturalists, and in the mid-1700s one successfully bred *Cannabis* to produce fibre in the central highlands. (This cultivar did not survive the farmer's death in the 1770s, however.[30]) Others kept trying, with modest success. In 1787 Mexican unfinished hemp exports to Spain reached 2,000 kg (4,400 lb), when a large ship required 100 tons of rope.[31] The colonial government spent heavily to develop hemp industries, but by the 1790s decided that the project was an expensive failure.[32]

Colombia and Peru were other important areas of early Spanish activity, and *sativa* failed in these low-latitude countries. Into the 1950s Colombian authorities lamented the absence of hemp, while bemoaning the presence of marijuana.[33]

The Portuguese had even less success. Colonial authorities in Brazil tried *cânhamo* without luck by the 1620s.[34] Plant-introduction efforts increased during the 1700s, when the Portuguese sought new sources of profit.[35] *Cannabis sativa* was seemingly grown in Portugal by 1710, when hempseeds were listed in a Portuguese herbal.[36] Official correspondence from northeastern Brazil in 1784 suggests *Cannabis*. The botanically uncertain letter-writer described a plant similar to that 'which the nations of the north . . . use for cordage'. The plant was probably *indica*, because there was enough of it to 'fill a ship'.[37] The Portuguese established a flax and hemp plantation in southern Brazil in 1783 that persisted for four decades, despite little success.[38] 'Hemp' was tried several other times before 1800; these trials failed, although in 1812 hempseeds (from *indica*?) remained locally available.[39] Brazilian *Cannabis* farmers exported a minuscule 255 kg (560 lb) of unfinished hemp in 1812.[40] The Portuguese did not successfully produce hemp even at home. In 1875 a scholar reported that 'hemp farming is unknown in Portugal'.[41] Portuguese enterprises relied on Russian hemp.[42]

Spanish and Portuguese settlers found other plants to meet local needs, although these did not satisfy imperial authorities. Mexican fibre mostly came from three *Agave* species: sisal, henequen and pita. The Spanish fleet along the Pacific coast relied on pita in the late 1700s, despite the fact that it deteriorated much more quickly than hemp.[43] Imported hemp was expensive, but its durability made it a long-term bargain – if one could pay for it initially.

Cannabis sativa did succeed along the temperate edges of Spanish America, in present-day Chile, Argentina and the U.S. In mid-latitude South America, the plant took root as early as 1545.[44] *Cannabis* hemp industries developed and have persisted into the present, mostly supplying regional markets for rope, sackcloth and hempseed. The moist climate of Chile suited *sativa* better than the drier climate of Argentina. In Spanish California, hemp farming began in 1795.[45] Production increased after 1805 when the Crown started subsidizing production to supply the Pacific-coast fleet.[46] Subsistence farmers valued the guaranteed market. In 1810, *Californios* produced 110 tons of hemp,[47] 50 times more than Mexico in 1787.

Farmers dropped the crop when subsidy ended with the Mexican War of Independence (1810–21), although some hemp farming

Argentine products from *c*. 1900: leather, wool, canned foods and hemp.

continued into the twentieth century. There is no evidence of hemp in Spanish New Mexico, where colonists met plant-fibre needs mainly with Native American fibre plants.

Russian hemp exports were hugely important globally from the 1700s, but this commerce weakly affected the distribution of *Cannabis* because hempseed was a minor commodity. *Cannabis sativa* farming was concentrated in Russia's western plains, extending into the Baltic Republics, Poland and Belarus.[48] Exports from the eastern Baltic began in the 1200s, when Livonian hemp (modern Estonia and Latvia) circulated in the Hanseatic League commercial confederation.[49] Early eighteenth-century social reforms enabled Russia to expand its international trade, and ship more hemp into the Baltic. International demand expanded opportunities for Russian hemp producers, who benefited from millennia of *Cannabis* expertise and a social structure that assured cheap labour.[50] Additionally, most of the Russian crop could be exported without affecting its relatively small navy. Russia undersold most exporting countries, and out-produced all.

Russian colonists did not farm *Cannabis* in imperial outposts along the Pacific coast of North America, which they occupied from the late 1700s to 1867. Many Eurasian crops were tried in Russian Alaska, including flax in 1796, but agriculture failed because hunting, trapping and fishing proved more profitable. Farming did better in Russian California (1812–41), although farmers focused on food. They made woollen clothing, and probably imported cordage from Russia.[51]

Despite its low cost, Russian hemp was of a high quality. Producers could afford the two years' labour required to produce the best fibre, and market overseers reduced fraudulent sales of low-quality hemp.[52] Russian hemp was mostly sold unfinished, which made imports even cheaper and enabled rope-making industries throughout the Atlantic. Hempseed and oil were minor exports.[53] The Russians also passed transport costs on to other countries by relying on foreign merchant fleets, first from the Hanseatic League, then Sweden and The Netherlands, then Britain and its American colonies in the eighteenth century.

Russian success can hardly be overemphasized. The British spent £10,000 per year on Russian hemp at the end of the 1500s, and £2,000,000 annually by the end of the 1700s.[54] During the Seven Years War (1756–63), Russia supplied 73,000 tons of hemp to Great Britain, whose colonies supplied just 2 tons.[55] Indeed, American manufacturers relied on Russian hemp trafficked through London.[56] In 1696 a politician complained that 'England is at Russia's mercy'

Promotional card representing retting of hemp and flax, France, c. 1910.

because of hemp imports,[57] which would only increase. One of Napoleon's motivations for disastrously invading Russia in 1812 was to force Russia to boycott British trade. The low cost of Russian raw material aided manufacturers, but discouraged farmers worldwide. In Spain, for example, first-quality Russian hemp cost 9 pesos per hundredweight in 1792, while comparable Spanish hemp cost 14–18 pesos.[58] Despite decades trying to develop *Cannabis* farming, Spain – and many other countries – could not afford to avoid imports. Further-more, shipbuilders and rope-makers objected to import tariffs meant to favour domestic farmers, because tariffs raised their costs and substitutes for Russian hemp were considered inferior.

France and Great Britain had the largest roles in *sativa* dispersal, because for centuries these countries attempted to establish hemp in mid-latitude settler colonies. *Cannabis* was vital in both countries by the 1500s, its importance registered in place names. In France, place names referenced hemp farming, retting and breaking.[59] In Britain, many place names, including 'Hemphill', refer to *Cannabis*, but other names are misleading. 'Hempstead' is from an early form of 'homestead'.[60] In the Americas, hemp place names date from the

Russian hemp rigging on a Russian ship. Lake Baikal, Russia. *c.* 1900.

1600s, because the plant was among the colonies' initial crops. *Cannabis* widely took root from these early introductions, but hemp industries developed very slowly.

The main difference between British and French hemp efforts was that French domestic supply more closely equalled domestic demand. Certainly, British growers and manufacturers developed robust hempen textile and cordage industries. Yet Britain continuously struggled to produce enough unfinished hemp, and the authorities constantly tried to induce production. In 1533 Henry VIII required farmers to plant a quarter-acre of hemp or flax per 60 acres of farmland; Elizabeth I renewed this requirement in 1563.[61] Henry also sought to recruit farmers by allowing clergymen to sell hemp or flax.[62] Land was too dear, however, for farmers to grow much hemp, which was effectively inedible, paid poorly and required much labour in processing. Beginning in 1576, poor laws reduced labour costs by requiring 'governors of the poor' to make their charges process hemp or go to jail.[63] This practice did not stimulate industry outside the poorhouses.

British trade policies proved disastrous for domestic and colonial hemp producers. Early in the 1600s, policies meant to favour British shipping required that imports arrive on British ships, or on ships from the same country as the goods on board. Manufacturers relied on Russian hemp, but Swedish and Dutch vessels dominated the seventeenth-century Baltic. Simultaneously, trade laws allowed the import of Dutch finished goods on Dutch ships. Dutch manufacturers enjoyed lower costs and a reliable supply of raw material, and dominated the British market. Other countries similarly took advantage of British trade laws, even France (via smuggling). In 1653, free-trade policies attempted to rectify the situation, allowing 'all persons in any ship and from any port' to bring hemp into Britain.[64] The revision came too late; trade networks did not change. Free trade further drove down prices for unfinished hemp, creating a thin, precarious profit margin for British farmers. British workers lost jobs to imports and protested, but to no avail.[65]

The British became irreversibly dependent on imported hemp by 1700, but authorities would not abandon *Cannabis* inducements. The government offered guaranteed prices for hemp beginning in 1705, but dropped the bounty by 1740 because it had had no effect on production, in Britain or the colonies.[66] Other attempts were made to encourage British and colonial hemp in the 1700s, but by the 1810s British manufacturers had closed or shifted to fibres other than *Cannabis*.[67]

The British hoped colonial hemp would alleviate supply problems. Settlers planted *Cannabis* in Virginia in 1616 with satisfactory results,[68] and by the 1630s *sativa* had been planted throughout the North American colonies. These introductions failed to germinate commercial industries. Although the empire had an acute hunger for naval stores, the colonists had to feed themselves. In Virginia in 1649, labour limited the production of hemp: 'Hands are wanting to this and other workes'.[69] *Cannabis* grew best in the colonies from Pennsylvania to Virginia, but few farmers planted it. Hempseeds were not considered food, and hemp could not guarantee income enough to buy food.[70] Edible crops were less risky, and other crops paid better. In Virginia in 1621, the best hemp prices were about two pence per pound, while tobacco averaged 3 shillings.[71]

Colonial *Cannabis* inducements began by 1619, when Virginia's authorities made hemp or flax cultivation compulsory and designated plant fibre as legal currency. Ten of the thirteen colonies that became the United States tried to induce *Cannabis* farming by 1700,[72] with little success. Many treatises promoting hemp were printed in North America and Europe during the 1700s and 1800s, but trade conditions still discouraged farming. American colonies could export only unfinished hemp and only to British manufacturers, who could buy Russian raw material more cheaply. Shipping bulky, unfinished hemp across the Atlantic was not economical, although more valuable Russian hemp was economically shipped to North America. Commercial rope-makers and weavers used Baltic hemp, and enabled North American shipbuilders to rig ships fully. Trade policies favoured colonial manufacturers of naval stores over colonial suppliers of unfinished hemp.

Colonial hemp agriculture reflected European practices. In Britain, *sativa* was anciently the main plant-fibre crop, but declined after flax arrived from continental Europe in the 1400s.[73] British farmers integrated *Cannabis* into sustainable agriculture. In new or newly manured

LA TELA — LA TOILE — THE LINEN

Promotional card depicting the weaving of hemp and flax into linen. France, c. 1900.

fields, farmers planted *Cannabis* to *decrease* soil fertility, to prevent the following grain crop from growing too rapidly and becoming top-heavy (grain is damaged if stems bend to the ground). *Cannabis* was often not a field crop but grew in 'hemp yards' next to cottages, where farmers planted turnips (*Brassica rapa*) after the autumn hemp harvest.[74] *Cannabis* supplied homespun linen, sackcloth and rope, or income if processed then sold to manufacturers.

In North America, *Cannabis* poorly suited settler agriculture. The weedy annual competed with another fertility-demanding annual, the food staple maize (*Zea mays*). 'Hemp requires such very strong Land to produce it, that it would consume all our Dung to raise it in any great Quantities[,] so that we should not be able to raise Bread Corn', wrote a farmer in Massachusetts in 1760.[75] Hemp promoters argued that *Cannabis* did not deplete soil fertility, but few farmers were convinced. In 1769 the Canadian colonies supplied Britain with about 23 tons of hemp, when annual consumption was 20,000 tons. When British authorities in Ontario made Russian hempseed freely available in 1790, farmers claimed 29 of 2,000 bushels – probably because *Cannabis* supplied only birdseed to Canadian settlers.[76]

Sometimes the plant did not cooperate. Hempseeds shatter easily and lose viability quickly, and were regularly in short supply in the Americas. Overland and transoceanic shipping did not improve germination rates. As Massachusetts planter in 1760 discovered, 'Old Hemp Seed will not grow, not so much as one Seed of it.'[77]

In Brazil, a trial in 1779 failed because birds ate the freshly sown seeds.[78] The prevalence of feral *Cannabis* across Eurasia and North America is largely because of seed-eating birds, which can carry viable hempseeds long distances in their guts.[79] Hempseed was important poultry feed by 1600, and probably earlier.[80] Canary lovers provisioned hempseed in France by the 1600s; later, British hempseeds fattened wild-caught blackbirds for the table.[81] In North America, songbird-keeping wives of U.S. army officers introduced hemp to Minnesota in the mid-1800s.[82] Hempseeds collected from feral plants were initially the main source of birdseed,[83] but in the early 1900s small quantities of hemp were grown for birdseed in Britain, the U.S. and Canada. China, France and Italy exported large quantities.[84]

Hemp also failed commercially in British colonies in South Africa, Australia and New Zealand. European settlers in South Africa widely grew 'hemp' during the 1800s,[85] but it is uncertain if *sativa* was ever actually introduced. *Cannabis indica* was present by 1713, and settlers may have tried producing fibre from drug cultivars. The earliest hemp in Australia was certainly *indica*, sent as seed from British India in 1802.[86] This introduction failed as hemp (but succeeded as marijuana 160 years later). Australians may have tried *sativa* later, but commercial hemp remained nascent in 1876,[87] when global demand had nearly evaporated. New Zealand did not need *Cannabis*, because the indigenous fibre plant harakeke, or 'New Zealand hemp', achieved commercial success in the 1800s.

France had marginally more success in its colonies. *Cannabis sativa* grew in Québec and Nova Scotia in the late 1600s, but proved unprofitable for subsistence-orientated settlers.[88] In French Louisiana, hemp *Cannabis* thrived, but domestic producers feared competition.[89] In 1721 colonial authorities prohibited *Cannabis* to favour metropolitan industries. Nonetheless, Louisianans still produced hemp for household use. The French re-legalized *Cannabis* in 1730. Spain acquired Louisiana in 1762, and dispatched experienced workers to develop the colony's hemp industry.[90] By the 1790s, ships visiting New Orleans could buy high-quality cordage,[91] but the industry declined rapidly. When Louisiana joined the U.S. in 1803, its plant-fibre industry centred on cotton, which was more profitable and had lower labour costs.

The relative success of *Cannabis* in Louisiana reflects the vitality of France's domestic industries. By 1500 France had the largest population in Europe, and remained primarily rural into the 1900s. *Cannabis* was integrated into smallholder agriculture,[92] similar to other European countries. Farmers sowed fallow fields with hemp to shade out weed populations before planting food crops, and sometimes intercropped hemp with food crops to maintain soil fertility. Sufficient labour and cooperative processing enabled hemp industries. Hemp-processing machinery also helped to reduce costs in some areas, especially after 1800. The integration of hemp (and flax) products into many aspects of French social life helped to sustain the industry, too. Cordage and textiles were always most important, and waste fibre – rags and old rope – had supplied papermakers since the 1200s. Neither *Cannabis* nor flax was grown specifically for paper, because new fibre was too expensive; wood pulp was not used until the late 1800s.[93] Hempseeds were used mainly for feeding poultry, although by 1818 French anglers used hempseed meal for fish bait.[94] Hempseed oil had various industrial uses. French practices became globally important via emigration. In particular, the exodus of Huguenots – religious minorities – from France in the 1600s and 1700s improved the hemp (and flax) industries in Britain, Ireland, North America and other adopted countries.[95]

French trade policies sometimes benefited and sometimes harmed domestic hemp. In contrast to Great Britain, France's trade policies usually impacted farmers and manufacturers equally. By the mid-1500s, spun hemp and flax were mostly exempted from domestic taxes,[96] encouraging trade between farms (where women spun thread) and fabric manufacturers. (Many other hemp processing tasks were also women's work across Europe.) Restrictions on exports, which

40 MŒURS ET TYPES BRETONS. — *Filant le Chanvre.* — LL.

Spinning hemp in Brittany, France, *c.* 1910.

'Ropemaking: Woman Eating Hemp', advertisement for a French string-maker, c. 1910, ostensibly based on a drawing from 1750.

strengthened in the 1500s and 1600s, negatively impacted both farmers and manufacturers, and production declined; by the 1620s, France imported hemp from The Netherlands.[97] All French industries declined in the 1600s and 1700s as public debt and taxes constantly rose. Domestic hemp persisted, and experienced growth again beginning in the 1730s. Still, imports continued into the 1840s, when Russian and Italian hemp supplemented domestic supply.[98] French colonists in Algeria had planted hemp by 1875, but no commercial industry developed there.[99]

Despite its poor commercial performance outside Europe, small, semi-managed patches of *Cannabis sativa* supplied homespun industries in North America beginning in the 1600s. Farmers clothed themselves with rough fabric made from wool, flax, hemp and cotton (which was mostly imported before 1800).[100] Cordage, textile and papermaking industries arose mainly after 1700, with the immigration of skilled workers and the increasing availability of Russian hemp. *Cannabis* followed European settlers across North America, because it was weedy rather than crucial. Researchers have dated European entry into Iowa by collecting *Cannabis*-type pollen from sediment.[101] The plant grew feral in Louisiana by 1758,[102] and across eastern North America by the 1850s. Summertime aridity limits its distribution in parts of the western U.S., and short growing seasons limit its northward diffusion in Canada.

Wild plant fibres were important in the North American colonies, comparable to nettle in Europe. Colonists learned indigenous fibre plants from Native Americans. A significant example is 'Indian hemp': dogbane. A British observer celebrated this plant's fibre in 1775, though it was never cultivated.[103] Wild harvesting could meet household needs, but could not sustain commerce.

Imported hemp was commercially vital, but represented a geopolitical vulnerability. Colonial plant exploration enabled the Global North to begin replacing *Cannabis* hemp in the 1700s. The first significant alternative was 'East India hemp' – often just 'India hemp' – meaning jute. *Cannabis* histories have understandably confused the common names for dogbane and jute with 'Indian hemp', a name for *Cannabis indica* coined in London in 1689. Common-name confusion has sustained the myth that George Washington grew (and used) marijuana. Washington acquired 'East India hemp' seeds for trial in 1794, and repeatedly wrote to confirm that his gardener was tending the crop. Washington understandably ordered the gardener to 'make the most' of the 'India hemp' seed,[104] because jute was a promising new fibre source. American ships carried cargoes of 'India hemp' by 1796, and in 1807 the British East India Company agreed to supply the imperial fleet with 'India hemp'.[105] At that time, a British writer hoped that 'we shall be independent of the Russian and Polish . . . supplies of hemp' (although a critic complained: 'To be dependent upon India would be worse than [being] dependent upon Russia').[106] Washington hoped 'India hemp' might replace *sativa* hemp; however, he was equally excited about the European forage crop sainfoin (*Onobrychis viciifolia*).[107] His gardener succeeded with jute, maintaining a plot into 1796.[108] Nonetheless, 'India hemp' was never adopted in the States.[109] Jute did not ultimately supply maritime-quality products, but it replaced *Cannabis* in cheap ropes, carpets and sackcloth.

During the American Revolutionary War (1775–81), British control of the Baltic made imported hemp more expensive, and thus encouraged domestic production.[110] *Cannabis sativa* was introduced to Kentucky in 1775.[111] Kentucky would become the centre of the American hemp industry, but American hemp never supplanted Russian hemp. After the Revolutionary War, U.S. merchants re-entered the Baltic trade independently and developed global commercial networks to supply goods (and specie) that Russian merchants would exchange for hemp.[112]

When hemp finally achieved commercial success in the U.S., it supplied the cotton industry. The invention of the cotton gin in 1793 reduced labour costs, and helped cotton to become the South's dominant crop. Kentucky grew little cotton, but its antebellum economy depended on sales of hempen baling twine, sacks and ropes to cotton growers. Domestic sailcloth was normally made from flax, but

A Kentucky Hemp Field.

Kentucky hemp field, c. 1910.

the Napoleonic Wars (1803–15) raised hemp prices to the benefit of Kentucky producers. *Cannabis* was an economic staple for the state by 1810, although the industry stagnated once European hemp imports recovered after 1815.[113]

U.S. commercial hemp industries grew slowly. Labour posed a constant problem: hemp work was unpopular, and free labourers avoided it. 'Without hemp, slavery might not have flourished in Kentucky, since other agricultural products . . . were not conducive to the extensive use of bondsmen.'[114] American producers never widely adopted water retting, because of the labour costs. Farmers considered retting a hazardous task, owing to 'the infectious nature of the air generated from th[e] putrifying [stalks]'.[115] Slave owners refused to send slaves into retting ponds, and free workers refused themselves. Producers supplied small quantities of pond-retted fibre into the 1850s, but the fibres were poorly processed and unusable. 'American hemp' became synonymous with low-strength, dew-retted fibre; no one considered it a safe substitute for Russian hemp.[116]

Entrepreneurs and government boosters repeatedly tried to improve U.S. hemp production, with little success. Hundreds of patents failed to produce an economically successful hemp-breaking machine;

retting with chemical solvents instead of water failed too.[117] The u.s. Navy built a rope factory in Tennessee, hoping to make maritime cordage and encourage water-retting, but the investment failed. In 1858, the finest Russian hemp cost $215 per ton in Boston, while inferior American hemp cost $445 per ton.[118] Farmers complained that foreign hemp glutted the market, but shipbuilders and rope-makers had more political clout. Imported hemp remained tariff-free. Although u.s. production persisted until 1958 and rose when wars temporarily increased demand, the American hemp economy peaked before 1860.[119]

Kentucky's success with dew-retted hemp encouraged commercial farming in other states, especially Missouri, whose production was poised to surpass Kentucky's in 1860.[120] However, the u.s. Civil War (1861–5) decimated the hemp industry in several ways.[121] First, Kentucky did not secede from the u.s., but its principal markets did. Hemp growers could not sell their produce to the rebel South; Missouri was similarly affected. Even before the war, cotton growers complained of their reliance on Kentucky, and invented cotton, wood and metal ties to replace *Cannabis* twine. The post-war cotton boom enabled a widespread shift to metal ties. Second, the u.s. government quit subsidizing domestic hemp in 1862. Growers could no longer economically transport a bulky raw material to eastern cities. Although war stimulated demand, this withered with peace. Third, after emancipation, freed slaves generally refused to return to hemp. Post-war hemp farmers sought labour-saving techniques to replace slave labour, but large farmers shifted to other crops (often tobacco) and hemp devolved to sharecroppers and poor independent farmers.[122]

In 1855 the u.s. *Cannabis sativa* hemp crop failed owing to the weather. The Kentucky state government dispatched an envoy to France to buy hempseed, but he could acquire only a fraction of the quantity needed. Planters tried Russian hempseed, but the crop was disappointing.[123] Then, in 1857, Kentucky newspapers began advertising 'cultivated Chinese Hemp Seed'.[124] Chinese hemp cultivars represent *indica*. European plant explorers encountered Chinese *má* in the early 1800s, and '*Cannabis chinensis*' was grown in botanical gardens in Austria

1094 - MAUVES (Loire-Inf.) — Rouissage du chanvre en Loire

Industrial retting of *indica* hemp during the First World War, Loire River, France, *c.* 1918.

(1827) and France (1846). Chinese hempseeds were widely distributed to French farmers from 1850.[125] In France, the taller Chinese cultivars outperformed *sativa* varieties, and hempseed producers provided a reliable supply for continued planting. In Western Europe, *indica* hemp became dominant across landscapes, so that farmers who still planted *sativa* saw the crop lose its valued characters after just one or two seasons through genetic outcrossing.[126] In North America, the abundance of feral *sativa* similarly encouraged outcrossing, and seed remained scarce for the preferred East Asian varieties.[127] Even in 1902 U.S. farmers required regular inputs of *indica* hempseed, including packets sent from American missionaries in China.[128] 'Kentucky hemp' was not a genetically stable cultivar, but a name indicating the conceptual centrality of the state in U.S. hemp history.

Kentucky hemp spread widely during the 1880s, when a last, minor boom forestalled the North American hemp collapse. Expansion of grain farming in the Great Plains states and Canadian provinces stimulated local hemp production to supply twine, burlap and rope for harvesting and shipping grain crops. Early producing states were Missouri (production lasted from 1835 until 1890) and Illinois (1842–1902).[129] Twine demand increased after 1879, when a key invention enabled agricultural machinery to tie cords and thereby encouraged *indica* hemp farming in Midwestern states.[130] California also received *indica* hempseeds by 1912.[131] As hemp spread, demand declined in Kentucky, where many farmers stopped growing *Cannabis*. Manufacturers everywhere shifted to imports. Even in 1843, Kentucky bought 1,600 tons of unfinished hemp from Missouri.[132]

U.S. hemp crashed in the 1890s, because Mexico-grown henequen replaced *Cannabis* in twine.[133] Henequen made smoother cords that were less likely to tangle in farm machinery. In 1905 a Kentucky historian wrote, 'Manufacturing of hemp has nearly disappeared.'[134] Wisconsin was the main producer in the moribund twentieth-century market, which focused on commercial twine (used to tie parcels) rather than more valuable agricultural twine.[135] By 1923 an American twine expert regretted his country's reliance on Mexican henequen,[136] but overall sisal, harakeke and abacá were more important. In 1927 *Cannabis* provided 0.47 per cent of cordage sold in the U.S.[137] *Cannabis* prohibition began ten years later.

Most societies worldwide shifted away from *Cannabis* hemp during the 1800s, replacing it with new technology. The decline of hemp in western Europe is apparent in lake sediments. In most landscapes, *Cannabis* pollen was most abundant in the early 1800s and disappeared almost completely by 1900.[138] By the 1830s, steel manufacturers made

PEORIA, ILL. AND ST. LOUIS, MO., JULY 9, 1889.

ROCK BOTTOM PRICES.

TO THE TRADE:—Owing to the large oat crop now to be cut, there will be a large demand for Binder Twine. We have a fair stock for prompt shipment from Peoria and Rockford, Ills., and St. Louis, Mo. We have a larger stock of Manila and Sisal running 550 feet to the pound, and to reduce the same, we quote you a special rock bottom price of 14½ cents; also to introduce Russian Hemp, which we guarantee to be equal to American Hemp, we quote you a special low price of 12½ cents. We will also make you as low prices as anyone else on corresponding grades of twine.

Above F.O.B. cars as above, payable Sept. 1st. If longer time wanted, to say one-third September, October and November, with interest from September 1st, at 8 per cent. it will be given. We solicit your immediate orders.

Respectfully yours,

KINGMAN & CO.

WE ARE MANUFACTURERS AND LEADING JOBBERS OF BINDER TWINE.

American agricultural twine advertisement. 1889.

wires and chains that could replace most types of hempen cordage. *Cannabis* retained value longest for specific nautical rigging. Ropes remained better than wires in fixed rigging as long as sails remained in use.[139] Cables were the last bit of rigging for which *Cannabis* retained value, but hempen cables were nearly obsolete by the 1890s, replaced with steel or abacá.[140] The last big sailing ships – the metal-hulled, five-masted windjammers introduced in the 1870s – used tiny

Top: A ship's cable 20 cm (8 in.) in diameter and 200 m (656 ft) long.
Bottom: Workers from the factory that produced the cable, c. 1890s.

quantities of plant fibre, whether *Cannabis* or not, compared with earlier, smaller ships. Coal-burning steam engines supplanted sails from the early 1800s onwards. Before the First World War, European Navies had mostly abandoned sailing in favour of fossil-fuel energy. Ocean-going steamships carried masts and sails for security into the 1900s, but the transition away from hemp was, like a sunset, gradual and irreversible. Technological change disfavoured hemp globally, even in Russia (where many producers had switched to flax by 1872) and France (where hempen cloth was a 'textile of yesterday' in 1896).[141]

The Industrial Revolution disfavoured hemp because *Cannabis* resisted mechanization. Machines replaced people in flax, cotton and other plant-fibre industries, driving down costs all around *Cannabis*. Although hemp had been a subsistence staple for centuries, purchased substitutes became more affordable and more desirable. In China, *indica* hemp had clothed the poor for millennia; silk, cotton and ramie signified greater wealth and status. In the 1890s cotton thread imported from India shifted Chinese textile industries away from hemp, but only for those with money to buy thread. By the 1920s, Chinese factories began selling cotton cloth less expensively than homespun fabric, but the poorest still had no cash. Hempen clothes became objects of ridicule, signifying backwardness as well as the onerous labour of hemp processing, which many people were pleased to abandon. By the 1950s, hemp clothing persisted only in the most marginal areas. Elsewhere hempen cloth was just for sacks. The communist state allowed people to exchange hempen garments for cotton in the 1950s, as a symbol of modernization.[142] Hemp had seemed outdated much earlier, too. Chinese officials had begun inducing people to replace hemp with cotton centuries earlier, by 1300 CE.[143]

Russian hemp disappeared from global markets with the Russian Civil War (1917–22). Hemp remained important domestically in the Soviet Union, where imported substitutes were often too expensive. Yet even Soviet authorities needed to coerce production. The state set quotas for collective farms, and awarded medals to farmers with particularly high production. Notably, Soviet statisticians tracked

Medal for
exemplary
hemp *Cannabis*
cultivation,
Soviet Union,
c. 1950s.

'southern hemp', meaning *indica* hempseed and fibre cultivars in
Turkmenistan, as well as 'northern hemp', meaning Russian *sativa*.
'Southern hemp' remained miniscule within the Soviet Union. It failed
in mid-latitude locations, while 'northern hemp' failed in the south.[144]

Vicissitudes in the supply of other plant fibres represented throes
in the global decline of hemp. The case of abacá – grown almost exclusively in the Philippines, Malaysia and Indonesia – is a key example.
U.S. merchant ships began using abacá in the 1840s. In 1869 American
manufacturers made more rope from abacá than from any other plant,
and in 1871 the U.S. Navy exclusively bought abacá,[145] although it again
bought Russian hemp later that century. Abacá proved nearly equal to
hemp, but was much less expensive. The U.S. became dependent on abacá
as the colonial power in the Philippines during the early 1900s. In
1927 some 79 per cent of U.S. cordage came from abacá.[146] When Japan
seized the Philippines during the Second World War (1939–45), abacá
imports ceased and the U.S. temporarily encouraged domestic hemp

again. Despite *Cannabis* prohibition, which began in 1937, farmers could still grow hemp by registering with the government and paying a nominal fee of $1.[147] The government's wartime 'Hemp for Victory' programme offered farmers guaranteed prices, and proved an expensive failure. In 1943 a U.S. business magazine called the programme a '$25,000,000 hemp headache'.[148] 'Hemp for Victory' was probably unnecessary, because plant-fibre imports from Central America and India increased to meet wartime demand. After the war, the U.S.

Monoecious hemp held promise for European farmers beginning in the 1930s,
as reported in this French magazine, *Life in the Country*, of 1957.

government sold its hemp investments at a loss.[149] *Cannabis* production sputtered along in Wisconsin until 1958.[150]

Cannabis prohibition was increasingly enforced worldwide after the Second World War. In the U.S., fears that hemp production contributed to marijuana trades were influential,[151] and the idea was exported through American political-economic dominance. By the 1960s, international hemp commerce had effectively disappeared, but domestic industries persisted in the Soviet Union, Italy, France, Yugoslavia, Romania, Hungary, Poland, Turkey, China, Korea and Japan.[152] When synthetics like rayon and polypropylene began replacing plant fibres in the 1970s, hemp *Cannabis* declined further. Ironically, European producers gained a profitable minor market from drug *Cannabis* beginning in the 1960s, when hempen rolling papers became fashionable in the Global North.[153] Among the countries where commercial hemp survived after 1950, cultivation had mostly ended or become illegal by 1990.

In the 1990s industrial hemp regained attention in the Global North as concerns about environmental sustainability caused people to seek renewable, plant-based resources. The so-called hemp renaissance has meant modest success for the plant. Cheap oil and the politics of prohibition continue to discourage industrial hemp. Small industries in several European and East Asian countries (and Canada) produce edible hempseeds, seed oil and fibre, which are used to manufacture foods, plastics, wood substitutes, cordage, fabric and animal feed. In a bow to prohibition, marketed hempseeds are commonly heat-sterilized to prevent germination. Current hemp industries mostly rely on highly selected *Cannabis* varieties from professional plant breeders. For instance, monoecious varieties (which were developed in the 1930s and have male and female flowers on each plant) offer greater uniformity among individuals, reducing processing costs.[154]

Hemp *Cannabis* experienced a long, steady rise in political-economic importance over the centuries before 1850, followed by a remarkably swift decline. In contrast, drug *Cannabis* has experienced nearly the opposite historical trajectory.

four

The Drug Goes Global

In contrast to hemp *Cannabis*, which dispersed as a commodity valued by political and economic authorities, drug *Cannabis* spread primarily with social underclasses.

The global diffusion of *indica* was an outcome of the way the drug affects users. Marijuana pharmacology is well established.[1] THC and other cannabinoids substitute for neurotransmitters produced within mammalian bodies that affect specific nerve receptors. The neurotransmitters and receptors together comprise the endocannabinoid system, which contributes to perceptions of pain, anxiety and hunger, and to memory processes, metabolism and thermoregulation. As a drug, *Cannabis* is particularly effective as an antispasmodic, an appetite stimulant and an analgesic. Importantly, at low doses, marijuana might stimulate appetite, but at high doses it can suppress hunger. Lethal overdoses are impossible owing to marijuana's low toxicity, although extremely high doses are unpleasant for anyone. In nineteenth-century Central Africa and Madagascar, traditional authorities meted out massive doses of *indica* as punishments.[2]

Drug *Cannabis* is psychoactive and mildly hallucinogenic. The folk species sativa – mostly associated with the *bhang* and *ganja* cultures – is generally a pseudo-stimulant, generating racing, expansive thought and manic action sometimes in accompaniment. The other folk species, indica, is a pseudo-depressant associated originally with *charas*. Indica commonly produces mellow, sensual thought, often accompanying

Half a gram of *ganja*, two strains, in a sealable plastic bag. UK, 2014.

lethargy and heightened sensitivity to physical sensations,[3] which might be pleasant or unpleasant. Indeed, either folk species can produce paranoid, violent and other unsavoury thoughts, possibly alongside uncomfortable physiological effects – elevated pulse and blood pressure, nausea and dizziness. Bad trips happen, even if marijuana is relatively safe.[4]

Genetic variation among people and plants makes subjective effects potentially individualistic. People experience drug *Cannabis* differently depending on personal health and genetics,[5] as well as environmental conditions. For instance, some people suffer chronic endocannabinoid deficiency, but others may benefit from exogenous cannabinoids only when malnutrition or stress impairs normal functions.[6] The plant's genetic variability expands the range of possible experiences. Farmers and plant scientists have developed many cultivars that each produce distinctive subjective effects.

People have always had diverse experiences on drug *Cannabis*. For instance, in the 1670s 'eight or tenne' British sailors tried *bhang* tea in eastern India. Two sailors experienced no effects (common among first-timers), one 'wept bitterly all the Afternoon', one was 'terrified with fear', one was 'quarrelsome', two 'Sat sweatinge . . . in Exceeding Measure' and four or five 'lay upon the Carpets[,] highly Complementinge each Other in high termes'. The sailor who described this party decided *bhang* was of 'Such a bewitchinge Sottish nature, that whoever Use it but one month or two cannot forsake it without much difficultie'.[7] In current societies, about 10 per cent of regular users develop behavioural addiction.[8]

The subjective effects of drug *Cannabis* are still more complicated because they depend on the setting of drug use and the mindset of the user, conditions that vary within and between societies in historically traceable ways.[9] Beliefs about marijuana's effects establish expectations for both users and observers; pharmacology remains important, yet social discourse is deeply part of a user's experience. Of course, no two individuals share identical attitudes and behaviour.

Since 1500, drug *Cannabis* has dispersed alongside labour underclasses because the drug enhances the ability of workers to endure lives of physically demanding but mentally dulling tasks, constant occupational hazards, poor nutrition and exposure to infectious diseases. At least, the *idea* that marijuana can be good for hard labourers has sustained the plant's migrations. A Dutch account in 1598 of India coarsely described *bhang*-using social groups as 'whores, . . . soldiers [and] . . . slaves'.[10] The centrality of sex workers, low-ranking warmakers and exploited labourers extends through *Cannabis* history. These underclasses were mostly silent in the historical record, although others wrote about the drug among the lowly as well as occasional middle-class experimentations. Since the 1960s, middle-class people in the Global North have adopted marijuana, but socially high-ranking users have always been uncommon. The global diffusion of *indica* illustrates that reality-altering drugs attract people whose lives are unhappy.[11]

The globalization of drug *Cannabis* began when Portuguese sailors travelled around the coast of Africa to India and encountered *bhang* in the western Indian Ocean. The Portuguese in India, like Galen centuries before, struggled to make sense of the familiar-looking plant with an unfamiliar use. In 1578, a Portuguese naturalist wrote: 'Bangue is a plant similar to *cáñamo*, . . . [and] the Canabis [*sic*] of the Latins, as Dioscorides described.' Faithful to precedent and knowing Dioscorides only in Latin translation, the writer attributed ancient Greek hempseed uses to sixteenth-century South Asians, but also described indigenous psychoactive use. He ultimately concluded: 'One should not confuse [*bangue*] with *cáñamo*, although [*bangue*] really looks like it.'[12]

By 1563 Europeans had certainly tried drug *Cannabis* in India, and adopted specific ideas about the drug. 'Many Portuguese . . . have taken it, and . . . experienced the same [effects]' as Indian servants, who used *bhang* 'so as not to feel work, to be happy, and to have a craving for food'.[13] By 1600 *bhang* was 'verie much used by the Indians, and likewise by some Portingales, but most by the slaves thereby to forget their labour'.[14] Drug *Cannabis* 'gives them strength and vigour', wrote a European traveller who was astonished at the loads borne by low-caste Indian porters in the 1670s despite paltry rations.[15] European sailors adopted and initially transported this labour–drug relationship.

Group of people preparing *bhang* tea and smoking water pipes, India, 18th century.

Portuguese sailors also encountered *indica* in eastern Africa, where the *bhang* culture had arrived centuries earlier. *Cannabis* spread most rapidly in East Africa's semi-arid woodland biome, which is ecologically similar to northwestern India. In 1500 *Cannabis* had not yet arrived in the southwestern woodland biome of Africa – which stretches from modern South Africa to Angola – and probably not west of South Sudan. Drug *Cannabis* slowly entered the humid forest at the centre of

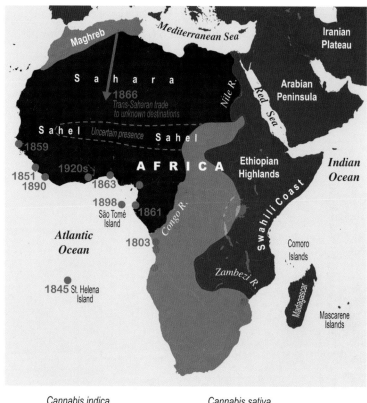

Cannabis indica
■ Distribution by c.1500 CE
■ Distribution by c.1850 CE
● Earliest documentation dates in western Africa
● Locations of cognate words to Portuguese *bangue/banga*
  (introduced likely between early 1500s and mid 1800s)

Cannabis sativa
■ West Eurasian culture
  c.1500 CE

Historic *Cannabis* distribution in Africa.

the continent, its distribution limit in 1500 perhaps the upper Congo basin. In the late 1800s European travellers considered it recently arrived in the lower Congo.[16] Drug *Cannabis* was first documented in East Africa about 1585; in Southern Africa in 1713; and in western Africa in 1803, although it certainly predated these European observations.[17]

Africans transformed *bhang*. Swahili-speaking traders drank *bhang* tea in the 1580s in Tanzania, but more widely *Cannabis* was taken into pre-existing drug ethnobotanies.[18] Smoking pipes were unequivocally invented in sub-Saharan Africa, independently of the Native American invention of smoking pipes for tobacco (*Nicotiana* spp.).[19] One particular technology, the African water pipe, became especially associated with *Cannabis*, but people first smoked *Datura* and, in Southern Africa, the original *dagga* (*Leonotis leonurus*).[20] 'Dagga' now means marijuana, and 'wild *dagga*' refers to *Leonotis*. After the introduction of tobacco, the New World smoke shared pipe bowls with Old World herbs.

Sailors on Portuguese ships first encountered and adopted smoking in southeastern Africa, and transported African technology and practices worldwide. Mortality, injury and morbidity rates for European sailors were notoriously high because they had poor diets, risky work and frequent exposure to infectious diseases.[21] In Portuguese ships on the Indian Ocean, European sailors were often a minority in crews comprised mostly of South Asian labourers.[22] Cultural exchange took place among sailors. In the Atlantic, the conditions European crews experienced on slave ships were sometimes little better than those of the slaves, a condition of marginality that contributed to violence on board.[23] Common sailors were crucial to mercantile shipping, but represented low socio-economic classes in their native societies.

'I don't smoke their kind of cigars – too strong!': postcard of a man smoking an antler-based water pipe, South Africa, c. 1900.

Portuguese authorities began collecting duties on *bhang*, as well as opium, in India by the late 1500s.[24] Alongside this official valuation, some individuals valued *bhang* for personal use. The Portuguese used *indica* in Ceylon (present-day Sri Lanka) during their occupation (1505–1658). The English sailor Robert Knox – marooned in Ceylon from 1659 to 1678 – drank *bhang* to treat gastrointestinal illness. He did not know the plant but reported that 'They call it in *Portugueze Banga* . . . and this we eat Morning and Evening upon an empty Stomach. It intoxicates the Brain, and makes one giddy, without any [negative] operation.'[25] The drug perhaps relieved cramps and encouraged eating despite illness. Thomas Bowrey, who plied the East Indies in the 1670s, enjoyed *bhang* recreationally, calling it the 'Soe admirable herbe'.[26] Given the dismal environments of European sailors, these positive reviews were probably not unusual. Middle-class Dutch traders in South Africa in 1713 sometimes filled their pipes with *dagga*.[27] In Brazil, upper-class society secretively smoked drug *Cannabis* in the late 1700s.[28] In nineteenth-century Mozambique, marijuana was called 'Portugal hemp'.[29] In 1851 a British physician in Sierra Leone stated: '[*indica*] is well known to the Portuguese on this coast [western Africa]'.[30] In 1948 an Argentine physician alleged that 'Portuguese sailors' had introduced marijuana to Cuba.[31]

Dagga farmers form *Cannabis* inflorescences into masses for storage, South Africa, *c.* 1925.

GUERRE 1914 – Au camp Hindous, «Le Fumoir »
Le Narguileh qui circule de mains en mains est fait avec une vieille bouteille

Indian soldiers smoking an improvised water pipe, France, 1914.

The language of sailors spread with their ships. During the 1500s, Portuguese-speakers adopted the interchangeable terms *banga* and *bangue* (from similar-sounding Hindi and Swahili terms). '*Bangue*' was a trade item in Indonesia by 1708, and '*bange*' and '*pango*' were used in Brazil by the late 1700s.[32] In other parts of the sixteenth-century Portuguese maritime empire, derivatives of *banga/bangue* remain in use: '*bangi*' in Malaysia; '*bange*' in Mozambique; '*banga*' in Cameroon; and '*bangué*', '*epangue*' and '*mpangu*' in coastal Angola.[33] These words represent a cultural inheritance from common European sailors.

Banga and *bangue* were borrowed into English. The first report of *indica* in the Atlantic World is from England in 1689, when Robert Hooke reported horticultural trials of '*Bangue*' seeds from South Asia.[34] By 1800, English-speakers used *banga/bangue* for putative botanical species in South Asia, hashish sweetmeats in the Levant and herbal marijuana in Madagascar and Southeast Asia.[35] As the English gained familiarity with India, *banga* and *bangue* were no longer considered borrowed Portuguese, but borrowed Hindi.

Portuguese trade stimulated population movement among other peoples. In western Central Africa, sailors brought *Cannabis* to the coast in the 1500s. Portuguese demand for slaves and material goods brought people westwards from eastern Africa. *Cannabis* moved with this migration, composed predominantly of enslaved people whose survivors entered the transatlantic trade. One instance of trade-mediated diffusion occurred in the early 1800s when Portuguese firearms dealers sent a representative to a previously isolated leader. 'Not only did the [trade representative] show his new friend how to use the gun . . . he also taught him how to smoke diamba, and told him wonderful stories about the white men and their riches.'[36] This particular introduction helped to produce a politico-religious move-ment – the so-called Bena-diamba ('marijuana brotherhood') – which devolved into the BaLulua ethnic identity in the 1880s.[37]

Multiple diffusion pathways for *Cannabis indica* remain evident in Central Africa. Coastal groups that were historic trade intermediaries use derivatives of Portuguese *bangue/banga*, while inland groups use terms traceable to eastern African languages.[38] The most important inland term is *diamba*, including cognates *liamba* and *riamba*, and plural forms beginning *ma-*. In many coastal areas, *diamba* became dominant as slavery brought more and more people from inland.

The economy that carried *indica* into the Atlantic depended on cheap labour. Common sailors were cheap, and the massive, forced migration of the slave trade was entirely about cheapening labour. Enslaved Africans shaped the subsistence economy of the tropical Atlantic World, which widely depended on African plants and know-ledge applied in new contexts. *Cannabis indica* was part of the subsistence ethnobotany of some slaves who entered the Middle Passage in coastal Central Africa.

The idea that drug *Cannabis* was introduced to the Americas – particularly Brazil – via the slave trade was proposed in 1867,[39] and has become widely accepted despite minimal research. The main evidence for African introduction is linguistic similarities between Brazilian Portuguese and Central African languages. Additionally, in the early 1900s a Brazilian naturalist collected folklore that supports linguistic inference: 'The seeds [were] brought by unfortunate captives [who] tied [the seeds] in pouches along the edges of their wraps and loincloths,

[and] who ultimately disseminated [drug *Cannabis*] to all of South America and the Antilles.'[40]

Although this story is not repeated in other collections of Afro-Brazilian folklore,[41] it is plausible. Slaves entered the Middle Passage mostly unprepared and often unclothed, but many crops crossed the Atlantic on slave ships.[42] There are similar tales of the concealed transport of rice seeds,[43] which are approximately the same size as hempseeds.

Indeed, the transport of drug *Cannabis* seed by a slave was observed in Gabon during the 1840s or '50s. The American observer did not encounter *indica* near the coast, 'but once . . . saw a few . . . seeds in the possession of a slave . . . He was carefully preserving them, intending to plant them in the country to which he should be sold.' Unfortunately, the American recorded few details because 'Hasheesh and the *Cannabis Indica* are so well known that it is not necessary to say anything about them here.' Instead, he repeated contemporaneous European drug discourse: 'Insanity is often its ultimate result', and 'the negroes' seemed unable to resist the drug plant's 'gradual but sure advances' into new areas.[44] The rare chance that an outsider observed and recorded *indica* seed-saving suggests that marijuana was not unusual among Central African slaves.

The provisioning practices of slavers probably facilitated *Cannabis* diffusion. Slavers sometimes allowed captives to smoke, in Africa, aboard slave ships and in the Americas.[45] The practice increased on ships during the 1700s for its presumed benefits to health and morale. Most accounts of smoking certainly describe *Nicotiana* tobacco, but others are unclear. One slaver, for instance, observed Central Africans surreptitiously smoking a pipe below deck in the 1820s, but could not identify what was smoked.[46] Angolan slave-ship captains encouraged the loyalty of their sailors by supplying brandy and 'tobacco', and presumably Angolan captives were at least rarely given alcohol and 'tobacco', in line with Dutch, French and English practices.[47] Slaves probably also shared *indica* directly with slave-ship sailors. In Jamaica in 1862, freed 'Congo' slaves called the plant by a Portuguese name, *fumo* ('smoke').[48]

Slavers may have unwittingly supplied marijuana because 'tobacco' was not necessarily *Nicotiana*. Names for *Cannabis* in Brazil, used by slaves and slavers, included 'Angolan tobacco' and *maconha*, borrowed from the KiMbundu plural term *ma'kaña* ('tobacco leaves').[49] Elsewhere drug *Cannabis* was called 'Congo tobacco' and 'African tobacco'.[50] *Cannabis* smoking was widely tolerated into the 1900s, but users also developed plant nicknames – including *maconha* – to escape the notice of authorities.[51]

The deforestation, erosion and other landscape changes that accompanied slave-labour industries suited the weedy *Cannabis*. By 1860 in central Brazil *indica* grew 'everywhere'.[52] *Cannabis* became a component of vegetation that supported the lowly and resisted colonial authority. Afro-Brazilians smoked drug *Cannabis* in the 1820s, slaves in Brazil's mines smoked in the 1860s,[53] and Afro-Brazilian folklore of *diamba* persisted into the 1960s. In the 1930s the Brazilian sociologist Gilberto Freyre proposed that sugarcane plantation bosses tolerated *diamba* because it enabled slaves to endure their labour.[54] Freyre claimed that marijuana was intercropped with sugarcane, an oft-repeated story with no further evidence. Slaves probably grew *Cannabis* on marginal land,[55] rather than competing for space and soil fertility with a cash crop.

Native Americans adopted *Cannabis indica*. Indigenous Amazonians smoked *diamba* in African water pipes by 1904,[56] and probably much earlier through contact with escaped slaves. Similarly, slaves had probably brought drug *Cannabis* to Central America by the 1700s. During the 1500s and 1600s, the majority of slaves who disembarked in Spanish Central America came from Portuguese Angola and the lower Congo.[57] By 1800 the plant had entered indigenous Central American ethnobotanies as far north as Mexico.[58]

Importantly, the word *marihuana* suggests slave agency, and a faint cultural inheritance from enslaved people shipped from coastal Central Africa. The Central American term *marihuana* is a borrowing of *mariamba*, the plural of *riamba*, an older pronunciation of *diamba*. Drug *Cannabis* spread in subaltern social networks in Central America. In Colombia in the 1980s, 'marimba' meant drug *Cannabis* in a community established by escaped 'Congo' slaves in the 1500s.[59] Cognates of *mariamba* also persist in Brazil.[60] The earliest documentation of any form of *diamba* is from 1843; the term was widespread in the Atlantic during the 1800s.[61] When *maríhuana* was first written in nineteenth-century Mexico, it was a 'Mexican' term without history.[62] The African origin of *maríhuana* has been overlooked because this derived form differs superficially from *diamba*, the form that currently dominates. At some point, 'Congo' slaves used plural nouns in the trade language KiMbundu to name smoked herbs – *ma'kaña* for tobacco (and *Cannabis*) and *mariamba* for *Cannabis* – and these plural forms became established locally in the Americas.

Cannabis histories commonly mention African slaves, but provide little more than overgeneralizations. For instance, a history from 2005 tells that 'Black slaves [in the U.S.] knew of it [marijuana] from their experience of *dagga* back in Africa.'[63] This phrase includes several major errors. There is no evidence of drug *Cannabis* among U.S. slaves; Africa is a diverse continent and slaves came from identifiable areas; and essentially no slaves came to the U.S. from South Africa (suggested by the irrelevant term *dagga*).

The subsistence-oriented diffusion of drug *Cannabis* traces the diffusion of a social group from coastal western Central Africa. Slavers called slaves from this region 'Congoes', one of many pseudo-ethnic identities created to classify people based on imagined and real linguistic, geographic and behavioural similarities.[64] These designations represent social groups – slaves placed in the same category – and not cultural groups that existed prior to the slave trade. Similarly, the *diamba* iteration of drug *Cannabis* was produced through the slave trade, after 1500.

European scholars began paying substantial attention to drug *Cannabis* in the 1800s, as abolitionist challenges to slaving gained force. Emancipation assisted the diffusion of *indica*. Colonial societies worldwide replaced slavery with other exploitative labour regimes, including indentured servitude, wage slavery, compulsory service and sharecropping. African, Asian and European labourers who migrated in these regimes functionally replaced chattel slaves, performing physically demanding, mentally dulling tasks in environments of risky nutrition and disease. Post-slave labourers were shipped within a

Anonymous, *Saartje the Hotentot Venus* (Saartje Baartman), British print, 1810.

British-dominated network that connected South Asia, sub-Saharan Africa, the Americas, Australia, China and islands in the Atlantic, Indian and Pacific oceans. These labourers travelled with some possessions, and had bare income enough to attract commercial *indica* markets.

Drug *Cannabis* spread with liberated slaves. After 1808, the British and American navies captured hundreds of slave ships, generally coming from Central Africa towards Brazil and Cuba. These so-called recaptives were resettled widely, especially in Sierra Leone but also in Liberia, Jamaica, Guyana, Trinidad, South Africa, the Bahamas, Cuba, the Lesser Antilles and Brazil.[65] Recaptivity was different from, even if no better than, slavery. The British trans-shipped many of the 160,000 recaptives through the South Atlantic island St Helena, a commercial shipping node since the 1600s. An English botanist identified 'Common hemp' on the island in 1813.[66] A British physician reported in 1845 that 'the negroes' on the island valued '*diamba*' as a multi-use medicinal herbs, although he did not know the plant's identity.[67] The observed people – from western Central Africa – purchased *diamba* from South Asian sailors '[who] procure it from India'. Other recaptives carried drug *Cannabis* into the Middle Passage. In West Africa, 'its seed was brought to Sierra Leone by Congoes captured by [British] cruisers' before 1851, while in Liberia 'Congo negroes' brought marijuana 'from their old home' before 1888.[68] (*Cannabis* histories say there is no evidence of marijuana in West Africa before 1945.) Slaves and post-slave labourers suffered many health problems from poor nutrition and injuries.[69] Most notably, 'negro cachexy' – fatal loss of appetite – was a common medical diagnosis among slaves, attributed to 'grief, despondency, poor diet, hard labor, and harsh treatment'.[70] This condition was well-documented among recaptives.[71] Marijuana, an effective appetite stimulant, had market value in recaptive holding camps and receiving societies.[72] (Cachexia resulting from chemotherapy is a primary indication for medical marijuana in modern societies.)

A different set of freedpersons came from Brazil, where authorities tried to forestall emancipation by sending troublesome slaves back to Africa. After a revolt in 1835, many Afro-Brazilians migrated to coastal Togo, Benin and Nigeria. In 1863 an English traveller in Nigeria associated *diamba* with towns that had large Afro-Brazilian populations,[73] suggesting a west-to-east Atlantic crossing.

In societies that received freed slaves, drug *Cannabis* was diffused socially and did not remain associated with any specific group. In Sierra Leone, by 1851 it was grown and smoked by 'Congoes' but also 'Akoos, Eboes, and many of the other liberated African tribes, and likewise by the Maroons, Settlers, and Creoles'.[74] Similarly, in other Atlantic locations, marijuana was associated with socio-economic classes, not cultural groups, although traditional *Cannabis* cultures persisted into the mid-1900s in Brazil, Jamaica, Angola, the lower Congo and South Africa.[75] Beginning in the 1840s, the British encouraged (then required) recaptives to become indentured labourers in the Caribbean, to replace slave labour and recoup some costs of naval patrols.[76] Indentured Sierra

Leoneans introduced marijuana to Jamaica by 1862.[77] Afro-Caribbean labourers carried *Cannabis* to Central America in the late 1800s; U.S. soldiers in Panama had learned to smoke marijuana by 1920.[78]

Military service exposed many people to marijuana. In the 1800s in southern Africa, indigenous forces used drug *Cannabis* before fighting, and recreationally between battles.[79] Early users in nineteenth-century Mexico were conscripts who shared a world view and material culture similar to contemporaneous criminal prisoners.[80] Brazilian slaves who gained freedom by volunteering to fight the Paraguayan War (1864–70) introduced Euro-Brazilian soldiers to marijuana.[81] Hookah smoking was common among French troops in colonial Algeria, Tunisia and Morocco, where they shared the drug with prostitutes.[82]

Like other labour underclasses, sex workers had unhappy lives, and drugs offered brief escapes. Recent sociological surveys show that prostitutes and pornography actresses have higher rates of drug use than other women.[83] Some pornography actresses reduce anxiety with marijuana before performances, as did Egyptian prostitutes in the 1960s.[84] Historically, in French colonial Morocco prostitutes had little freedom, and spent half their income or more on *kif*, alcohol and tobacco.[85] In Europe, the enslaved South African Saartje Baartman – exhibited in Britain and France as 'Hottentot Venus' in the 1810s – smoked a *dagga* pipe while she was ogled.[86]

Drug use was entangled in broad social transformations within colonialism. As European authority expanded in South Africa, Baartman's Khoisan culture declined. Its population spiralled downwards with drug use, escaping brutal realities with copious amounts of imported alcohol and tobacco, and locally grown wild *dagga* and *indica*. The first documentation of drug *Cannabis* in South Africa (1713) described it as 'wild hemp, which the [Dutch] plant . . . principally for the usage of the Hottentots'.[87] The Dutch paid the Khoisan with drugs rather than food, goods or cash.[88]

The agency of African labourers in the diffusion of marijuana has been overlooked because colonial authorities focused on drug use among South Asian indentured labourers.[89] After 1834, the British transported South Asians globally to provide post-slave agricultural labour, particularly on sugar plantations in Mauritius, South Africa, the British Caribbean and Australia.[90] These labourers transported drug *Cannabis*, following innumerable Lascars – South Asian sailors on European ships – since the 1600s. In the Caribbean, British authorities knew about drug use among labourers through their experience in colonial India. As South Asian labour migration grew, so did the salience of *indica* use in receiving societies, especially Jamaica, Trinidad and Guyana.[91] Authorities adopted the Hindi term *ganja* in laws to control the plant, and the legal vocabulary established the primary common name for marijuana in the region.[92] In nineteenth-century India, *ganja* was not socially equivalent to *bhang*. *Ganja* was a substitute for hashish and sometimes opium among labour underclasses.[93] *Ganja* had replaced *bhang* in the drug–labour relationship the Portuguese encountered in the 1500s. *Bhang* had become more of a social tonic, somewhat like tea or coffee in Europe.[94]

Ganja first experienced maritime diffusion after 1500, around the Bay of Bengal. In South Asia, *ganja* dispersed along the eastern Indian coast to Ceylon. The drug's name was 'comsa' in Sinhalese in the late 1600s, although a more ancient name – *sanal*, a recognizable form of the Indo-European root *śāṇa* – persisted at least until 1870.[95] *Ganja* had crossed the Bay of Bengal to Southeast Asia by the 1600s. Thomas Bowrey found that '*Bangha* . . . groweth in many places of this coast [central eastern India]; but Gangah is brought from the Island Sumatra.'[96] Common names for cannabis are Hindi loan-words in many Southeast Asian languages, including Bahasa Malay *ganja* (first recorded in the late 1600s) and Thai *kạn chā* and Vietnamese *cầnsa* (terms known from the 1900s).[97] Separately, Chinese *má* culture entered the Southeast Asian highlands, anciently and in the 1700s, when persecution drove minority groups from China. In the Hmong language, cannabis is *maj*.[98] European botanists in Southeast Asia recognized *Cannabis* widely in the 1800s, as both drug and potential source of hemp.[99] These observers liked the fibre qualities of some drug strains,[100] suggesting a mix of *má* genetics and *ganja* practices.

Customers visiting hookah proprietors, Bangladesh, *c.* 1910.

The archaeological and historical record for *Cannabis* in Southeast Asia is poor. Fibre uses remain important in artisanal textile industries in the highlands. In lowland, coastal areas *indica* has for centuries been primarily a drug crop, although not a particularly prominent one. Other fibre crops performed better in the lowlands, and other drugs were more popular.

By the 1600s around the Bay of Bengal *ganja* was a stronger alternative to *bhang*, especially because *ganja* was increasingly smoked rather than eaten. In eastern India, Bowrey found *ganja* smoking 'a very Speedy way to be besotted'. It had 'a more pleasant Operation' than *bhang* tea, and was considered a more effective aphrodisiac. Users paid five times more for imported *ganja* than for local *bhang*.[101] Travelling labourers preferred *ganja* probably because it carried more psychoactivity by weight and volume than *bhang*, ideal for people with limited personal space. South Asian users have carried pouches of *ganja* since at least the 1200s.[102] Hashish similarly has a favourable psychoactivity-to-volume ratio, and the drugs were often interchangeable.[103] However, *ganja* was more characteristic of the eastern Indian areas where most indentured labourers embarked. Hashish also does not include seeds – it did not directly aid the dissemination of *Cannabis*.

Drug markets developed to supply post-slavery labour under-classes, including populations with and without a history of *Cannabis*. In 1828 small-timers began advertising local marijuana in Brazilian newspapers.[104] In Senegambia in the 1850s, a French traveller recorded '*diamba*' as 'tobacco' among Manding-speaking merchants from Gambia.[105] People became increasingly reliant on international markets for food and medicine, including drug *Cannabis*, during the nineteenth century. In the 1870s, 'Arabs' in East Africa bought *bhang* from Bombay.[106] Ethnic Chinese traders imported *ganja* to Guyana, presumably from India via London.[107] Portuguese Angolan exporters supplied marijuana to Gabon in 1870, advertised in Brazil in 1883, and sold 'notable quan-tities' to labourers in São Tomé by the 1890s, even though the plant grew 'abundantly around the living quarters' of the indentured Angolan workers.[108] Brazilians also exported 'tobacco' to West Africa's Slave Coast (present-day Togo, Benin and Nigeria).[109] In Mexico, herbal-ists sold *marihuana* to prisoners and military conscripts, among other medicinal plants.[110] Migrant labourers – of African, Asian, European and Native American descent – were important in developing infor-mal markets, which became black markets as *Cannabis* prohibition unfolded. In the 1920s and 1930s, Sierra Leonean mariners dispersed marijuana in West Africa between Gambia and Ghana. Lascars carried *ganja* and hashish to London.[111] New York City police caught sailors with the drug, both Sierra Leoneans (1938) and South Asians (1940).[112]

The earliest certain introduction of marijuana to the U.S. was by immigrants from southwest Asia.[113] In 1895, 'Arabs . . . Armenians [and] Turks' grew *Cannabis indica* in central California to supply hash to compatriots in San Francisco, and to smoke 'kiff' themselves.[114] This 'kiff' might have been herbal marijuana straight, or mixed with tobacco. The Arabic term *kif* is associated nowadays with a mixture smoked in northwestern Africa's Maghreb region.[115] However, *kif* is also a nickname of *indica*, roughly meaning '*the* high'. *Kif* is a mental state – which has been translated as 'blessed repose' – recognized across the Islamic Mediterranean and into Iran.[116] There are many pathways to *kif*, including music, meditation and drugs. In the mid-1800s in the

Maghreb, *takrouri* was the proper name of herbal drug *Cannabis*, despite its common appellation *kif*.[117]

The history of *Cannabis* in the Maghreb is poorly known.[118] Moorish documents from the Islamic Golden Age do not mention it. In the earliest European documentation (1840s), *Cannabis* was well integrated into society. The name *takrouri*, whose etymology is unknown, is unlike other Mediterranean names. In other contexts, the Arabic term *takruri* has layered meanings. In the early 1900s it was a pejorative term for West African pilgrims to Mecca; *Takrur* was the name of the ancient Ghana Empire (800s–1200s CE) in the western Sahel.[119] These significations suggest quite tenuously that Sahelian Africans introduced drug *Cannabis* to the Maghreb. The history of *indica* in the Sahel is unknown. Pre-Columbian smoking pipes are known from Mali.[120] By the 1860s, Algerian merchants annually sold 17,000 kg (37,000 lb) of drug *Cannabis* into trans-Saharan caravans towards the Sahel.[121]

In any case, Levantine *kif* did not endure in California, although plants may have escaped cultivation. Instead, drug *Cannabis* entered the U.S. in the early 1900s in two primary ways. First, merchant sailors carried marijuana to Atlantic ports. From ports in the southeastern U.S. from about 1910 marijuana spread among labour underclasses, which were predominantly African-American as a result of slavery and segregation. In New Orleans, prostitutes adopted marijuana, as did musicians who provided other entertainment in bordellos. These musicians created jazz. Lyrics celebrated marijuana in the 1920s, and as musicians travelled to perform, so did drug *Cannabis*.[122] By the 1930s, *Cannabis* commerce extended from Central America to the northeastern U.S., supplying participants in the jazz scene, where marijuana smokers were 'vipers' and alcohol drinkers were 'lushies'.[123]

In the western U.S., *marihuana* arrived overland from Mexico. Herbalists sold it in northern Mexico by the 1890s and prisoners tried to smuggle it into an Arizona jail in 1897,[124] but the main diffusion happened after 1900. In California the authorities became increasingly concerned about 'locoweed'.[125] During the 1910s, demand grew

151   Nègres au Café Maure   Collections ND Phot

Sahelian men playing a board game at an Algerian café, c. 1910.

sufficiently to support commercial sales in New Mexico and Texas, where storekeepers advertised *marihuana* leaves and inflorescences.[126] The imported drugs included seeds, which enabled outdoor production in several states by the 1920s, as far from the border as Kansas.[127] By 1930, limited quantities were grown in California, where it was stereotypically associated with 'Negroes and Mexicans', although much 'was smuggled [in] on fruit boats from South America'.[128] Marijuana production remained negligible in the U.S. until the late 1970s.[129]

However, medicinal *Cannabis indica* was widely grown long before the 1960s marijuana boom. Colonial test farms included *indica* in Portuguese Angola (beginning in 1803), and French Senegal (late 1800s).[130] The U.S. government provided instructions to herbal medicine farmers in 1915, although plots had been sown a decade earlier in Texas, Virginia and South Carolina, where production continued into the 1930s.[131] The Texas farm acquired its seeds from Mexico. Kentucky and Illinois produced medicinal marijuana in the 1920s from *indica* hemp that had no commercial value as fibre.[132] Additionally, the U.S. army planted marijuana in Panama in the 1920s for testing its effects on soldiers.[133]

As marijuana became popular in the Global North, people increasingly noticed feral *Cannabis*. Once established, self-seeded *Cannabis* is nearly impossible to eliminate. Small, dispersed stands easily escape humans, but not seed-eating birds.[134] Songbirds carried drug plants far and wide in the 1800s and 1900s, though people did not initially realize this. In 1891 North American bird lovers were advised to cut birdseed costs by growing their own hemp, 'in the garden or any out of the way corner'.[135] At the turn of the twentieth century, North American birdseed came from *indica* hemp, as did supplies imported from East Asia.[136] In New York City in 1938 police hoped to catch people planting marijuana in empty lots, but discovered that the culprits were birds. The authorities soon required birdseed sold in the city to be heat sterilized.[137] Elsewhere, *Cannabis*–bird interactions were unhindered. In the 1960s North American marijuana aficionados learned to collect feral *Cannabis*. The quality was low, but the plants contained up to 2 per cent THC; commercial marijuana has about 8–23 per cent THC.[138] Beginning in the 1980s the U.S. government spent millions annually to uproot ditchweed, focusing particularly on states that had once produced Kentucky *indica* hemp.

In Australia the authorities have considered drug *Cannabis* a noxious weed since the 1930s, coincident with the global rise of prohibition, but

A rough field guide to feral marijuana. U.S., 1960s.

Anti-drug police insignia patch, U.S., 1990s.

the plant first arrived in 1802 as *indica* seed shipped from India to New South Wales as a potential fibre crop. Although hemp failed, the plant survived. A hemp promoter observed feral *Cannabis* in New South Wales in 1846, but no one else noticed until 1938, when *indica* grew up and down the east coast.[139] At that time, some Queensland farmers reportedly 'supplement[ed] their incomes' by supplying 'certain Afghans, who had brought the habit [of smoking *Cannabis*] from their home country'.[140] Australian authorities blamed the noxious weed on U.S. prohibition: 'The ban [on] hemp in Hawaii [shifted production to Australia because] a large proportion of the supplies for the East had previously emanated from [Hawaii].'[141] *Cannabis indica* grew on the islands by 1934, but no evidence exists for a Hawaiian drug trade,[142] unlikely given British India's well-established commerce. Although agronomists contemplated whether medicinal *indica* horticulture 'might be encouraged . . . to augment dairying [profits]',[143] Australians lost interest in *indica* again until 1964, when authorities and marijuana experimentalists realized that self-seeded, high-THC *Cannabis* occupied 200 hectares along the Hunter River valley. The so-called Hunter Valley infestation initiated the marijuana boom of the 1960s, and its War-on-Drugs backlash, in Australia.[144]

Liamba...

psychic drug of the jungle

Drug *Cannabis* was an exotic Brazilian herb to readers of *Fate*,
a pulpy American magazine of the supernatural (1952).

Charas also travelled widely after 1500, but its expansion did not
directly affect *Cannabis* distribution. Napoleon's troops discovered
hashish in Egypt in 1798.[145] Perhaps drug *Cannabis* was known earlier
in Europe, but it did not become an enduring part of society.[146] (The
Pantagruélion herb of the sixteenth-century French scholar François
Rabelais is a common conjecture, but he describes hemp rope on
ships.)[147] When Napoleon's troops returned to France, hashish imports
followed, and others learned to enjoy drug *Cannabis*. In the early 1900s,
India was the primary supplier, relying on smugglers to bring hashish
through the Suez Canal into the Mediterranean.[148] Marijuana was hardly
known in Europe before the 1950s, when popular media carried images
of the drug from the Americas. *Cannabis indica* farming in Europe did
not clearly exist until the 1970s, and only in the 1990s did domestic
production begin to match imports in some countries.[149] Until the
1990s, drug *Cannabis* in Europe was almost exclusively hashish; *ganja* has
become popular recently.

Phone credit card, U.S., 1994.

Les femmes qui fument.

LE NARGHILÉ

AHK
326

Quel bizarre instrument ! que fume-t-on la dedans ?
Du tabac d'Orient   On aspire fortement par le bout de
l'appareil qui correspond par un canal souple à un réser-
voir rempli de liquide parfumé.   La sensation est délicieu-
se mais le narghile à un autre avantage....... Ah ! Lequel ?
Quand on a fini de fumer on peut se nettoyer la bouche
en ouvrant simplement le robinet inférieur.

'Women who Smoke':
a European soldier
uses sexual innuendo
to teach a European
woman about
'Oriental tobacco',
France, *c.* 1915.

The twentieth century's human turbulence provided ideal conditions for the weedy plant's diffusion. Warfare produces major population shifts for large groups of young men, whose military service can produce bleak world views alongside diverse physical risks. Depending on the sociocultural context, *indica* can offer recreational escape, solace for psychological trauma or enhanced aggression.[150] *Cannabis* provided just one option, of course, alongside alcohol, opiates, cocaine and other substances. Fighters in the Mexican Revolution (1910–20) taunted the other side with allegations of marijuana use.[151] British and French troops in North Africa appreciated hashish during the First World War;[152] colonial South Asian troops brought hashish to Europe, as did Greek refugees fleeing Turkey. In the 1910s, U.S. soldiers adopted marijuana along the Mexican border, and in Panama too. Moroccan troops brought *kif* to the Spanish Civil War (1936–9).[153] U.S. troops encountered *indica* globally during the Second World War.[154] In West Africa, more veterans brought home *wee* ('weed') than the number of liberated slaves who had introduced *diamba*.[155] In the Vietnam conflict (1963–75), U.S. troops were either 'potheads' or 'juicers', according to their preferred self-medication (marijuana or alcohol).[156] In 1967 about 30 per cent of American soldiers had tried marijuana, half within two months of arriving in Vietnam; by 1970, 50–80 per cent of soldiers smoked pot. Smokers had seen more combat than non-smokers.[157] Vietnam-era troops in Europe valued hashish.[158] Volunteers in the U.S. Peace Corps – unarmed Cold Warriors – transported marijuana globally, helping to establish *indica* in several Pacific island nations.[159] U.S. and allied soldiers in Afghanistan (2001–present) have used drug *Cannabis*, and also synthetic cannabinoids.[160] In sub-Saharan Africa, the controllers of child soldiers have plied their captives with drugs.[161]

Practitioners of ritualized warfare also appreciate marijuana and other drugs.[162] Professional American football players are young men who experience violence, emotional stress, authoritarian overseers and severe injuries.[163] In 1972 one professional football player guessed that 75 per cent of his peers used marijuana, while another player thought 50 per cent in 2012.[164]

Prohibition complexly affected *indica* biogeography. Drug *Cannabis* was included in the 1925 Geneva Opium Convention, mainly as a result of international political manoeuvring between post-colonial Egypt and South Africa, and Great Britain. U.S. support was important, although the Americans were mainly advancing an agenda unrelated to *Cannabis*.[165] Anti-marijuana concerns in the U.S. intensified after 1935, culminating in the prohibition of drug *Cannabis* in 1937. Since then, political authorities have increasingly sought to limit the plant's distribution, although with little success.

Marijuana boomed globally in the 1960s. Social unrest abetted *indica* in the Global North, where it became a symbol of anti-establishment sentiments among disenfranchised, middle-class youth. American exiles helped drug *Cannabis* to gain popularity in Canada and western Europe,

American and British marijuana advocacy patches, 1960s–70s.

and increased demand in the ancient *indica* zone in Africa and Asia. In the Global South, political and economic elites controlled access to schools, jobs and opportunities, and denied young people the chance to gain status within their societies.[166] Such conditions of political-economic marginality encouraged drug use North and South, and marijuana often represented a chic, new option. Popular music and other media encouraged marijuana use, and people increasingly grew the plant to supply themselves or others.

In 1973, U.S. President Nixon responded to the marijuana boom with 'an all-out global war against the drug menace'.[167] The War on Drugs encouraged the latest major dispersal of drug *Cannabis*. In the 1970s, anti-narcotics efforts caused marijuana shortages in the U.S., which relied on imports. Middle-class users developed the technology to grow

In the U.S., *Big Jim McLain* fought communists; in the dubbed
German release, he battled *Marihuana* (1952).

plants indoors, perhaps earliest in California and Arizona.[168] The need
to grow plants in confined spaces favoured the shorter indica folk
species over taller sativa.[169] Indoor agriculture has enabled *indica* to
travel far beyond its outdoor range, especially in the Global North[170] (and

aficionados have dreamed online of indoor grows on space stations). Indoor farming has enabled new commerce; Canada now exports several tons of drug *Cannabis* annually to the U.S.[171]

Authorities and users contest the plant's distribution. In the 1960s, the Moroccan government generated violent opposition by trying to eliminate *Cannabis* farming; Morocco remains among the world's largest producers.[172] International forces in Afghanistan have worked to eradicate *Cannabis* (as well as opium) since 2001, but production remains vibrant.[173] In the U.S., authorities annually uproot millions of ditchweed plants, clear thousands of outdoor plots and shutter numerous indoor operations, but supplies remain abundant. Indoor production continues to increase as states have mounted legal challenges to prohibition. Colorado and Washington legalized recreational marijuana in 2012, and eighteen other states have medical *Cannabis* programmes. The only federally legal production comes from a medicinal garden in Mississippi, first planted in 1965, where scientists conduct basic research on herbal supplements.[174] This garden has a federal appropriation around U.S.$2 million.[175] In contrast, the expanding U.S. marijuana market is conservatively estimated to exceed U.S.$10 billion.[176]

Cannabis indica is big business – seemingly an unlikely culmination of an economic history that for centuries centred on the lives of poor labourers. The apparent contrast is misleading, though. Its value reflects its expansion further into social margins, where it now attracts users whose health needs and political-economic desires remain peripheral to broader society. Similarly, despite the success of indoor horticulture, users in the Global North still depend on farmers in the Global South for the bulk of their supply. This relationship reflects the ancient biogeography of *indica*, which has not been effaced. Simultaneous antiquity and modernity characterize both species of *Cannabis*.

five
Things to Make
With and For *Cannabis*

T he material cultures of *Cannabis* encompass a basic opposition. *Cannabis* is an ancient crop that supplies anciently valued products, yet since the mid-1900s it has entered input-intensive, globalized agriculture. Although small-scale, traditional production persists minimally, *Cannabis* epitomizes modern farming.

The desire to drive down the costs of hemp caused *Cannabis* to enter early industrial farming. Densely planted hemp fields were a sensory spectacle, 'conspicuous, brilliant, [and] strange . . . masses of living emerald'.[1] Their 'balsamic, startling . . . smell' was pleasant to some, but 'strong and disagreeable' to others.[2] Initially, farmers harvested male and female plants separately, by thinning males from fields where females produced hempseed.[3] This practice was described in England in 1580, when farmers harvested 'fimble [hemp] to spin, and the carl [hemp] for her seed'.[4] Contemporaneous French farmers had similar practices, but by 1617 they grew fibre and seed plants separately.[5] Farmers harvested all stems in fibre-plant fields in the summer after male plants released pollen. Pollen-bearing plants were pulled from seed plots, which were harvested in the autumn. Farmers grew seed plants in well-spaced mounds of manured soil, to ensure abundant and large hempseeds. Fibre plants may produce few, small hempseeds, called 'lint seeds', useful only as birdseed.[6]

Farmers densely sowed fibre plants to produce tall, unbranched stems. Branched stems produce kinky fibres that are harder to process.[7]

In densely sown fields, seedlings must grow straight up towards sunlight, or die in the shade of others. *Cannabis* captures sunlight so effectively that farmers widely used hemp to kill weeds in fields before planting food crops.[8] Densely planted fields also offer refuge, for animals and people in hiding.[9] During the English Civil War (1642–51), a group of women 'hid themselves in growing Hemp, and there lay on the Ground almost 20 Hours' to escape attack.[10]

The tools of hemp production were historically iconic. In most locations, fibre-processing tools were not specifically for *Cannabis*, but used for other fibre plants too. Everywhere, hemp was labour-intensive. From planting to spinning, traditional processing had about ten major steps, each with distinct material elements.[11]

In Europe, the most iconic tool was the hemp break, a wooden lever used to crush *Cannabis* stalks and loosen fibre from dried pith after retting. Linguistic evidence suggests that the break originated along the southern Baltic; it diffused west after 1500. The archaic English spelling *hemp brake* more closely reflects medieval German.[12] The earliest documented English name for the tool was 'prichell' (known from 1593); the surname 'Hemprick' seemingly derives from this term.[13] In 1642 a minor English noble named Hampson established a crest featuring a hemp break.[14] The tool was soon afterwards described in Dutch and French.[15] Earlier workers had broken hemp with mallets, or peeled the stalks by hand.[16] In Hungary, workers broke stalks around large spools.[17] Although wind-, water- and animal-powered hemp-breaking mills were medieval inventions, these were not generally successful but locally important across northern Europe.[18]

Hemp field, France, 2000s.

Hemp fieldwork, France, c. 1900.

Textile and rope-making technologies changed little over long periods of time. Rope-making equipment in China remained static from ancient times into the 1900s, while the last major European innovation before the Industrial Revolution came about 1500.[19] Across Eurasia, rope was made in ropewalks, long, narrow buildings or straight paths where workers could twist great lengths of yarn. The American poet Longfellow meditated on rope-making in 1854: 'Human spiders spin and spin, / Backward down their threads so thin / Dropping, each a hempen bulk.'[20] Rope-making was the earliest hemp-related task adapted to steam-powered machines, in the 1850s.[21]

Cannabis resisted mechanization. Steam-powered textile mills were developed in the early 1800s, built for flax or cotton. *Cannabis* fibres are thicker, tougher and less flexible, and hemp performed poorly on machines designed for other plants. Hemp's nineteenth-century decline discouraged *Cannabis*-specific machinery, and the old, manual tools were increasingly used just for hemp. In Great Britain in 1905, for instance, 77 per cent of spindles in spinning mills carried flax threads, 20 per cent jute and 3 per cent hemp.[22]

Fully mechanized hemp production was proven in the U.S. during the First World War, when foreign supplies dwindled. Agronomists in

Wisconsin developed a system that needed people only to operate machines. Technical innovation was as important as technology, however. The agronomists decided that hemp was profitable only with cooperation among producers, to reduce costs for equipment and transport.[23] Such cooperation did not develop. Instead, by the 1940s mill owners rented equipment to farmers, and contractually designated which fields – the best – farmers would plant. Yet even then hemp was technologically primitive; Kentucky producers used hand breaks into the 1940s.[24] Other countries slowly adopted petroleum-based, industrial production after the Second World War, although full mechanization did not become standard until the 1970s.

Cannabis hemp products are diverse. The commonly repeated figure of 25,000 uses comes from an eager hemp promoter in 1938.[25] Nonetheless, in 1758 a French promoter celebrated 'the diversity of its uses, which are still known quite imperfectly'.[26] The most valuable products came from long stem fibres; other parts found minor uses. Most important were shives (short, broken fibres), which were mixed with adhesive to make oakum, used for caulking ships. But other sources of fibre could substitute for shives, including bits of old rope. Waste fibre primarily supplied paper-makers. Hemp made high-grade paper, but parchment (made from animal skin) was the standard for durable

Promotional card depicting hemp, rope-making, linen and hempseed oil, France, *c*. 1900.

documents into the late 1800s; flax paper mostly replaced it, if only because hemp had already generally declined.[27] *Cannabis* histories tell that the U.S. Declaration of Independence was printed on hemp, but it was not.[28]

People have made many *Cannabis* fabrics. 'Canvas', of course, is related to *Cannabis*, which can also provide the lighter fabric linen, a name derived from Old Latin *linum* ('flax'). Both fabric names refer to types of cloth, not plants of origin. Hempen linen and flaxen canvas are ancient. Cloth names sometimes indicate geography: for example, 'denim' comes from the French phrase *serge de Nîmes* ('serge from Nîmes, France'). One anecdote tells that the original denim was *Cannabis*,[29] but it was not. Serge was anciently woollen.[30] Producers at Nîmes innovated by using cotton instead.

Cordage products are diverse. Rope and twine are mundane, yet crucial for many tasks. Historically, ropes secured sails, hoisted loads, restrained animals and hanged people at the gallows. Many plants have been made into rope. In Europe, hemp supplied the most valued cordage, especially for maritime ropes and heavy cables. In China, hemp rope was important, but bamboo provided the strongest cables

String factory, France, c. 1918.

Serbian hemp used as a death threat — religious leader Lukijan Bogdanović
was later assassinated. Serbia, 1913.

for ships and civil engineering.[31] Around the Indian Ocean, many plants
provided cordage; coir (from coconut, *Cocos nucifera*) was preferred for
nautical applications.[32]

Hemp *Cannabis* has many non-fibre uses. The green, aromatic oil
is edible but its taste and odour were unpopular across Eurasia. From
ancient times, hempseed oil was the primary medicine from *sativa*,
used to treat ailments in people and animals.[33] Hemp-oil varnish was
made in tenth-century China.[34] In Europe, hempseed-oil-based paints
were developed in the 1300s in northern Italy.[35] Painters always preferred linseed oil (from flax) and used hempseed oil as a substitute, or
'only for mixing up the coarser paints'.[36] Unscrupulous vendors cut
linseed oil with hempseed oil, which otherwise could fuel lamps or
make 'beautiful green' soap.[37] Hempseed oil sometimes retained value
longer than hemp fibre. In Turkmenistan, people grew *Cannabis* for
oil into the 1870s, although Russian hemp had mostly supplanted local
fibre.[38] Turkmen cultivars represented *indica*; male plants provided
fibre, and females provided both hempseed and *bhang*.[39]

Hempseed foods were widely unpopular. In China, hempseed
reached its culinary pinnacle more than 3,000 years ago, although it

remains a minor food. In East Asia, hempseed foods remain perhaps most important in North Korea, whose impoverished farmers depend on reliable crops.[40] In western Eurasia, Polish people made various hempseed foods after 1500, but ate them mainly for tradition, not taste.[41] Russian peasants ate hempseeds with peas into the twentieth century, and substituted hempseed oil for animal fats during Christian religious fasts.[42] European *Cannabis* cuisine was most developed in the Baltic Republics. In the 1950s Estonians and Latvians made flour from roasted hempseeds, ate hempseeds with peas and flavoured porridge with hempseed milk (made from crushed seeds soaked in water).[43] Hempseed milk had uses beyond food, too. Seventeenth-century Spanish women washed with hempseed milk; eighteenth-century French bird keepers nursed ill canaries with it; nineteenth-century French cheats used hempseed milk to cut cow's milk.[44] (Despite this history, companies in the Global North have manufactured highly palatable hempseed foods since the 1990s.)

During twentieth-century wars, materials engineers used plants, including hemp, to substitute for metals, petroleum and wood. *Cannabis* found many new applications, but it was never particularly crucial. For instance, in 1941 the U.S. carmaker Henry Ford unveiled an experimental car made from plant-based plastics. Hemp histories have portrayed this car as entirely *Cannabis*, but Ford actually used flax, wheat, sisal, hemp and wood pulp, bonded with resin from other plants.[45] The vehicle never made it to market. Proofs-of-concept for new hemp products were regularly reported beginning in the 1800s, but novel uses were insufficient to halt hemp's global decline.

The products of drug *Cannabis* have been less diverse than those of hemp. The plant has supplied drugs and pharmaceuticals, although Chinese farmers have used powdered *indica* leaves to discourage pests in stored grain.[46]

Cooks have concocted diverse *Cannabis* drug foods. *Ganja* or hashish were ingredients in three major categories of sweet developed across southwestern Asia and North Africa: *majun*, a flour- and butter-based paste; *dawamesk*, a pistachio-based paste; and *halva*, a dense, glutinous

sweetmeat.[47] These names are Arabic loanwords. Recipes varied
between cultures and over time.[48] People chewed roasted *ganja* mixed
with spices in South Asia from ancient times into the 1900s, while
Southeast Asian cooks continue to make savoury soups laced with *ganja*.[49]
People have mixed South Asia's milk-based *bhang* for millennia. *Bhang*
sales remain legal in India with a government permit. Alcohol tinctures
of *indica* were mixed into spiced fruit jams in Central Asia.[50] In Jamaica,
middle-class consumers drink *ganja* tea and scorn *ganja* smoking.[51] THC
is not water soluble, so great volumes of tea are necessary for any
psychoactive effect.[52]

Europeans have had vague knowledge of *indica* edibles since Galen's
first-century account, but drug foods were not adopted in Europe until
the 1840s, when artists, writers and others discovered *dawamesk*. Some
experimenters published their experiences, inspiring others. One result
was short-lived commerce in 'hasheesh candy', sold as medicine, in
the U.S. North during the 1860s. Newspapers advertised brands including Gunjah-Wallah, a representation of the Hindi phrase 'ganja seller'.
These sweets failed commercially because they 'produced none of the
desired symptoms of intoxication'.[53] Even P. T. Barnum considered
them a scam.[54] Drug *Cannabis* foods have been minor components of
subsequent marijuana fads in the Global North, where established
desserts, such as brownies, were adapted to incorporate *indica*. Since the
1990s, small industries have manufactured THC-laced foods that
mimic mainstream, non-drug foods.

Oral consumption of drug *Cannabis* declined with the global
expansion of smoking after 1500. Different smoking traditions have
distinct paraphernalia. Marijuana paraphernalia is 'an aspect of historical research that has long been neglected', 'usually mentioned [only]
as an aside in [studies] primarily concerned with tobacco'.[55]

Beginning about 400 CE, African cultures have developed two
broad types of smoking paraphernalia – dry pipes and water pipes. The
African water pipe is particularly important for *Cannabis*. This technology consists of a hand-held container for water, fitted with a
normally straight-necked pipe bowl, and fashioned with a hole from

which to draw smoke. Ancient pipe bowls have been found across sub-Saharan Africa, including examples with cannabinoid residue from fourteenth-century Ethiopia. Europeans first described African water pipes in the Comoro Islands in 1626, and soon afterwards in Madagascar.[56] Water-pipe containers were commonly antelope horns in Southern Africa, coconut shells along the East African coast and bamboo stems or calabashes elsewhere.[57]

Smoking-pipe historians have considered African water pipes derivative of Asian technology, reflecting the stereotype that Africa is technologically backward. The basic design of the African water pipe was patented in the U.S. in 1980 as 'Water Pipe or Bong'. The patent credits prior art in Asia, describing 'the oriental bong' as derivative of 'the Persian hookah'.[58]

Evidence of Eurasian smoking prior to the sixteenth-century introduction of tobacco is scant.[59] People purposefully inhaled plant smoke, with inefficient technology – fumigated tents, incense and face-sized chimneys. Smoking-pipes enable precise control of dosage and efficient use of smokable herbs. Pipes may have been invented independently in highland Southeast Asia around 1100 CE, but this technology is barely known.[60] The earliest pipes in southwestern Asia – in Yemen and Iran – are from the 1400s and 1500s.[61] These pipes are ceramic versions of the coconut-based African water pipe, which diffused through Indian Ocean maritime trade. From the Levant to the Bay of Bengal, coconut-shaped ceramic water pipes persisted into the twentieth century.

The Persian water pipe was associated with hashish from India to North Africa. This technology employs flexible hose for the drawing tube, and a free-standing glass or ceramic container with a large, upright bowl. This technology was developed after the introduction of tobacco in the late 1500s.[62] Its name is *nārghile* ('coconut' in Farsi), indicating derivation from the coconut-based water pipe. In English, the Persian water pipe is often called 'hookah', after Arabic *huqqa* ('jar'). Europeans first described jar-based pipes in South Asia in 1616, when smokers burned tobacco.[63] Hookah-smoking spread quickly in the

'Hashish Smoker'
with coconut-shaped
water pipe. Egypt.
c. 1905.

FUMEUR DE HACHICHE

seventeenth-century Levant, with pipe bowls holding tobacco, hashish, *ganja*, opium, datura and other plants. From North Africa to India, elaborate Persian pipes remained in use alongside simpler water pipes.

In Southeast Asia, bamboo-container water pipes became dominant. Modern smokers use these pipes for tobacco, marijuana and opium.[64] The Southeast Asian water pipe may be an independent invention, or a development of the coconut-based pipe in areas far from the coast. In the 1960s American troops encountered Southeast Asian water pipes, and adopted the technology along with the name 'bong', which entered the U.S. vocabulary about 1972.[65] This name probably comes from Khmer *babong*, which means 'water pipe' in Cambodia.[66] The patented bong uses plastic pipe to mimic bamboo.[67]

In the Atlantic World, calabash-based water pipes accompanied marijuana. This association arose in coastal Central Africa after 1500. The link between *Cannabis* and calabash is strong for some cultures. For instance, BaVili people in the lower Congo River basin counselled appropriate behaviour with the proverb, 'Put tobacco in the pipe, *liamba* in the calabash'.[68] A German account of Liberia of 1888 called the calabash-based technology 'hemp-pipe', or the 'common pipe type available from anywhere in [coastal western Africa]'.[69] In the Americas, the earliest account of African water pipes is a 1645 Dutch description of an escaped slave settlement in Brazil.[70] Europeans reported nineteenth- and twentieth-century calabash pipes from Brazil and Jamaica.[71] People have for more than a century improvised water pipes with bottles and other containers.[72] Commercial pipes mimic bulbous calabash containers with plastic or glass. All forms of water pipe have succeeded commercially in the Global North since the 1960s.

Dry pipes are simpler and generally smaller than water pipes. People can easily carry a dry pipe, a fact that facilitated the early globalization of smoking. Marijuana dry pipes have a history distinct from that of tobacco pipes, invented in Native America.

Men with calabash-based water pipes and European-style
dry pipes, Congo-Brazzaville, c. 1910.

130

NES et TYPES. - Arabe fument le Narguileh   Collection Idéale P. S.

Man with Persian-style water pipe and tea, probably Egypt, *c.* 1917.

Marijuana dry pipes came initially from southeastern Africa, and were dispersed initially by sailors on Portuguese ships. Most European languages use words recognizably similar to English *pipe*. In contrast, 'smoking pipe' in Portuguese is *cachimbo*, which was borrowed from an African language,[73] most likely KiNyasa, now spoken in southern Malawi and neighbouring areas. KiNyasa includes terms for calabash- and bamboo-based water pipes, two dry pipes and various expedients (including 'earth pipes' formed in soil). KiNyasa *kachimbo* means 'ordinary [smoking] pipe'.[74] Portuguese sailors first encountered KiNyasa during a treasure hunt along the Zambezi River in 1514.[75] Before tobacco arrived later in the 1500s, African pipes contained marijuana and other plants. However, sixteenth-century European smoking practices in southeastern Africa are unknown. The Portuguese 'who were in closest contact with Africans and [best knew African] languages were themselves illiterate or poorly educated, and [thus their]

Sailor with *cachimbo*-style dry pipe, Portugal, 1904.

knowledge . . . contributed little' to the written record.[76] The earliest global diffusion of pipe-smoking was led by 'the "lower orders" of society – slaves and seamen – [rather than] those who knew the art of writing'.[77]

The loanword travelled widely. *Cachimbo* appeared in a Spanish-language book of 1642 about a banquet in the Portuguese court, which included 'cachimbo-tobacco addicts, or . . . tobacco-*cachimbo* addicts'.[78] Around 1700, Portuguese ethnobotanical treatises recommended *cachimbo*-smoking to administer several plant medicines, and a 1718 Dutch–Portuguese dictionary defined *cachimbo* as 'A tobacco pipe, or [any smoking] pipe, because [the Portuguese] smoke some herbs'.[79] *Nicotiana* tobacco became the preferred smokable worldwide, but early European pipes often carried herbal mixtures.[80] From Portuguese, *cachimbo* entered French, Basque and Occitan, in which *cachimbau* was a sailor's pipe.[81] In Spanish *cachimba* has been considered an American dialectal word, but it is actually an Atlantic word. In western Africa, 'cachimbo' was spoken in Portuguese Creole, but regional African languages have terms for 'smoking pipe' that are unrelated to *cachimbo*.[82]

In areas of initial Portuguese and Spanish contact in the Americas, smoking pipes were rare, if present, before 1500.[83] Additionally, the Portuguese had used *pipa* to mean 'barrel for storing liquid' since

1152, the usage passing into Spanish by 1402.[84] The English 'pipe' –
meaning smoking pipe – dates from a 1588 description of Native
Americans in Virginia, who invented the technology that became the
iconic English white-clay pipe.[85] This pipe form was copied widely,
including in sub-Saharan Africa. Cognates of 'pipe' passed into other
European languages in the 1600s, including the Spanish *pipa* in 1644.[86]

Similar terms spread with European tobacco smoking and English-
style white clay pipes, which had large bowls integrated with long
stems. *Cachimbo*-type pipes had small, red-clay bowls with short, wooden,
removable stems. Their compact, simple design was ideal for travellers.
Over time, *cachimbo*-type pipes increasingly held only tobacco, but
into the 1800s Europeans commonly characterized *cachimbos* as smelly,
suggesting other herbs. In Uruguay in 1890 *pango* was 'an herb that
blacks smoke in place of tobacco in a . . . *cachimbo*'.[87] In European

Man with bamboo-
based water pipe,
Assam region,
northeastern India,
c. 1960.

Spanish *pipa* signified polite smoking; *cachimba* was less genteel. In 1908 a Spanish writer sarcastically advised aspiring poets to 'let your hair grow a little and smoke a *cachimba*'.[88] In the 1990s, *cachimbo* meant 'water pipe for crack cocaine'.[89] As people gained a preference for tobacco, Portuguese *cachimbo* became simply a small pipe. Elsewhere, small dry pipes became *Cannabis* paraphernalia, though the name *cachimbo* disappeared (except in Costa Rica, where '*cachimba de Don Juan*' is a marijuana pipe).[90]

Other marijuana pipes succeeded elsewhere. In India, *chillum* pipes are common. This simple technology – a conical tube – originated as the removable bowl of a Persian water pipe.[91] In North Africa, *kif* is smoked in *sibsa* pipes,[92] which have long, wooden stems and small, red-clay bowls – a long-necked *cachimbo*-type pipe. The origins of *sibsa* pipes are unknown. European merchants traded 'long pipes' in Africa during the 1700s; an historic representation of a long-stemmed pipe in Senegal looks similar to a *sibsa*.[93] Long-stemmed pipes were also portrayed in 1950s Global Northern popular media about marijuana in Brazil.

Cigarette smoking was originally Native American – tobacco rolled in cornhusks or other leaves. Tobacco cigarettes became fashionable worldwide in the late 1800s, and the smoking of pipes declined. *Cannabis indica* entered North America mainly in cigarettes. North African *kif* filled cigarettes in the early 1900s. *Cannabis* cigarettes have generated innumerable nicknames worldwide, including *muggles* and *joint* in English. South Asian *bidi* cigarettes are not *Cannabis*, but tobacco–herbal mixtures rolled in tree leaves.

Since the 1960s, drug *Cannabis* cigarettes in the Global North have commonly been rolled in hemp *Cannabis* paper. This trend helped to revive French commercial hemp farming, which had nearly collapsed.[94] Commercial rolling papers have cleverly suggestive brand names – like 'hemp' or 'cannabis' – that indicate the paper fibre, but are also slang for marijuana. Manufactured tobacco cigarettes have been dominant since the early 1900s; marijuana cigarettes are hand-rolled. In the 1970s the U.S. Drug Enforcement Administration tracked rolling-paper sales to estimate marijuana consumption.[95]

The only brand of manufactured marijuana smokes flourished in the late 1800s. The French pharmaceutical firm Grimault globally sold packs of 'Indian cigarettes' made of 'Cannabis indica'. Grimault's newspaper ads provide the first record of marijuana in several countries. These cigarettes were among several types sold to treat asthma; other brands, such as Cigares de Joy, used datura.[96] Both plants (and also belladonna) are medically effective in treating asthma.[97] Despite their medical credentials, many people smoked asthma cigarettes recreationally. In 1895, a New Zealand newspaper joked that 'those who smoke Indian cigarettes say it is "Paradise Found".'[98]

Grimault's product persisted for decades, although experts questioned its contents. Advertisements listed only 'Cannabis indica', but in 1880

62. - KABYLIE. - Fumeur de Kif

Man smoking *kif* in a *sibsa* pipe, Algeria, *c.* 1920.

Cannabis-themed rolling paper packaging, U.S., 1970s.

a German pharmacist found that the cigarettes 'consist chiefly . . . of belladonna leaves, contaminated (we might almost say) with a few fragments of cannabis, and of two other species of leaves'.[99] Belladonna overdoses produce physical illness alongside 'agitative, combative, confused, and disoriented' behaviour.[100] A subsequent French study concluded that the manufacturer had mislabelled the contents because belladonna, unlike *Cannabis*, was a controlled substance.[101] A German pharmacy reference of 1909 reported Grimault's cigarettes carried one part *indica* to six parts of a mixture of datura, belladonna and henbane; the plants were soaked in a weak solution of opium and cherry laurel water (a perfume).[102]

Grimault's Indian cigarettes faced little opposition. The Austro-Hungarian Empire prohibited them in 1882 for 'social reasons',[103] although they were sold globally into the 1910s. Grimault had little competition. In 1886 a Belgian business trademarked packaging for roll-your-owns with Indonesian *Cannabis*,[104] but the brand seems not to have gone to market. Medicinal smokes were particularly popular in Australia,[105] where nineteenth-century newspapers carried many more Grimault advertisements than any other information on drug *Cannabis*. In 1898 paid articles in New Zealand repeatedly decried the 'Hardship on the Afflicted' imposed by a 44 per cent import duty,

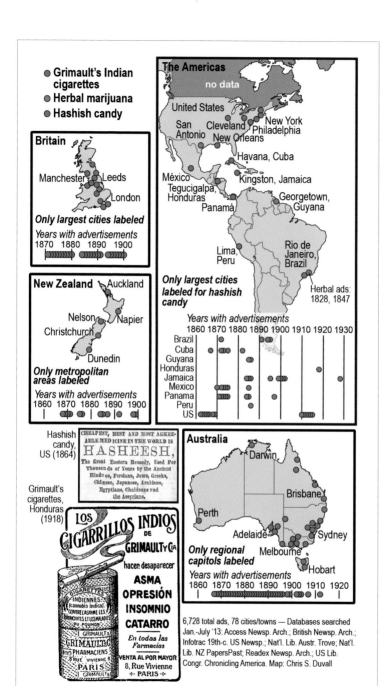

Marijuana ads from around the world.

because the cigarettes were 'the only prompt means of relieving asthma, difficulty of breathing, and insomnia'.[106] Duties were high elsewhere too. In 1885 the U.S. established a 50 per cent duty, while buyers paid 70 per cent in Guatemala.[107] In the U.S. in 1901, 144 cigarettes retailed for U.S.$4.50, while pharmacists could buy herbal marijuana for U.S.$0.45 per pound.[108]

Many in the Global North first experienced marijuana through medicines. Grimault's cigarettes gained global popularity, but 'Cannabis indica' extracts had greater medical acceptance. Tinctures entered commerce in the 1840s, and persisted in national formularies into the 1960s.[109] Cannabis indica pharmaceuticals were valued to treat tetanus and milder muscle spasticity, pain, asthma and insomnia, among other minor uses.[110] Manufacturers produced patent medicines with Cannabis, marketed for people of all ages, pets and livestock. Companies over-represented indica content to de-emphasize more dangerous opiate, alkaloid, bromide and other ingredients.[111] Nonetheless, the toxicity of patent medicine was blamed on Cannabis in the build-up to prohibition.[112] Topical treatments for corns included indica into the 1930s, but the plant was commonly just a colorant.[113]

People took patent medicines recreationally. Fitz Hugh Ludlow, the first U.S. user to publish his experiences in 1857, tripped on a tincture. 'For the humble sum of six cents I might purchase an excursion ticket all over the earth . . . contained in a box of Tilden's extract.' He encouraged his college chums to try it, too.[114] The first Australian experimentalist, Marcus Clarke, likewise got his high from a pharmacist.[115] Recreational use of Cannabis indica medicines flourished decades before indica was recognized on the continent. Australia's Northern Territory prohibited extracts and tinctures of 'Indian hemp' (alongside cocaine and morphine) in 1928, ten years before official concern about herbal indica.[116]

Historic commercial production of drug Cannabis was best described in India, where robust industries supplied unfinished indica for domestic and export markets.[117] Colonial authorities tried to regulate the trade closely, though illicit commerce was common. Pharmaceutical companies could legally purchase what they needed. Herbal drug production was not particularly labour-intensive, but commercial hashish needed significant processing. From North Africa to Central Asia, labourers used simple sieves to produce mountains of hashish. Less efficient methods were used locally. In Pakistan, workers in confined spaces beat dried plants with sticks, collecting the copious resinous dust on hanging sheets while wearing respiratory masks.[118] Current hashish production in Afghanistan uses a similar technique.[119]

Commercial hashish production was massive in the early 1900s. In 1933 China's Xinjiang region exported 98,000 kg to India, which shipped 30,000 kg into global markets. Minority-dominated Xinjiang includes the Tarim Basin, where archaeologists unearthed 2,500-year old Indo-European mummies with marijuana. The Han-dominated Chinese government outlawed the Xinjiang hashish trade in 1934, following a century of nationalist, anti-drug attitudes generated by British India's opium traffic.[120] The colonial Indian government did not seek to ban the Xinjiang trade, because it collected import duties.[121] The Chinese action created opportunities for South Asian producers, where hash production persists.

The British Indian government taxed *Cannabis* commerce. Other governments similarly profited. Pre-colonial Moroccan rulers sold annual monopolies to the *kif* trade; French Tunisia followed suit.[122] British India, Portuguese Angola and Mexico exported herbal marijuana, and publicized the product at nineteenth-century world's fairs.[123] In 1885 promoters thought the Belgian Congo should enter the trade.[124] Two years later the Portuguese colonial bank acquired colonial Angola's marijuana-producing test farm.[125] Returns on the investment are unknown.

Currently, marijuana economies are big but mostly illegal. In the Global North, high-tech, indoor horticulture dominates.[126] Indoor farming requires significant capital. Outdoor conditions are replaced with electric lights, ventilation fans, irrigation pumps, pipes, ducts, cords and electricity. Police have discovered grows based simply on energy consumption. Growers provide (synthetic) fertilizer in hydroponic solutions

Cannabis under grow lights, 2000s.

or partly synthetic soils. Indoor farms also require security systems. All this equipment is manufactured somewhere, transported elsewhere and powered somehow. High-tech indoor horticulture has a significant ecological footprint.

The economic importance of *indica* became salient when a business data company started monitoring U.S. medical marijuana in 2010.[127] The taxable marijuana economy includes over 1,700 medical dispensaries, mostly in California and Colorado.[128] In 2014 Colorado's legalized recreational sales began with long queues of customers. A successful argument for legalization in Colorado and Washington State was to generate local and state taxes from marijuana sales. In states where marijuana is fully illegal, it is sometimes taxed to increase drug-law penalties, by charging arrestees with tax evasion as well as drug possession. Taxes also accrue from hydroponics suppliers (1,000 in the U.S.) and paraphernalia shops (nearly 1,400 businesses).[129] The U.S. federal government taxes the income generated even from illegal drug sales.

Peripheral industries are small relative to the crop itself. Since the 1970s the news media have placed drug *Cannabis* among the most valuable crops in the U.S., worth many billions of dollars in 2010.[130] In 2006 an anti-prohibition advocacy group argued that *Cannabis* is the most valuable U.S. crop, based on legal agriculture statistics, law-enforcement data and street prices for weed.[131] The growth of U.S. markets is expected to continue.[132]

Current hemp farmers mostly participate in globalized agriculture, serving distant markets through mechanized agriculture. Agronomists treat hemp *Cannabis* like other industrial crops, the focal cog in agro-ecosystems that can be manipulated to improve production. In recent decades, China has produced about 40 per cent of global hemp, with South Korea, France, Chile, Italy, Hungary and Russia growing signifi-cant quantities.[133] Hempseed and hempseed oil have become globally more valuable than fibre. Nearly all hempseed used in the U.S. is grown in Canada, where nearly all the crop is exported south.[134] Despite a U.S. government forecast in 2000 that hemp would continue to decline, hemp industries have grown ever since.[135]

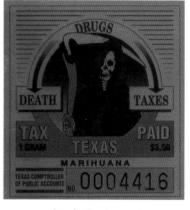

In several U.S. states, marijuana taxes help to increase penalties for illegal possession, 2000s.

Growing *sativa* is like growing *índica*, so hemp agricultural science benefits marijuana growers. Marijuana how-to books show that indoor production is highly technical. Commercial producers in the Global North rely on intensive selection of psychoactive and physical characters, practised by skilled (but untrained) plant scientists. Bioprospectors visit the Global South to acquire new genetic material. Seed companies reach globally via Internet commerce, although seeds are becoming less important to growers, who instead plant cuttings. These genetic clones preserve valued characters between plant generations.

Marijuana cultivation has been illegal for decades in the Global North, so outdoor production has been in marginal or hidden spaces. Indoor growing is, of course, a means of hiding. The earliest known indoor grow dates from 1929, when a man in New Mexico 'took the roof off [a] room and cultivated marijuana' in a dirt-floored house. He broke local *Cannabis* prohibition and received a year in jail.[136] Recent U.S. outdoor growers cultivate remote sites, including those in national forests and parks. Growers haul in farming equipment, fertilizer, living supplies and security devices. Guerrilla farming is environmentally damaging because farmers make minimal investment in impact management.[137]

Indoor farming has decimated outdoor production in the Global North. For instance, in northern California, high-quality marijuana came from the 'Emerald Triangle' growing region during the 1970s and 1980s, providing 25–50 per cent of local income. This economy has nearly disappeared since the 1990s, when medical marijuana initiatives stimulated indoor horticulture statewide. Indoor growers now dominate California's production.[138]

Outdoor-grown marijuana in the Global North has always come mainly from the Global South. Central America supplies U.S. demand; southern Asia and Africa supply Europe; Pacific Island nations help to supply Australia. Rural areas supply cities in Brazil and South Africa, countries with great economic disparity. The production–consumption divide in Brazil separates the 'Marijuana Polygon' in the northeast from the country's wealthier southeast.[139]

Harvesting hemp, France, 2000s.

Prohibition makes marijuana a potentially enriching, high-risk crop. The risks farmers face from law enforcement are complex. For example, in the 1970s and '80s, U.S. anti-narcotics police sprayed Mexican and Colombian fields with the herbicides paraquat and glyphosate.[140] Paraquat kills plants slowly, and 1970s Mexican growers learned to harvest immediately and sell contaminated weed. U.S. smokers feared 'Paraquat Pot', but the growers probably faced greater danger. The herbicide is highly toxic through skin exposure, but combusts into harmless components. U.S. smokers reported no injuries from Paraquat Pot,[141] but no data was collected about the farmers. *Cannabis* farmers in the Global South accept such risks out of economic desperation due to income inequities. Southern Africa exemplifies the conundrums inherent in international marijuana markets. *Dagga* demand in South African cities provides poor farmers in South Africa, Lesotho, Swaziland and elsewhere with a cash crop that can thrive on marginal land. However, *dagga* farming depresses food production and is illegal. Police action threatens each year's earnings until the crop is sold. Illegality maintains high prices; if *dagga* were legalized, current farmers would likely suffer as prices dropped and production increased elsewhere (as in California's Emerald Triangle).[142]

Globally, marijuana transporters – smugglers – control business with growers because value accrues through transport to urban centres. Transporters are often also territorial wholesalers; organized crime can be a vertically integrated business. Industrial consolidation and minimal profit for farmers broadly characterizes other export crops in the Global South.

Ultimately, differences between availability and demand drive marijuana production. When demand is relatively low and availability high, farming makes poor economic sense. In nineteenth-century Brazil, for instance, *indica* grew with little human assistance, and herbalists sold *Cannabis* inflorescences alongside wild-collected species.[143] With increased demand, cultivation increases. In the 1970s Western tourists brought demand along the 'Hippie Hash Trail' circuit between Morocco and Nepal. Vast fields covered with iconic plants created ideal land-scapes for drug-filled vacation snapshots.[144] In Afghanistan, drug production exploded with tourist demand. Before 1970 *Cannabis* and opium were minor crops, mostly exported to Iran. By 1973 over 5,000 'hippies' lived in Kabul, whose market demand improved national pro-duction capacity, enabling Afghanistan to become a major drug supplier.[145]

The 1960s marijuana boom in the Global North materially transformed drug *Cannabis*. Hashish producers now use specialized implements, including mechanical sifters. High-end herbal producers primarily supply closely manicured *ganja*. Small companies make specialized equipment for trimming seed leaves from inflorescences, but manual processing remains dominant.[146] Mass production and organic chemistry have spawned a new concentrate of drug *Cannabis*. 'Hash oil' has THC content of up to 70 per cent, many times greater than hashish or *ganja*. Manufacturers concentrate THC by washing low-quality hashish with organic solvents – acetone or butane – which cannot be completely filtered from the finished product.[147] Hash oil is a hard drug, relating to marijuana as heroin relates to opium, and cocaine to coca leaves.

Material cultures of *Cannabis* are in many ways ancient, yet inescapably modern. Water pipes still have plant-shaped containers, although few recognize their shapes as calabashes, coconuts or bamboo. Hemp is an antique crop whose current cultivation relies on mono-cropping and heavy processing; indoor marijuana is even more input-intensive. In the Global South, marijuana still thrives in low-input farming, but its economics are as unfair as those of most tropical export crops. Commercial *Cannabis* epitomizes modern globalized agriculture, depending on non-renewable resources, and creating disparity between farmers and consumers. The plant stands apart from other crops, however, because of the unusual set of symbolic meanings it has borne.

six

Symbolism Starring *Cannabis*

People enlist plants as symbols. *Cannabis* has borne many meanings. It has represented sanctity, health, enjoyment, productivity, beauty, foulness and poison. Symbolic cultures intertwine complexly with material cultures. Plants are interpreted through subjective value systems that validate symbolic meanings and support judgements based upon them. People may be judged by how they use plants and plants by how people use them.[1]

People–plant relationships are sometimes interpreted as person-to-person interaction when plants personify human values.[2] In China, beginning in the 100s CE, the Taoist goddess *Mágū* ('hemp maiden') represented beauty, longevity and tantalization.[3] In nineteenth-century France, children learned kindness to animals in the tale of Prince Chènevis ('Prince Hempseed'). The animal-loving prince's coarse servants mockingly called him 'hempseed' because he scolded them for failing to feed the chickens.[4] Fundamentalist Christian anti-drug crusaders have made *Cannabis* into monsters, as in Robert James Devine's book *The Moloch of Marijuana* (1943), in which marijuana was a false god that demanded the sacrifice of young people.[5] More often, drug *Cannabis* has personified desirable companionship (at least from a heterosexual male perspective). Nineteenth-century Mexico had *Mariajuana*, while twentieth-century Americans have known Mary Jane and others. Jazz musician Louis Armstrong recalled, 'Mary Warner, honey, you sure was good.'[6] Thirteenth-century

Islamic poets similarly portrayed hashish as an enjoyable female companion.[7]

Cannabis has represented the intentions people might have for particular uses of the plant. In English, from the 1600s to the mid-1900s, 'hemp' could mean 'death by hanging'. English colloquial names for *Cannabis* included 'neck-weed'.[8] Perceived justifications for hempen violence were projected onto the plant. The promotional poem *The Praise of Hemp-seed* (1620) assigned British prosperity, sovereignty and security to *Cannabis*, because it

> yeelds good whips & ropes, for rogues & theeves . . .
> 'Tis not . . . the letter of the Law
> That [keeps] theeves rebellious wills in awe . . .
> [It is instead] a hempen string . . .
> [Hemp] is a bullwarke to defend a Prince,
> It is a subjects armor and defence.[9]

Yet execution can operate in the opposite direction. 'Hemp [is] a plant with which they make *ropes*', wrote a political prisoner who died in British custody. 'Never did the cultivation of *hemp* deserve more encouragement than in . . . 1794,' he continued, 'when the horrible

'Hemp for traitors' during the U.S. Civil War, *c.* 1862.

147

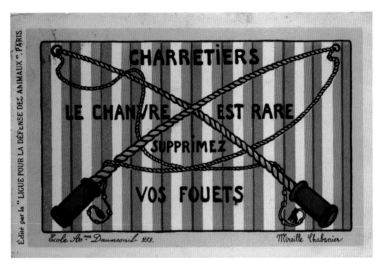

'Wagoneers . . . get rid of your whips': hemp lashed beasts of burden, to the
consternation of animal-rights advocates in France, c. 1921.

crimes of the aristocracy seem to be preparing punishments [requiring]
a vast consumption of the above *salutary* vegetable. The *Guillotine* is not
yet introduced into England.'[10] Hemp has enabled extreme judgements
against perceived violators of public laws or social rights.

More commonly, judgements about *Cannabis* use have reflected
stereotypes of human–plant interaction. These stereotypes have divided
societies into groups representing concepts of patriotism, race, social
class, mental attributes, spirituality and criminality.

Racial meanings of drug *Cannabis* originated in European ignorance
of genetic diversity within the genus. European scholars gained
knowledge of drug *Cannabis* slowly, mainly after 1800, and only in non-
European locations. Anciently, Galen described psychoactive *Cannabis*
as different from 'our cannabis'.[11] More recent experts theorized that
the difference between European hemp and the Other *Cannabis* was that
non-European environments activated the plant's psychoactivity.
European knowledge of marijuana developed alongside 'the tropics',
'the Orient' and 'the Dark Continent' as imagined geographic regions.[12]
Initial English knowledge of drug *Cannabis* arose mostly from travel
writings,[13] including the sailor Robert Knox's account of Sri Lanka in

the 1670s. The scientist Robert Hooke, who met Knox back in England, decided that the sailor had experienced 'only *Indian* hemp'. Hooke reported that '*Indian* hemp' was tried in English gardens, but the seed 'hath [in England] lost its Vertue, producing none of the effects fore-mentioned'. The English environment could not reproduce the foreign character of a plant otherwise 'so like . . . Hemp in all its parts'.[14] Psychoactivity reflected the presumed character of temperate England versus that of tropical India. Physical conditions – particularly day length during the growing season – limit *indica*'s outdoor range and productivity, especially *ganja* and *bhang* cultivars from low latitudes. This physical reality supported ideas of tropical Otherness; *Cannabis* chemistry was absolutely unknown until the mid-nineteenth century.

Nonetheless, the aesthetics of drug *Cannabis* developed quickly. In particular, *indica* came to represent a darkness of the Orient, as in this poem of 1836:

> Now in the East the ruling demons are
> *Morphion*, who seeks his prey with many doses
> Of bitter opium, fleeting dreams producing.
> *Banga*, his partner, fury of Hempseed,
> Both leading to a premature old age,
> Producing folly, madness and deceit,
> Insanity and crimes producing often.[15]

Often the two drugs merged rhetorically into one. Into the 1900s, writers commonly confused *Cannabis* drugs with opium, although the source plants are different and the drugs have different effects.[16] The generalized notion of drug *Cannabis* as an Oriental object was strengthened in Orientalist European paintings, in which hookahs and hashish became iconic.

The most influential motif in Orientalist portrayals of *Cannabis* is the etymological tale of the word 'assassin'. The literature on this word's history began in 1603, and *Cannabis* entered its history in 1809.[17] Standard etymologies begin with a semi-legendary group of

Rudolf Ernst, *Arab Smoking a Water Pipe on a Sofa*, 1894.

adherents to the Nizari Ismaʿili branch of Islam. In the eleventh century, Ismaʿilis in northeastern Iran developed a new tactic of warfare: dispatching stealthy, solitary cut-throats to eliminate enemy leaders. These killers were supposedly called *Ḥashshāshīn*, an Arabic word meaning 'users of hashish', reflecting belief that the drug fuelled their grim pursuits. Mispronunciation of *Ḥashshāshīn* produced *assassin*.

Other etymologies are plausible – perhaps the root word meant 'to slaughter people' – but regardless of its validity, the Assassin story is a central trope in *Cannabis* literature.[18] It has been retold frequently, and deconstructed severally.[19] Assassins were important in Orientalist thought beginning in the medieval period, when European Crusaders developed stereotypes of violent, fanatical Muslims. Crusaders learned the Assassin story through hearsay, primarily from members of rival Islamic groups. By spreading dark stories, rival groups advanced their religious politics and intimidated Crusaders as a favourable by-product. People in Central Asia also told medieval European travellers similar tales of drug-induced fanaticism amongst unseen neighbours. European storytellers added embellishments. The Assassin story has been a favourite of the 'Muslim (and later European) *imagination*' for a millennium.[20]

The Assassin story also reflects medieval Arabic language. In the 1100s and 1200s, Arabic-speaking poets used the verb 'to kill' as an idiom for hashish intoxication.[21] In medieval Islamic societies, many believed that habitual hashish consumption produced physical and mental deterioration, a figurative killing of the user. For example, one poet described a sorry-looking Muslim ascetic:

> This poor one whom you see
> Like a chick thrown to the ground featherless
> Has been killed by hashish intoxication,
> Killing being the custom of hashish.[22]

Poetic puns about killing and hashish contributed to the belief in marijuana-induced violence.

POUR OUBLIER L'ANDALOUSIE
ON S'ABRUTIT AVEC DU KIF

A colonialist view of Morocco, 1909: 'To forget Andalucia' — which the Spanish
won back from the Moors in 1492 — 'we stupefy ourselves with *kif*.'

Assassin etymologies have reflected shifting beliefs about drug *Cannabis*. In 1809 the French scholar Antoine Sylvestre de Sacy popularized the Assassin story. He believed that 'The drunkenness produced by hashish propels [one] into a type of ecstasy similar to that which the orientals gain from . . . opium.'[23] Thus, the leader of the Assassins lured young men into suicidal missions with hashish-induced, ecstatic visions of the hereafter. However, in the 1930s the Assassin story represented belief that marijuana produces maniacal violence.[24] A word historian in 1972 disagreed, arguing that because the Ismaʿīlis cutthroats 'were intended really to kill . . . it is most illogical to assume that they were hashish smokers, as hashish addicts soon become lax, lazy, and debilitated . . . drug addicts have no "fight" in them.'[25] The Assassin story reflects meanings projected onto *Cannabis* more than knowledge of historic *Cannabis* cultures.

The Assassin tale mingled with other Orientalist stories. The travel writer Richard Burton was important for creating English-language impressions of drug *Cannabis*. Burton embraced stereotypes of Orientalist lasciviousness, laziness and immorality. Lurid examples come from his version of the Thousand-and-One Nights folk tales (1885–8). Hashish was a recurrent motif that complemented Burton's salacious fascination. In one tale, the drug begets delusional dreams of wealth and sex: 'Are thou not ashamed, O Hashish-eater', scolds one character, 'to be sleeping stark naked with a stiff-standing tool?'[26] Burton established *Cannabis* themes decades before his Arabian Nights, after soldiering in British India during the 1840s. In 1851 he decided that *bhang* was not for clear-headed, productive people. Indian users of drug *Cannabis* were a 'laborious, merry-hearted, debauched, and thoroughly demoralised [that is, without morals] set of half savages'.[27]

Drug *Cannabis* remained Oriental far from Asia. A travel writer in 1873 portrayed a (fictional) British physician residing in Sierra Leone who 'moderately smok[ed] the *liamba*, or African haschisch'. The doctor 'possessed an Oriental temperament, and shunned the . . . social restrictions of the North [Europe]', even though he had 'resided in Africa all his life'.[28] Far away in New York, a newspaper in 1914 told that *maríhuana* was a 'Mexican' addiction that represented the 'Oriental character of the Mexican's mind'.[29] The Oriental stereotype provided overarching meaning for *Cannabis* worldwide, parallel with the out-of-Asia biogeography that had been established by 1870.[30]

Scientific, aesthetic and news media combine to develop society-wide meanings for biological objects.[31] European representations of marijuana in 'Oriental', 'Mexican' and 'African' contexts propelled a rhetorical theme linking *indíca* and violence. This theme emerged in European popular literature in part because *indíca* was embedded in colonial violence in locations where journalists filed reports of drug use among the natives. One widely republished story about the Congo Free State (modern Democratic Republic of Congo) in 1900 told of a murderer trimming his victim's skull to make 'a bowl [for mixing] tobacco and diamba'.[32] Simultaneously, Americans were discovering marijuana along the U.S.–Mexico border. An 1894 magazine article about the Rio Grande reported that female Mexican 'herb doctors' – 'nefarious . . . witch[es]' – sold marijuana to 'discarded women for . . . wreaking a terrible vengeance upon recreant lovers'.[33] The article was entitled 'The American Congo', because of the similarly 'degraded, turbulent, ignorant, and superstitious character of [the] population[s]' along the North American and Central African rivers.[34]

The intermingling stereotypes supported broader environmental determinism. The idea that environment produces *Cannabis* psycho-activity paralleled the idea that race reflects environment. In 1983, a paper on ultraviolet radiation in *Cannabis* evolution began with the 'casual observation that the sun-drenched areas growing the most potent Cannabis [are] populated by native peoples of the darkest complexions'.[35] This observation is inaccurate, but validates the social construction of race as a product of environment. The language of race was explicit in *Cannabis* taxonomy in 1976, when botanists distinguished 'the northern [fibre and oil] races' from 'the southern, intoxicant races'.[36]

Skin colour has been salient in portrayals of *Cannabis*. Black slaves served hookahs to lighter-skinned characters in European Orientalist

After hours, a Portuguese explorer's porters smoke 'the fatal *liamba*', Angola, 1881.

paintings. The *liamba*-smoking doctor in Sierra Leone had a 'harem' of African women 'and often declared he could see no beauty in a white woman'.[37] In the U.S., sensationalist newspapers that excoriated *Cannabis* during the twentieth-century rise of prohibition saddled the plant with anti-black racial stereotypes, while also striking an anti-Latino chord by adopting the Spanish term *maríhuana*.[38] In 1965, an international expert on crime told that 'different races of people vary in their susceptibility to marihuana'. His list of marijuana-induced crimes carried just one racial identifier, 'Negro'.[39]

Such stereotypes sustain the idea that cultural heritage explains marijuana use.[40] Although specific *Cannabis* cultures are traceable, for centuries the drug has diffused socially within labour underclasses.

Despite its social embeddedness, ancestry has served to explain drug use since the 1700s. A *Cannabis* history published in 2012 suggests that Louis Armstrong used marijuana because he was black, like various African 'tribes' that have *Cannabis* traditions.[41] The cited African peoples – Tsonga, Zulu, Sotho, 'Bashilenge', a 'Bantu tribe' and 'Hottentots' (the latter three are inappropriate terms) – have scant historical connections, and had no influence in Armstrong's early twentieth-century American South.

Ideas of race and class developed together. Since 1500, representations of drug *Cannabis* were often conditioned through overseer–labourer relationships. Some European employers considered drug *Cannabis* benign. 'I have never perceived any adverse effects of hemp [smoking]', wrote a German traveller whose Central African canoe-rowers were 'remarkably strengthened' following 'a few draws' of marijuana smoke.[42] A few European employers used the drug, including a British officer with Indian experience who smoked 'bang' like his guides while hunting in Mozambique in 1868.[43]

During the 1800s, Europeans struggled to decide if drug *Cannabis* was good or bad for societies. Many observers negatively characterized marijuana to denigrate labourers, yet until the 1900s Europeans also generally tolerated its use among their employees. Opinions about drug *Cannabis* depended upon opinions about labour. In East Africa, the explorer Henry Morton Stanley, for example, considered *indica* smoking 'the most deleterious [of all drug habits] to the physical powers'. He was incessantly frustrated with his retinue of porters, whom he claimed faltered physically because of 'excessive indulgence'. Yet he did not apparently prohibit marijuana use, and overlooked the role of onerous tasks and risky environments in producing 'their weakened powers . . ., their impotence and infirmities'.[44] Indeed, when he was not boss, but booster of the Congo Free State in 1885, Stanley listed drug *Cannabis* 'among the many minor items available which commercial intercourse would teach the natives to employ profitably'.[45] European merchants seemingly took his advice, and sold marijuana in Central African trading posts.[46]

The plant's social and economic role was often less salient than its perceived morality. European observers in colonial Algeria saw cafés where coffee and *indica* stimulated conversation, and saw *Cannabis* grown in 'gardens surrounding the towns'.[47] Nonetheless, drug *Cannabis* represented moral hypocrisy, not economic botany. 'Despite [Islamic] religious prohibition, the Arabs smoke daily', a French observer avowed, adding sarcastically that 'the good Muslims [smoke only] in their homes, where they are seen only by their wives and slaves'.[48] Drug *Cannabis* was purportedly valued as a 'powerful aphrodisiac', because Algerians were supposedly 'a people who[se men] passionately love the women so much'.[49]

In contrast, Europeans in North Africa had clear-headed reasons to try the drug. A French officer in Morocco smoked *kif* in the 1850s because of the 'increased intellectual power [it] afforded him, [which enabled him to] combat successfully the subtle plots of the Arabs'.[50] French troops and colonists in Algeria had a more scientific reason to sample *kif* – 'to become acquainted with its effects'.[51] Perhaps to complete such experiments, French troops frequented North African red-light districts,[52] and mailed postcards of prostitutes

Au MAROC — 120. Mauresque dans Fumerie de Kif   Coll. Louÿs

In the *kif*-smoking lounge, Morocco, c. 1915.

smoking *Cannabis*. Ribald humour and pornographic imagery are ancient associates of *indica*.[53]

Marijuana was widely tolerated into the 1930s, although many people had perceived negative social impacts of its use. Immorality was projected upon the plant, as well as insanity and psychopathy. The notion of *Cannabis*-induced madness circulated widely amongst nineteenth-century European scholars, who retold anecdotes often with no evidence of focal events.[54] By the 1880s newspapers widely republished stories of marijuana-crazed violence, establishing symbolism far beyond the plant's range. Descriptions of drugged-out behaviour were presented without context, divorcing events from circumstances. Between May and June 1907, major newspapers in New York and Washington, DC, recounted a rampage that happened 'the other day' in central Mexico.[55] In 1925 fourteen newspapers across Australia reported that a *marihuana* smoker had killed six in Mexico.[56]

Scientists had little evidence of *indica*-induced insanity. Few cases came from colonial psychiatric hospitals. Many cases actually reflected ethnocentric and stereotypical interpretations of non-European behaviour.[57] British physicians in colonial Egypt, India and South Africa increasingly just presumed drug use when admitting disturbed patients, biasing health statistics. Studies began with the premise that drug *Cannabis* produces madness, and not surprisingly found supporting evidence.[58] A 1920s study of marijuana among U.S. troops in Panama found no evidence of drug-induced madness, but the army doctors nonetheless concluded, 'Morons and psychopaths . . . constitute the large majority of habitual smokers.'[59] Just after prohibition began in the U.S., the Surgeon General's office issued guidelines for police unfamiliar with marijuana: 'the drug is mostly used by [mentally] unstable people' and its use is 'likely to lead to insanity' (based on statistics from India and Egypt), yet 'insanity due to marijuana is rare' in America.[60]

Despite the science, societies in Southeast Asia, Central America and North Africa considered *indica*-induced insanity a real condition. This belief was epitomized in the initially Malay notion of 'running amuck', a violent, temporary insanity that *ganja* could produce.[61] The idiom was first published in de Sacy's version of the Assassin story, as a stereotyped behaviour of 'Malays and Indians'.[62] The narrative circulated with embellishments. In 1885, decades before marijuana entered the remote U.S. state of Montana, a newspaper republished a story from London that 'running amuck' was a 'hysterical affection of certain races inhabiting oriental countries'. Brought on by 'the extract of hemp called bhang, ganja, or charras', the condition epitomized the 'bitterest and most relentless dogmas' of Islam. 'Once started on the "death run", [the] only thought [of a person running amuck] is to "kill and kill and kill".'[63] English-speakers widely adopted the idiom, although applying it in situations milder than murderous rampages.

The marijuana–violence association partly arose from social discourse, which establishes expectations for users and observers alike.[64] Paranoid, angry mindsets and parallel representations of *Cannabis* led some few users to believe they entered an alternate, violent reality. Not all users experienced this, even if they were aware of the discourse. In the 1940s, U.S. authorities suspected that arrestees claimed marijuana madness to reduce their criminal culpability.[65]

Stereotyped marijuana violence also had roots in pharmacology. Drug *Cannabis* increases the likelihood of psychotic episodes, especially among users who first try the drug during adolescence.[66] Users with genetic predisposition to psychosis face a 54 per cent greater risk; users without such predisposition have a 2 per cent increased risk.[67] The absolute number of users affected in this way is small, but not negligible.

Additionally, the global practice of mixing *Cannabis* with other drugs and spices likely produced disturbances that were incorrectly attributed to marijuana.[68] All forms of drug *Cannabis* have been mixed with other substances for effect or flavouring. Historically, the most important admixtures for *Cannabis* were opium and four plants from the alkaloid-heavy Solanaceae family: tobacco, henbane, belladonna and datura, which supposedly has 'ganja-like effects'.[69] *Datura*'s several species are as widespread as drug *Cannabis*; the two have been associated across Asia, Africa, South America and North America. In Malay, 'berhulam ganja' is indica mixed with datura, or, as an idiom, 'poison mixed with poison'.[70] Since the 1960s, marijuana has occasionally been mixed with harder drugs, from cocaine to PCP, and miscellaneous other adulterants. Historically, flavouring agents were common. People in New Mexico mixed marijuana with alcohol, perfume, sugar and 'sometimes a dash of red pepper' in 1925.[71] Nutmeg, cloves, ginger, cinnamon, cumin, cardamom, black pepper and other ingredients came with drug Cannabis in South Asia.[72] Grimault sweetened their Indian cigarettes, first with the Native American plant Epilobium and later with perfumes. The firm also added saltpetre to improve combustion.[73]

Drug Cannabis is fairly safe, but many additives are not. Opiates and alkaloids are quite toxic and can cause physical dependence. In seventeenth-century India, Mughal emperors administered slow capital punishment with increasing doses of opium mixed into datura-laced bhang tea.[74] Tobacco has long-term health effects, but datura, henbane and belladonna are riskier in the short term. In recent years, people trying datura recreationally have been gravely sickened.[75] In 2010, accidental poisoning caused a three-year-old Tunisian girl to become 'agitated and aggressive with purposeless movements, delirium, and hallucinations: she saw wild animals, a man who wanted to beat her, and various other things'.[76] Some minority of historic marijuana smokers likely suffered similarly with datura-, henbane- or belladonna-laced Cannabis.

Marijuana came to represent laziness and carelessness. The notion of marijuana sloth was a moral judgement on social underclasses. Since 1500, marijuana has been consistently associated with exploitative labour relationships in which workers needed little skill but much physical strength, had minimal autonomy and experienced emotional duress.

Overseers considered sloth common in social underclasses. Hard labourers were often deemed lazy, particularly those who used marijuana. In 1832 an English writer generalized about 'the negro' in Central Africa. 'When he awakens he regales himself with his cachimbo which is his pipe. [Pipe-smoking and other] habits of the negro render him

Marijuana sloth in Brazil. Sheet music from France, c. 1955.

easy to control, but [make it] difficult to get him to work as a carrier.'[77] The traveller who inspired this portrayal employed hundreds of porters, including several to haul him in his sedan chair.[78] In South Asia, Richard Burton denigrated labourers, who were inevitably non-British drug users. At a canal excavation, for instance, 'The head man . . . lies dozing drunk [while] at least half the diggers are squatting torpidly on their hams . . . at a certain time each man applies himself to the bhang, of which he has been dreaming all the morning.'[79] Labourers were lazy because of *bhang*, while upper classes 'smok[ed] themselves "screwed"' on hashish while wasting time with flowery conversation. In general, '[Pakistan's Sindh region], is an Eastern Ireland on a large scale. [Their populations] would rather want with ease than be wealthy with toil.'[80] Burton similarly portrayed drug *Cannabis* as a cause and indicator of backwardness in East, West, Southern, Central and North Africa, and Brazil.

Stereotypes were even embedded in paraphernalia, especially in the Atlantic, where slaves maintained distinct, 'African' smoking practices.[81] In European languages other than Portuguese, *cachimbo* meant 'pipe of blacks' by the 1800s.[82] Sometimes this meaning recalled the introduction of pipe-smoking by African slaves, as in Puerto Rico.[83] More widely, the usage simply reflected the racialization of labour. In Cuban Spanish, *cachimbo* meant 'the ordinary smoking pipe that field negroes use'; 'The unhappy slave finds some solace in his *cachimbo*, which they all smoke.'[84] In Central America, *cachimba* became a pejorative meaning 'arrogant negro'.[85]

For centuries, labour underclasses have used drug *Cannabis*. These people have had little reason to work hard except for threats of violence, economic hardship, arrest, imprisonment or enslavement.[86] Perceptions of laziness suggest slowdowns, purposeful inefficiencies and other forms of everyday resistance, whether drug-induced or not. The notion of marijuana sloth persists in the 'amotivational syndrome' described in the 1960s and questioned since the 1970s.[87] Popular media portrayals of underachieving potheads advance this idea, and some researchers still find evidence of low motivation among

Harvesting hemp, U.S., 1910s.

long-term users.[88] Governments and employers complain of lowered productivity caused by *Cannabis* and other drugs,[89] but aficionados appreciate marijuana's relaxing effects.

Drug *Cannabis* complexly affects work. Studies in Jamaica show that labourers are mechanically less efficient, but remain productive and have greater job satisfaction.[90] The drug can increase risks associated with dangerous tasks by impairing concentration, short-term memory, physical coordination and judgement.[91] Historically marijuana is likely to have contributed to work-related injury and death among labourers, though *indica* is less risky than other factors, particularly alcohol, fatigue and malnutrition.

Early laws against drug *Cannabis* served to control labour, and thus carried racial meanings depending on context. Local laws prohibited marijuana in Brazil beginning in 1830, when a botanist characterized users as 'Ethiopians [that is, Afro-Brazilians, who] extract from [*Cannabis*] powerful poisons and anodynes . . .; incense from the leaves is reported to be the best remedy against hangovers'.[92] Early legal controls on *Cannabis* targeted South Asian labourers in Sri Lanka (1867), Guyana (1885) and Mauritius (by 1898); African slaves in Angola and Mozambique (about 1875); African and South Asian labourers in South Africa (1870); South Asian sailors in Britain (after 1900); and 'Mexican', 'Black' and 'Poor White' workers in North America (mostly after 1900).[93] Concern about poor whites and *dagga* similarly arose in South Africa, where one expert hoped to list *Cannabis* as a 'noxious' weed to hinder drug use.[94] In Panama and New Mexico, marijuana symbolized indolent soldiers.[95]

Cannabis hemp has also borne anti-labour meanings, especially in Great Britain and the U.S. Hemp workers were marked racially, economically and criminally. Race was most important in the U.S. In 1836, a Kentucky farmer complained that it was 'nearly impossible' to hire whites for hemp work, so that 'of course it is entirely done by slave labor'.[96] Besides, there were other incentives to keep hemp a slave crop. 'Owing to their high birth rate, the slaves increased faster than they were needed. Sale of the surplus blacks to the lower South brought welcome revenue', and led to charges that hemp growers were slave breeders.[97] The interests of elites in Kentucky hemp society were nostalgically celebrated as morally noble (in explicitly Christian

William Hogarth, *The Harlot Beats Hemp in Bridewell Prison*, 1732.

scriptural terms) in James Lee Allen's novel *The Reign of Law* (1900).[98] When hemp expanded to other U.S. states, hemp workers remained racially defined. In 1887 Nebraska's first hemp-producing company 'brought hand brakes from Kentucky and colored laborers to operate them'.[99] Sharecropping functionally replaced slavery after emancipation, and hemp represented racialized underclasses as long as the industry survived. In 1926 Kentuckians considered *Cannabis* 'a "nigger" crop' because only sharecroppers still grew it.[100]

Hemp promoters apparently had no qualms about labour conditions, for *Cannabis* maintained entirely positive meanings. The plant represented the patriotic effort needed to sustain nations. In Britain, the failure to self-supply cordage and cloth was 'the greatest Shame to the nation' in 1742, because it 'necessitate[s us] to have these commodities from those who would destroy [us]'.[101] This moralism extended to North America. In 1765, an expert from Boston believed that 'It is [a] matter of reproach . . . that the importation of Hemp . . . has not already annually decreased.'[102] Another colonist considered hemp 'worthy of the serious attention . . . of every man, who truly loves his country'.[103] Although hemp labourers were below consideration, hemp labour could sustain national sovereignty and improve domestic society. In 1808, an Englishman argued that 'hemp ought to be grown here, in England, where we have plenty of land and plenty of hands'.[104] Imports took jobs. More jobs meant fewer burdensome paupers. 'Hemp is one of the most profitable productions . . ., as it employs a great number of poor people in a very advantageous manner', wrote an American in 1771.[105] Indeed, from 1576 inmates of British poorhouses were made to learn work ethics by processing hemp.

Criminals could learn via hemp too. In 1724, Virginian colonists proposed a penal labour county, called 'Hempshire', where land was 'fit to produce hemp and flax'. Not coincidentally, the proposal also promised 'better Supply of cordage in our Naval Stores'.[106] Criminal prisoners sentenced to hard labour in Victorian Britain processed raw hemp and tore apart old ropes – which 'cuts and blisters their fingers' – to make oakum.[107] Prisoners in Kentucky made hempen

Prison twine plant with *Cannabis* field inside the walls. U.S., c. 1915.

sackcloth before the Civil War.[108] Nine U.S. states and one Canadian province operated twine-spinning plants in prisons from the 1880s into the mid-1900s. Cheap labour enabled penitentiaries to undersell private manufacturers, to whom 'prison twine' symbolized unfair competition.[109]

In the 1900s, *Cannabis* increasingly symbolized crime. Prohibition represents drug use as a criminal rather than health concern. Prohibition diametrically transformed the meaning of hemp worldwide, following the U.S. precedent. Hemp still meekly symbolized American sovereignty and productivity in the 1930s, even though marijuana had been vilified.[110] The U.S. prohibition law of 1937 exempted *Cannabis* stalks, seeds and oil, though hemp remained economically unattractive. Hemp briefly represented military victory during the Second World War, although by 1950 it represented the evil of marijuana.[111] The last U.S. hemp producers ceased operating in 1958. In 1970 hemp *Cannabis* came under the control of the U.S. anti-narcotics agency, which gained authority to issue hemp-farming permits (but did not do so).[112] By 1976 U.S. and Canadian anti-narcotics agencies were goading taxonomists to label hemp *Cannabis* as indistinguishable from marijuana.[113] Hemp became criminal – an inconsequential side effect of drug prohibition.

Drugs represented moral and religious struggle in *The Moloch of Marihuana* (1943).

U.S. anti-drug agents burning hashish, Afghanistan, 2008.

Other countries eventually agreed. For instance, despite millennia of use, Germany outlawed hemp in 1982 (but re-authorized it in the 1990s hemp renaissance).[114]

Drug *Cannabis* gained much stronger criminal meaning. Experts – particularly Harry Anslinger, head of U.S. anti-narcotics efforts from 1930 to 1962 – adapted older narratives of marijuana madness, sloth and immorality to new contexts. Anslinger's 1937 article 'Marihuana, Assassin of Youth' successfully transferred the medieval Orientalist tale to the twentieth-century U.S.[115] He followed with several pulpy books about gruesome drug dangers. Nearly all articles about *indica* in mainstream English-language publications from the 1930s to the 1990s focused on crime, although often the drug seems to have been merely in the wrong place at the wrong time, in the pockets of lawbreakers. Anti-drug scholars and authorities represented marijuana as a gateway to crime, harder drugs and degeneration.[116] The gateway hypothesis has been fundamental to U.S. drug-control policies, yet it erroneously ignores social and geographic context.[117]

During the 1900s, *indica* was really associated with violence as its commerce was outlawed. Criminal enterprises fought for control of black markets. Many police officers, their opponents and bystanders have died through black-market violence.[118] Battles among drug-dealing criminal groups and governments have killed tens of thousands in Mexico, Colombia and elsewhere.[119] The Central American black-market trade to supply the U.S. has produced such heavy costs that sitting presidents of Guatemala, Honduras, El Salvador and Costa Rica, and former presidents of Mexico, Colombia and Brazil, have called to end the War on Drugs so that the commerce can be less violently controlled.[120] In 2013 Uruguay became the first country to reject the war on *Cannabis* by legalizing the drug within its borders.

Political-economic authorities responded severely to real and perceived marijuana crimes. This severity has been portrayed in belligerent language since 1907. In Mexico, near the end of the Porfirio dictatorship, the unpopular government absolutely prohibited drug *Cannabis*. A New York newspaper called this policy 'War on Marihuana Smoking'.[121] Similarly, the 'War against Mariahuana Users' described the 1917 efforts of an army commander in New Mexico, who blamed

Marijuana smoke-in protest, Australia, *c.* 2005.

the 'Asiatic plant' for dereliction among soldiers who 'took to the drug as a substitute for liquor, which ... anti-drink regulations are making increasingly hard to get'.[122] A discourse of righteous violence propelled prohibition: 'the "dynamite" of God, the gospel of Christ, is the greatest weapon that can be wielded in the battle against the dynamite of the devil – marihuana'.[123] Righteousness persisted even without religiosity. In 1973 U.S. President Nixon declared global war on 'the drug menace' in language similar to Cold War discourse.[124] In the U.S., this effectively meant war on marijuana, by far the most common illegal drug.[125] Draconian punishments have destroyed scores of marijuana law-breakers, and battle-clad narcotics agents regularly conquer burning heaps of *Cannabis* in photos of the drug war.

Marijuana law enforcement reflects historic stereotypes. The best statistics are from the U.S., but similar bias exists elsewhere.[126] African-Americans face ten times the rate of drug-related arrests as whites in the U.S., although the racial groups use marijuana at statistically identical rates.[127] War-on-Drugs law enforcement has been called 'the new Jim Crow',[128] recalling historic segregation. The international group Human Rights Watch concluded that the U.S. drug law system's 'human[,] social, economic and political toll is as incalculable as it is unjust'.[129] In Brazil, human rights advocates consider the War on Drugs 'pointless' and a 'war on people'.[130] Police particularly target Afro-Brazilians and Native Americans.[131]

The drug war has generated angry responses, with marijuana symbolizing justified revolt. Marijuana growers are embedded 'guerrilla' farmers in Global Northern societies.[132] Hemp and marijuana activists antagonize the system through lobbying, legal complaints and protests.[133] Mostly peaceful public smoke-ins annually annoy the authorities in cities worldwide.

Law-enforcement violence has spurred counter-violence, real and rhetorical. The musical genre of *narcocorridos* arose in the 1930s, eventually expressing world views of drug-trading young men in Mexico, Colombia and the U.S. *Narcocorridos* celebrate violence within gangster economies, and anger against authorities.[134] This genre foreshadowed

U.S. gangsta rap, which originated in the 1980s among African-American men in cities embroiled in the drug war. Protest songs like 'Fuck Tha Police' (U.S., 1988) challenged a legal system that was biased against blacks. Rappers gave marijuana anti-establishment symbolism with lines like, 'Since I was a youth I smoked weed out' and 'We do not just say no, we too busy sayin' yeah!'[135] U.S. President Reagan intensified the War on Drugs in the 1980s; its youth anti-drug programme was called 'Just Say No!' and rallied around the colour green.

Drug *Cannabis* has always had meaning to its users. We lack direct knowledge of what these meanings were before the twentieth century, other than from ancient South Asian texts, medieval Arabic poetry and early modern travel accounts by British sailors. We have no direct accounts of drug use from social underclasses in Asia, Africa, Europe or the Americas, until musicians began singing about *indica* in the 1920s.

Drug *Cannabis* has carried religious meaning. In South Asia, mystics and ascetics maintain faint echoes of ancient Indo-European practices around the Hindu Kush.[136] Muslim *fakirs* and Hindu *sadhus* have used high doses of drug *Cannabis* to sustain fasts and gain spiritual awareness. *Sadhus* were commonly depicted with *bhang* tea and water pipes in early modern Indian paintings. Medieval Arabic-speaking poets commonly portrayed *fakirs* as *Cannabis* users, and later European travel writers considered these devotees morally corrupt because of their drug use. A *fakir* supplied *bhang* for Thomas Bowrey's initial drug experimentation in India in the 1670s.[137] Muslim societies generally came to consider *indica* an illegitimate path to spirituality.[138] Hindu users in India and the worldwide diaspora associate the drug with the gods Shiva and Indra.[139] *Cannabis* remains sacramental in Hinduism and other South Asian religions.[140]

Other religious uses are relatively recent. In the Americas, Native Americans in Amazonian Brazil use *indica* in spiritual contexts,[141] but the plant arrived there after 1500. In Central Africa, marijuana has been mostly mundane, but sometimes serves to provide spiritual clarity and transformation.[142] Such use survived among descendants

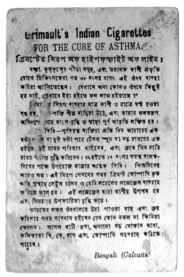

Promotional card for Grimault's Indian cigarettes; the Bangla text
advertises cough syrup. India, c. 1900.

of liberated slaves in Jamaica into the 1900s.[143] In the 1880s colonial
violence and arms trading in Central Africa helped generate the Bena-
diamba ('marijuana brotherhood') politico-religious movement,
which became more an ethnic identity than a religion. Stereotypes that
sub-Saharan *indica* was 'truly ceremonial', 'a staple of African shamanism', or transported inside 'magical talismanic dolls' are inaccurate.[144]
Ganja is famously a Rastafarian sacrament enabling spiritual insight.
Rastafarianism arose in Jamaica in the 1930s, when its followers melded
South Asian and Central African beliefs in their Caribbean context.
Rastafarian *ganja* uses have been transported and transformed glob-
ally through Jamaican reggae music, most influentially in the work of
Bob Marley.[145]

Middle-class users in the Global North have created meanings
for drug *Cannabis* since the mid-1800s. The French *Club des Hashishins*,
a group of artists and writers who ate *dawamesk* during the 1840s,
imagined themselves entering the experience of Assassins and other
stereotypical characters. The psychiatrist who founded the club, Jacques-
Joseph Moreau, believed that drug *Cannabis* could both treat and cause

mental illness. Moreau pioneered mental health considerations of *Cannabis*, framed in Orientalism. 'Anyone who has travelled to the Orient knows how widespread the use of hashish is, especially among the Arabs.'[146] Moreau's novices influentially portrayed the drug's effects, particularly books by Charles Baudelaire, who preferred alcohol and morphine.[147]

Drug *Cannabis* has stimulated many creative artists. In the 1900s musical genres worldwide praised *indica*, including Greek *Rebétiko* music (beginning 1920s), U.S. jazz (1920s), rock and roll (1950s), Jamaican reggae (1960s) and other genres elsewhere.[148] Marijuana music reflects its social context. In the hedonistic 1920s of the U.S., 'reefer' represented creative inspiration and escapist recreation.[149] In Greece, where many users in the early 1900s were Greek refugees from Turkey, hashish symbolized the effects of social marginalization: 'Five years, I got, in Yendi-Koule jail / Ball and chain turned me on to the *argílé* [water pipe].'[150]

Political-spiritual meanings propelled the marijuana boom of the 1960s. In the U.S., counter-cultural writers and musicians turned many people on to drugs. A few hipsters in the 1940s and '50s used marijuana, and Beat Generation writers portrayed it.[151] Drug use exploded in the mid-1960s. In 1966 Allen Ginsberg challenged 'the great marijuana hoax' perpetrated by U.S. authorities. 'The actual experience of the smoked herb has been clouded by a fog of dirty language perpetrated by a crowd of fakers who have not had the experience and yet insist on downgrading it.'[152] For the psychologist Timothy Leary, the magical medicine of marijuana could enable the better society that progressive agitators promised.[153] 'There are three groups who are bringing about the great evolution of the new age', he asserted, 'the DOPE DEALERS, the ROCK MUSICIANS, and the underground WRITERS and ARTISTS.'[154] Non-celebrities similarly projected progressive meanings upon marijuana,[155] often in underground comics and newspapers.

Importantly, the marijuana boom of the 1960s advanced neo-Orientalist stereotypes of *Cannabis*. Writers emphasized experiences in

Paul McCartney was arrested for drug *Cannabis* possession in Japan, 1980.

southern Asia and North Africa.[156] Ginsberg wrote that marijuana was a way of entering into 'consciousness described in the Prajnaparamita Sutra central to a Buddhist or even Christian or Hindu view of Kosmos'.[157] Leary's ideal guide for novices was '[Middle Eastern] Sufis, [who are] cannabis alchemists and magicians'.[158] Other celebrities embraced neo-Orientalist meanings for drugs, including The Beatles.[159] Neo-Orientalism benefited from superficial consideration of marijuana history. An aficionado wrote in 1969 that 'A strange historical reverse is going on: Americans are being accused of turning on . . . innocent native population[s]! (We in North America inherited the practice from our black [and] Mexican . . . brothers.)'[160] The parenthetical statement might be broadly true, but it neglected the dynamics of the global marijuana boom, whose leaders were white North Americans. Instead, the aficionado anachronistically adopted the 1930s prohibitionist discourse that minorities were spreading marijuana among whites.

The progressive marijuana politics of the 1960s peaked in the 1970s. In the U.S., marijuana symbolized infringed civil liberties for its advocates, who practised civil disobedience at public smoke-ins. Several jurisdictions decriminalized marijuana. Nonetheless, *indica* still represented immorality to most authorities. Prohibition laws remained in place and were enforced, even against critically ill patients for whom marijuana represented medicine.[161] New laws criminalized drug paraphernalia and literature.[162] Marijuana was fully re-stigmatized in the 1980s, when President Reagan intensified the global War on Drugs. Conspiracy theories about prohibition sprouted in *Cannabis* histories, belying paranoia among marijuana aficionados.

The anti-establishment meaning of drug *Cannabis* produced the iconic, stereotyped drug dealer. Since the 1930s, political authorities had portrayed 'marihuana peddlers' as morally corrupt predators of weak-willed users,[163] but popular portrayals have been kinder. The French smuggler Henri de Monfreid, who trafficked hash to Europe in the mid-nineteenth century, glorified drug-smuggling (and gun-running) in numerous adventure books.[164] Timothy Leary called dealers 'the new Robin Hood' for challenging anti-drug laws.[165] Nonetheless, in the 2000s, some U.S. dealers considered marijuana users to be dupes, wasting themselves with the drug.[166] Dealers in the U.S., Colombia and elsewhere sometimes gained respect in their communities for succeeding against biased political-economic systems.[167] Yet authorities in some countries established the death

Cannabis advocacy designs on personalized postage stamps, The Netherlands, 2010s.

penalty for dealers, and moralistic politicians elsewhere called for similar intolerance.[168]

Hemp similarly came to symbolize state oppression. In 1980, activists complained that 'British farmers could face 14 years in jail' if they tried to emulate successful French farmers.[169] Unlike pre-prohibition promoters, recent activists blame governments, not people, for the sorry state of industrial hemp. In the U.S., activists have planted hempseeds as an act of civil disobedience,[170] while police enforce the criminal meaning of hemp. In 1999 the U.S. Drug Enforcement Agency (DEA) ordered Canadian farmers to recall tons of birdseed after zealous testing uncovered a THC content of 0.0014 per cent in a truckload of hempseed.[171] A promising trial of East Asian hemp cultivars in Hawaii ended in 1999 because the DEA constructed insurmountable bureaucratic obstacles, despite the state's blessing.[172] Successful legal challenges to state authority have centred on the meaning of hemp, rather than the portrayal of marijuana as criminal, dangerous and useless. In 2004 a U.S. court decided that the DEA had unlawfully extended the meaning of 'marijuana' to include 'hemp' in anti-drug policies.[173]

Cannabis was resurgent in the 1990s. Hemp was burdened with environmental symbolism in its renaissance. Marijuana has represented patient-centred healthcare. The populist medical marijuana movement has been most successful in the U.S., and portrays *indica* as an unethically forbidden medicine.[174] Medical marijuana laws tend to focus on debilitating illnesses, suggesting the struggles of past advocates. Many medical users, however, are not critically ill. In states with liberal laws, such as California, drug *Cannabis* is authorized for debilitating conditions and 'any other illness for which marijuana provides relief'.[175] Some patients admit that marijuana only marginally relieves their ailment, but nevertheless find that getting high makes life better – 'I am a more loving, attentive and patient father when I take my medication.'[176] To opponents of medical marijuana, the drug represents 'snake oil', a front for illegal, unsafe and unnecessary recreational use.[177]

Understanding *Cannabis* in current global society is challenging because symbolic meanings that are often substituted for empirical information. For the past two centuries, people have too often avoided undertaking original research, because symbolic cultures of *Cannabis* have seemed either unassailable, or not worth assailing.

Hemp, weaving and seed-eating birds, France, *c.* 1900.

seven

How Do You Know *Cannabis?*

K nowledge of plants does not arise simply from observing how plants interact with their environments. Instead, it is the outcome of social processes, which might or might not value specific observations. Whether or not a particular observation is deemed to produce legitimate knowledge depends upon subjective methods of research and learning, as well as needs within societies for creating order, conformity and predictability.[1]

The unusual character of *Cannabis* – a cosmopolitan genus with two cryptic species and two symbolically charged uses – has strongly shaped how people have generated information about it. Initially, ethnocentrism shaped knowledge production. European scholars who first paid attention to *Cannabis* after 1500 came from societies whose world views gazed down from imagined pinnacles of sociocultural supremacy. Their science supported the broad project of European colonialism.[2] The portrayed weakness of non-Europeans for drug *Cannabis* was one of many ostensible facts justifying extension of authority from the Global North over the South. In the twentieth century, political-economic elites increasingly controlled *Cannabis* by narrowly delimiting legitimate from illegitimate knowledge about the plant, thereby preventing outsiders from gaining authority over it. Knowledge is power.

Observers have for decades recognized that official knowledge of *Cannabis* serves mainly to establish the moral supremacy of prohibition.[3]

Yet anti-prohibitionists have also produced unscientific science to establish moral supremacy. Under prohibition, very little *Cannabis* expertise has been accrued through formal study. Personal experience provides expertise too, though individual experience usually does not extend beyond a limited social group. Current *Cannabis* expertise is compartmentalized within global society. Several subcultures of expertise overlap minimally, yet share practices of knowledge production due to the shared constraints of prohibition.

One similarity is the need to establish sub-cultural expertise explicitly. Recitations of experience signify credibility in *Cannabis* media, indicating reliability independently of evidence or argument. A hemp activist postures, 'I started learning about hemp as a teenager.'[4] A researcher blesses the writer of *The Science of Marijuana* (2000) 'as a scientist who works on understanding how drugs act on the brain'.[5] Other scientists simply list degrees, titles and affiliations. Marijuana aficionados flaunt illegal expertise with obvious pseudonyms like 'S. T. Oner'; singers of *narcocorridos* and gangsta rap trumpet

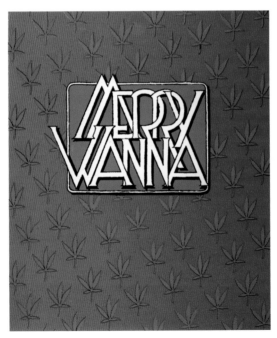

Christmas greetings card, U.S., 1990.

underworld experience. Conversely, anti-*Cannabis* authorities trumpet legal credentials: '[The Food and Drug Administration] is the sole [U.S.] agency that approves drug products as safe and effective for intended indications.'[6] Clearly, such markers of status are meaningful only within particular subcultures.

The need to establish credibility reflects the general lack of knowledge about *Cannabis*, despite its past and present importance. Learned knowledge of *Cannabis* has developed slowly. Agriculturalists have explicated hemp for centuries, but most readers avoid formal agronomy. Hemp promoters sell more books with advertising copy, given in titles such as *A Way to Get Wealth* (1676) and *Hemp: What the World Needs Now* (2010).[7] The regular publication of how-to books alongside constant farming inducements suggests that few people have gained enduring knowledge of hemp from paper.

Hemp knowledge can not be separated from marijuana knowledge. European scientists significantly began paying attention to drug *Cannabis* in the 1840s. Nineteenth-century pharmacists did not know cannabinoid chemistry but simply applied established methods of preparing herbal extracts. Into the 1900s, chemists could not reliably differentiate psychoactive and non-psychoactive *Cannabis*. Pharmacists estimated a plant's psychoactivity based on provenance, and debated whether 'Indian hemp' not grown in India could be useful.[8] This debate persists in the form of botanical field experiments – planting seeds from one location in another, then testing cannabinoid content (or fibre potential). THC was not identified until 1964, and chemical tests were slow, expensive and imprecise into the 1980s.

Given this lack of knowledge, *Cannabis* psychoactivity was historically attributed to human behaviour rather than plant biology. By the 1700s, European travellers considered marijuana a wasteful use of a familiar-looking plant with presumed potential for fibre production. In 1797 an Englishman in South Africa complained that the 'common hemp' he observed was squandered as a 'substitute for tobacco'.[9] In 1803 *Cannabis* agronomic trials began in Portuguese Angola under the belief that marijuana was a 'terrible and disastrous' use of '*cânhamo*',

Ash tray, probably U.S., c. 1970.

or European *sativa* hemp.[10] Simultaneously in British India, botanists unsuccessfully tried making rope from *ganja* plants,[11] and dispatched *indica* seeds in the hope of initiating an Australian hemp industry.

The notion that psychoactive marijuana is simply a use of European hemp persists. Anti-prohibitionists elevate the historical status of marijuana by maintaining that George Washington used the drug, because he farmed hemp. European *sativa* hempseeds did not somehow germinate psychoactive plants on Washington's Virginia plantation, and presentist presumptions are unnecessary to understand his agricultural practices.

Of course, for East Asian *indica* hemp, marijuana *can be* just another use. The nineteenth-century switch from European *sativa* to East Asian *indica* hemp in the U.S. and Europe has been mostly forgotten. Nonetheless, in the U.S. before 1945, experts recognized that for then-dominant *indica* fibre cultivars, the difference between marijuana and hemp was simply the manner of use.[12] Even fieldworkers seem to have discovered this in late nineteenth-century Kentucky by smoking female hemp flowers.[13] In China, current anti-narcotics literature simply calls the plant *ta má* ('great hemp'), which in ancient times distinguished hemp uses from drug uses. This modern usage reflects the reality that context rather than appellation determines the legality of Chinese *Cannabis*.

This same logic was embedded in U.S. prohibition laws, although the formal appellation *Cannabis sativa* L. envelopes two cryptic species. *Cannabis* specimens cannot be reliably determined psychoactive or non-psychoactive, *indica* or *sativa*, based on physical characters. This has always been the case. A nineteenth-century French botanist confessed that physical differences between French *chanvre* and Algerian *kif* were 'easier to notice in the field than to express precisely through a botanical description; for [the differences] reduce . . . to simple nuances [which] are not always perfectly clear'.[14] When prohibition began in the U.S., certain uses were allowed and disallowed, not specific types of *Cannabis*, because taxonomists were then, and remain, unable to distinguish the two species visually. This situation offered a fairly obvious legal loophole. Anyone arrested could avoid conviction by claiming possession of only hemp, whose status remained a grey area in drug law. All *Cannabis* material became more unquestionably illegal once all

Anti-drug public awareness postcard, China, 2011.

plants were assigned to one species. Of course, the idea that *sativa* – European hemp – is the central concept of *Cannabis* simply reflects the origins of scientific taxonomy on a Baltic seashore in the 1750s.

The historical coincidence that science adopted European hemp as the prototypical *Cannabis* has supported a Eurocentric biogeography. *Cannabis* histories map Europe as the origin of drug *Cannabis* populations outside the Old World, under the belief that non-Europeans initiated a novel use of a temperate Eurasian plant. This conceptual error allowed *Cannabis* drug use to represent cultural difference, rather than biological diffusion from Asia or Africa.

The variety of *Cannabis* stereotypes betrays a lack of knowledge about human–*Cannabis* relationships. Historic European scholars knew much about certain *sativa* cultures. Confidence in the general relevance of this knowledge prevented careful observation of other cultures. The first robust study of a non-European *Cannabis* culture came in the 1894 report of the Indian Hemp Drugs Commission, which studied *bhang, charas* and *ganja* in British India.[15] No subsequent study of drug *Cannabis* within a society has been as thorough, although recent works have improved understanding of the plant in scattered societies. Global Southern societies are vastly underrepresented in the literature, which focuses on biochemistry, pharmacology and epidemiology in Europe and North America.[16] We know that New York City residents used more marijuana following the attacks of 11 September 2001,[17] but we do not know how survivors of violence in the ancient *indica* zone might use the drug. The *Cannabis* cultures of the Global South are undervalued human resources.

Repetitiveness in the *Cannabis* literature has been frustrating for decades, and practised for centuries. Trenchant reviews have described *Cannabis* books as 'highly incestuous' (1975), 'stuffed with rehashes of well known materials . . . that read wearisomely for the expert' (1977), and 'less . . . careful scholarship than a polemic' (2007).[18] A pattern of plagiarizing information about *Cannabis* arose in sixteenth-century European scientific botany, following more than a millennium of rehashes of Dioscorides and Galen.[19]

Many *Cannabis* 'facts' have become established through repetition.
The dangers of marijuana use have been amplified since the early 1800s
via retellings of key stories, and embellished hearsay. For decades, Harry
Anslinger shared anecdotes from his 'gore file' of sensationalist news
clippings, and opened his file for writers who parroted him as far away
as Tasmania.[20] Prohibitionists have chanted the mantra that drug
Cannabis has no medicinal use,[21] despite its historic appearance in legal
pharmacopoeias, and studies in the 1800s and since the 1970s show-
ing its effectiveness for treating various conditions.[22] Pro-marijuana
literature has also generated truth through repetition.

Received wisdom flourishes through poor citation of sources.
The traceable bibliographic trajectories of *Cannabis* anecdotes can be
remarkable. For instance, marijuana advocates maintain that seven early
U.S. presidents used drug *Cannabis*, including one allegedly addicted to
hashish. Recent recitations seem to trace to *The Great Book of Hemp* (1996),
a mostly reliable reference work that cited a 1975 source not listed in
its bibliography.[23] The 1975 citation was in fact a Neo-Pagan spiritual-
ist magazine that had borrowed the article 'Pot & Presidents' from
another vaguely identified source, which was a page of pro-marijuana
humour in an underground newspaper of 1972 from New Mexico.[24]
Other anecdotes can be traced back to advocacy materials. George
Washington's association with marijuana seemingly began with a poster
in 1973.[25] Among U.S. presidents, only Barack Obama has admitted
getting high.[26] One of Queen Victoria's many physicians published

Graffiti on U.S. currency, 1995.

185

the unremarkable nineteenth-century view that *Cannabis indica* had (limited) medical usefulness.[27] There is no evidence that he prescribed *indica* for the Queen – a quite unlikely event – but her use of it became fact through pro-marijuana ads in *Playboy* magazine during the 1970s.[28] Harry Anslinger was puritanically intolerant of marijuana, and ruined many people through his influence. Marijuana advocates have understandably vilified him, although sometimes with unfair tactics. A hemp activist, for instance, ostensibly paraphrased 1930s prohibitionists as saying '[marijuana] mak[es] the "darkies" think they [are] as good as "white men"'.[29] Other activists attribute the unsavoury quote to Anslinger, although it was written in the 1980s to promote hemp.

People have learned about *Cannabis* primarily through experience with unwritten practices. Since the early 1800s, laws against drug *Cannabis* further deepened the historical shadows cloaking the marginal populations who used the plant, and pushed knowledge underground. In southern Africa, twentieth-century users smoked earth pipes – tubes formed in the ground – to dispense with incriminating paraphernalia.[30] Users in New York City in the 1930s smoked in rooms sealed so tightly that they risked suffocation.[31] A common experience of marijuana aficionados in the Global North has been to acquire 'some nameless pot [from] the weird dude on the corner'.[32] A guiding principle in current marijuana horticulture is to 'never tell anybody about any garden [and] never trust anybody – friends, family . . . even your mother!'[33]

Knowledge of drug *Cannabis* has been communicated secretly for centuries, following millennia of informal discussions. The language of drug *Cannabis* has (purposefully) impeded the formalization of knowledge. Historical scholars struggle to identify *Cannabis* in antiquarian texts because it had so many names.[34] Since the 1800s, drug *Cannabis* has travelled under assumed names, whether 'tobacco' throughout the Atlantic or 'locoweed' in North America, a name that also referred to certain other plants that sicken livestock.[35] The number of nicknames generated after the North American marijuana awakening of the 1920s stumped the authorities, who needed dictionaries of 'criminal slang' to understand.[36] In the Caribbean, people developed

Advertisement (detail) from *Playboy* magazine:
Queen Victoria smoking a joint, U.S., 1977.

Flyer for a 4 20 event, Madison, Wisconsin, 2012.

hidden vocabularies to conceal their activities, calling *indica* 'gully weed' and 'kaya' among other names.[37] The marijuana boom of the 1960s generated a diverse lingo whose evolution continues.[38]

Marijuana has become an open secret across the Global North, and hidden language has become as much stylistic as concealing. One example is the number '420' – pronounced 'four-twenty', and including the time '4:20' and the American-style date '4/20' – names without naming marijuana. The code word originated among California teenagers in the 1970s, but has become internationally important.[39] *Cannabis*-friendly commerce peaks around 20 April, a popular day to celebrate marijuana (and hemp) and protest prohibition. The Internet readily yielded directions to dozens of 4/20/2014 events in countries across Europe, the Americas and Oceania. Even the authorities take notice: on 20 April 2006, the U.S. Food and Drug Administration reiterated its view that drug *Cannabis* is medically useless.[40] Global ambivalence towards *Cannabis* might become salient each April, but polarization permeates knowledge of the plant.

Humans have excellent practical knowledge of *Cannabis* uses, yet limited understanding of its sociocultural consequences, whether past or present. Global Northern authorities had little idea what marijuana was when outlawing it in the early 1900s; in 1919 a fire-department physician stated, 'hashish . . . is produced by the burning of jute' and is more deadly than the 'yellow fumes of [burning] sulphur'.[41] Prohibition created insurmountable obstacles to research,[42] and cast *Cannabis* as a disreputable or dangerous object of study. As a result, *Cannabis* experts often rely on ideas believed to be true rather than those known to be true, a quality called 'truthiness'.

Truthiness is common in debates about drug use generally,[43] and marijuana specifically, as well as hemp. Governments order commissions to study marijuana, then ignore, disavow or suppress reports that do not support established policy. Hemp activists make inaccurate claims because they believe authorities have conspired to obscure the plant's value. Governments inaccurately undersell real hemp economies because prohibition posits that *Cannabis* has no value. Journalists, police and anti-marijuana physicians misrepresent marijuana to support pre-existing ideas about the drug's dangers. Marijuana advocates concoct stories to elevate the drug's historical status, and overlook its real risks (which are imperfectly known because prohibition has stunted research).

The consequences of false claims are both material and symbolic. Histories carry symbolism, and pseudo-histories belittle real human experiences. For instance, a hemp activist scored a symbolic victory on 4 July 2013 by having a hempen flag raised over the U.S. Capitol Building.[44] This flag was meant as 'a reminder of the role hemp played in the founding and early days of the country'. The activist illustrated hemp's historic value with the canard that the first U.S. flag was made of hemp. The first flag disappeared in the 1700s. The story of its creation emerged in 1870, and included nothing about the cloth; in any case, most flags were made of lightweight wool bunting in the 1700s and 1800s.[45] In the early days of the country, slave-grown hemp sackcloth

A Kentucky Hemp Field.

Hemp breaking in a Kentucky field, c. 1913.

wrapped slave-grown cotton bales. Low-quality hemp was woven with low-quality wool, jute and cotton to make 'negro cloth', used to clothe slaves.[46] Hemp's role in slavery should be recalled amid cheerleading for its revival, especially in a setting as symbolic as a national capitol building.

Cannabis has been valued for millennia, and past societies developed multiple ways of managing it. The policy of prohibition represents one globally normative option, simple in principle but difficult to implement because it reduces the complexities of human–*Cannabis* interaction to a binary good–bad choice. This oversimplification under-lies the belief that prohibition unquestionably benefits society, or is unquestionably irrational. For decades, progressive, populist factions and reactionary, authoritarian elements have debated these irreconcil-able views. The debate has become more important than knowledge production; pro- and anti-*Cannabis* discourse has changed little for decades.

It is difficult to assign good *or* bad labels to any of the plant's uses. Both hemp and marijuana encompass unresolved contradiction. Hemp's conundrum is that of modern agriculture. It has untapped potential as a renewable resource, capable of replacing wood, petroleum and animal-based foods. Yet the environmental friendliness of hemp is poorly tested,[47] and its commercial production is as input-intensive as any modern agriculture. Ancient environmental costs still exist: retting requires water, and can pollute water sources; commercial cultivation requires copious fertilizer; processing requires considerable labour, or energy-intensive machinery. Hemp's overall impact is not necessarily higher or lower than that of competing crops,[48] but any agricultural transition carries unforeseen costs. Attempts to create bio-fuel economies based on other plants have proven energy-inefficient, and taken fields from food crops.

The long-standing arguments that hemp generates employment and enhances national sovereignty remain active (and perhaps true for any crop). A 2010 book asks: 'Can you visualize an America [that uses]

'Hemp for Fuel' patch, U.S., c. 1990s.

Fake money with marijuana theme, U.S., 2013.

hemp-based methanol produced in the U.S., by local workers? It is a practical . . . vision [that] will dramatically reduce the U.S. dependency on foreign-owned oil.'[49] Hemp industries provide employment, but historically this work was unpopular and unprofitable. In the U.S., hemp's potential profit margin is thin,[50] a fact that would favour large agribusinesses if the crop became legal. Furthermore, before prohibition the favoured hemp cultivars represented *indica*; the activists' argument that hemp is inherently drug-free is not entirely correct.

The trickiness of marijuana exceeds that of hemp. Drugs in global society encapsulate a deep-rooted problem: pleasure is to be pursued, but within limits.[51] The limits can be unpopular and difficult to enforce. Extremely ill people have found relief in marijuana, but many more have simply found a good time. Marijuana is not terribly dangerous compared to other illegal and legal drugs, but it is not risk-free. The legal control of drugs is a fundamentally progressive idea in human history, even if control policies have been self-serving, prejudiced and unsuccessful.[52] The failure of prohibition to control marijuana is globally salient. *Cannabis* is the most widely used illegal drug, despite a War on Drugs that has cost trillions of dollars over the last 40 years, and impedes global development goals.[53] Prohibitions have other perverse effects. Negatively framed anti-drug messages encourage some people to try the negated behaviour,[54] even as prohibition creates obstacles to understanding this use. In India, drug prohibitions imposed by the United Nations in 1961 have damaged millennia-old medical, religious and cultural norms that reduced drug risks, while also shifting consumption away from *Cannabis* towards harder drugs, such as crude heroin.[55]

The currently fraught status of *Cannabis* can obscure and distort millennia of human experience. Broad patterns of human–*Cannabis* interaction have been remarkably consistent for very long periods of time. Focusing entirely on whether prohibition makes sense nowadays overlooks important reasons why *Cannabis* acquired its current status. Despite the trite aphorism about repeating history without knowing it, the lack of historical knowledge in current debates does not promise that the human–*Cannabis* relationship is indeed moving forward, regardless of legal and political changes since the 1990s. Hemp initially gained success as a weed, and enjoyed enduring agricultural success only where people were satisfied to grow it in small quantities, or where large-scale production was subsidized through exploitative labour relationships, unfair market conditions, or (very recently) fossil fuels. Drug *indica* also first succeeded as a weed, and gained global popularity by offering momentary escape from difficult realities, an escape nuanced with medicinal activity, sensual pleasures and spiritual meanings. By providing escape, marijuana has enabled social marginalization rather than opposition to it. It remains unproven that hemp is sustainable, or that marijuana has escaped the social margins.

Many people appreciate marijuana for enabling spiritual awareness outside formal religions, including as an aspect of recreational use. Informal, drug-enhanced spirituality has been disregarded, ridiculed or negatively framed as hedonism, hallucination or mental illness. Nonetheless, one insight drug *Cannabis* offered in one society should be considered more broadly. In the early twentieth century, Sesotho-speaking *dagga* smokers in South Africa sang, 'We smoke it and . . . remember the miracles of the world / We remember those far and near / We remember.'[56] Whether hemp or drug, *Cannabis* has a complex history that should be remembered, accurately.

Timeline

55 to 65 million years ago	*Cannabis* evolves to become a distinct genus during this long period
11 million years ago	Regional climate change in Central Asia separates *Cannabis* into two populations; subsequent geological uplift selects for THC production in the southern population
130,000 years ago	Earliest physical evidence of *Cannabis*: pollen from sediment in Lake Baikal, Russia
30,000 to 10,000 years ago	*Cannabis* follows early human migrations across Eurasia
5500–5000 BCE	*Cannabis sativa* is used for fibre across northern Europe, but it is not clearly farmed
4000 BCE	*Cannabis indica* domesticated by this time in East Asia
2600–1700 BCE	Indo-Iranian civilizations flourish around the Hindu Kush mountains, and possibly use *Cannabis indica* in sacramental beverages
16th century BCE	Hempseeds are one of five staple grains during China's Shang Dynasty
16th century BCE	*Cannabis indica* domesticated by this time in South Asia; earliest physical evidence of *Cannabis* in lowland South Asia

7th to 6th centuries BCE	Indo-Iranians in the Tarim Basin include *Cannabis indica* flowers among grave goods
6th century BCE	*Bhang* provides a sacramental beverage in Hinduism, Buddhism and other South Asian religions
5th century BCE	Thracians produce hempen fabric and Scythians burn hempseed at funeral ceremonies; Herodotus takes note
5th to 1st centuries BCE	*Cannabis sativa* enters Europe as a domesticated fibre crop as an outcome of Roman expansion
2nd century BCE	Paper-making invented in China, with *Cannabis* waste fibre
1st century BCE	Chinese writers describe psychoactive uses of *Cannabis indica*, which enter the Chinese pharmacopoeia
2nd century CE	Galen and Dioscorides write about *Cannabis*
10th to 13th centuries	Regional hemp markets and water- and animal-powered hemp mills appear in France
11th and 12th centuries	Increased evidence of pipe smoking across eastern Africa suggests the diffusion of *Cannabis indica*
12th and 13th centuries	Arabic poets in North Africa and the Levant begin writing about *hashish*; Islamic physicians begin to mention psychoactive *Cannabis* explicitly
14th century	Venice establishes a European precedent of controlling hemp production to ensure naval power
14th century	Baltic hemp enters international trade through the Hanseatic League
15th century	African water pipes arrive in the Arabian Peninsula, and subsequently in South Asia and the Levant

16th century	Sailors on Portuguese ships encounter smoking in Mozambique, and *bhang* throughout the western Indian Ocean; sailors bring their knowledge into the Atlantic
16th to 19th centuries	Enslaved people bring knowledge of *diamba* from eastern Africa to western Africa, and throughout the Atlantic via the transatlantic slave trade
16th to 19th centuries	Spain, Portugal and Great Britain increasingly rely on imported Baltic hemp, and try to increase domestic production
17th and 18th centuries	Commercial hemp industries fail in North American colonies, but *Cannabis sativa* persists in subsistence production
1689	Scientist Robert Hooke decides sailor Robert Knox had used 'Indian hemp' in Ceylon, and reports that 'Indian hemp' seeds do not produce psychoactive plants in Britain
18th and 19th centuries	Russian hemp dominates global supply
1753	Taxonomist Carolus Linnaeus names *Cannabis sativa*
1784	Taxonomist Jean-Baptiste Lamarck names *Cannabis indica*
1790s	Commercial hemp production peaks in Spanish Louisiana, and begins in Kentucky
c. 1800	Napoleon's troops learn about hashish in Egypt; Europeans try to make rope from drug *Cannabis* cultivars in British India and Australia, and Portuguese Angola and Brazil
1809	Antoine Silvestre de Sacy popularizes the Assassin tale, which establishes hashish in Orientalist discourse
1829	Rio de Janeiro, Brazil, establishes the first law controlling *Cannabis indica* use

1830s	British physicians in India evaluate the medicinal potential *Cannabis indica*; 'Cannabis indica' becomes an accepted pharmaceutical in Western medicine
1834–1920	Indentured South Asian labourers carry *Cannabis indica* to many locations worldwide, particularly around the Caribbean
1840s	The French *Club des Hashischins* experiments with drug *Cannabis*, and the club's members popularize drug use through subsequent publications
1840s	Mexican authorities first become concerned about *marihuana*
1850s	Hemp *Cannabis* peaks globally; East Asian *indica* hemp introduced to Europe and North America
1870s–1910s	Multiple colonial and independent states in South Asia, southern Africa and the Americas prohibit recreational drug *Cannabis* use in order to control labourers
1880s–1930s	Anti-drug authorities portray drug *Cannabis* as certainly inducing madness and violence in users
1910s–30s	*Marihuana*, *locoweed* and *reefer* gain limited popularity across the U.S.
1925	*Cannabis indica* is included as a controlled substance in the International Opium Convention
1938	*Cannabis* drug prohibition begins in the U.S.
1950s	Commercial hemp production is moribund in Europe and ceases in the U.S.; the Chinese state discourages hemp
1961	The Single Convention on Narcotic Drugs standardizes legal controls on drug *Cannabis* among United Nations member states
1960s–70s	*Cannabis indica* gains global popularity as part of social and political upheavals; celebrities popularize drug use in music, literature, film and art

1960s–present	The popularity of hand-rolled drug *Cannabis* cigarettes creates demand for hemp *Cannabis* rolling papers
1973	U.S. President Richard Nixon declares a global War on Drugs, which continues today
1990s–present	The 'Hemp Renaissance' develops as people seek renewable sources of raw materials; several countries worldwide re-legalize hemp production
1996	In the U.S., California and Arizona legalize medical marijuana use; eighteen states (and Washington, DC) follow by 2014; other countries allowing some medical use include Austria, Canada, Finland, Germany, Israel, Italy, the Netherlands, Portugal, Spain and Sweden
2012	In the U.S., Colorado and Washington State legalize recreational marijuana
2013	Uruguay legalizes the cultivation, sale, distribution and use of *Cannabis indica*
2014	Colorado's government-regulated recreational marijuana market opens; the state reports $14 million in sales and $2 million in taxes during the first month of business

References

1 What is *Cannabis*?

1 John M. McPartland and Karl W. Hillig, 'Early Iconography of *Cannabis Sativa* and *Cannabis Indica*', *Journal of Industrial Hemp*, XII (2008), pp. 189–203; Robert C. Clarke, *Marijuana Botany* (Berkeley, CA, 1981), pp. 157–8.

2 Carl Linnaeus, *Species Plantarum: A Facsimile of the First Edition* [1753], reprint edn (London, 1957), vol. II, p. 1027.

3 Giovanni Anton Scopoli, *Flora Carniolica* (Vienna, 1772), vol. II, p. 263.

4 Kenneth J. Sytsma, Jeffery Morawetz, J. Chris Pires, Molly Nepokroeff, Elena Conti, Michelle Zjhra, Jocelyn C. Hall and Mark W. Chase, 'Urticalean Rosids: Circumscription, Rosid Ancestry, and Phylogenetics Based on *Rbcl*, *Trnl-F*, and *Ndhf* Sequences', *American Journal of Botany*, LXXXIX (2002), pp. 1531–46; Zhekun Zhou and Bruce Bartholomew, 'Cannabaceae', in *Flora of China*, vol. V (*Ulmaceae through Basellaceae*), ed. Z. Wu, Peter H. Raven and D. Y. Hong (Beijing and St Louis, MO, 2003), vol. V, pp. 74–5; Paul G. Mahlberg, 'Laticifers: An Historical Perspective', *Botanical Review*, LIX (1993), pp. 1–23.

5 Ivan Ivanovic Martinov, *Techno-Botanical Glossary, in Latin and Russian Languages* [in Russian] (St Petersburg, 1820), p. 99.

6 Alfred Barton Rendle, *The Classification of Flowering Plants: Dicotyledons* (Cambridge, 1925), vol. II, p. 56.

7 Norton G. Miller, 'The Genera of Cannabaceae in the Southeastern United States', *Journal of the Arnold Arboretum*, LI (1970), pp. 185–203.

8 Legislative Counsel Committee, 'Chapter 475 – Controlled Substances; Illegal Drug Cleanup; Paraphernalia; Precursors', in *Oregon Revised Statutes* (Salem, OR, 2011), vol. XII.

9 Sytsma et al., 'Urticalean Rosids'.

10 Anita Radini, 'Palaeogeography and Palaeoethnobotany of European and African Nettle Trees (*Celtis australis* L. and *Celtis integrifolia* Lam.) in North Africa', Association of American Geographers 2012 Annual Meeting, New York, 2012.

11 Karl-Ernst Behre, 'The History of Beer Additives in Europe: A Review', *Vegetation History and Archaeobotany*, VII (1999), pp. 35–48.

12 Clarke, *Marijuana Botany*; Michael Starks, *Marijuana Chemistry*, 2nd edn (Berkeley, CA, 1990); Richard Evans Schultes and Albert Hofmann, *The Botany and Chemistry of Hallucinogens*, 2nd edn (Springfield, IL, 1980).

13 K. W. Hillig, 'Genetic Evidence for Speciation in *Cannabis* (Cannabaceae)', *Genetic Resources and Crop Evolution*, LII (2005), pp. 161–80; Karl W. Hillig and Paul G. Mahlberg, 'A Chemotaxonomic Analysis of Cannabinoid Variation in *Cannabis* (Cannabaceae)', *American Journal of Botany*, XCI (2004), pp. 966–75.

14 Brent Berlin, *Ethnobiological Classification: Principles of Categorization of Plants and Animals in Traditional Societies* (Princeton, 1992).

15 Arun Agrawal, 'Dismantling the Divide between Indigenous and Western Knowledge', *Development and Change*, XXVI (1995), pp. 413–39.

16 Ernest Small, 'American Law and the Species Problem in *Cannabis*: Science and Semantics', *Bulletin of Narcotics*, XXVII (1975), pp. 1–20; William A. Emboden, 'The Genus *Cannabis* and the Correct Use of Taxonomic Categories', *Journal of Psychoactive Drugs*, XIII (1981), pp. 15–21.

17 Richard Evans Schultes, W. E. Klein, T. Plowman and T. E. Lockwood, '*Cannabis*: An Example of Taxonomic Neglect', *Harvard University Botanical Museum Leaflets*, XXIII (1974), pp. 337–67.

18 S. T. Oner, *Cannabis Indica: The Essential Guide to the World's Finest Marijuana Strains* (San Francisco, CA, 2011); S. T. Oner, *Cannabis Sativa: The Essential Guide to the World's Finest Marijuana Strains* (San Francisco, CA, 2012).

19 Isaac Campos, *Home Grown: Marijuana and the Origins of Mexico's War on Drugs* (Chapel Hill, NC, 2012), pp. 74–7; Alan Piper, 'The Mysterious Origins of the Word "Marihuana"', *Sino-Platonic Papers*, CLIII (2005), pp. 1–17.

20 Yeda Pessoa de Castro, 'Towards a Comparative Approach to Bantuisms in Iberoamerica', in *Africamericas: Itineraries, Dialogues, and Sounds*, I. Phaf-Rheinberger and T. de Oliveira Pinto, eds (Madrid, 2008), pp. 79–90, see p. 86; Nicolás del Castillo Mathieu, 'El Léxico Negro-Africano de San Basilio de Palenque', *Thesaurus*, XXIX (1984), pp. 80–169, see p. 143.

21 Brian M. du Toit, *Cannabis in Africa: A Survey of Its Distribution in Africa, and a Study of Cannabis Use and Users in Multi-Ethnic South Africa* (Rotterdam, 1980).

22 E. J. W. Barber, *Prehistoric Textiles: The Development of Cloth in the Neolithic and Bronze Ages with Special Reference to the Aegean* (Princeton, NJ, 1991), pp. 36–8.

23 James L. Butrica, 'The Medical Use of Cannabis among the Greeks and Romans', *Journal of Cannabis Therapeutics*, II (2002), pp. 51–70.

24 F. E. Dussy, C. Hamberg, M. Luginbühl, T. Schwerzmann and T. A. Briellmann, 'Isolation of delta-9-THCA-A from Hemp and Analytical Aspects Concerning the Determination of delta-9-THC in Cannabis Products', *Forensic Science International*, CIL (2005), pp. 3–10.

25 Pedanius Dioscorides, *De Materia Medica: Libri Sex*, trans. of Marcellus Vergilius (Florence, Italy, 1518), p. 218; Indalecio Lozano Cámara, 'El uso terapéutico del *Cannabis Sativa* L. en la medicina Árabe', *Asclepio*, IL (1997), pp. 199–208.

26 Claudius Galen, *De Alimentorum Facultatibus, Libri Tres* (Lyon, France, 1547), pp. 84–5.

27 Lozano Cámara, 'El uso terapéutico'; Lozano Cámara, 'Terminología científica Árabe del cáñamo', in *Ciencias Naturaleza en Al-Andalus*, ed. C. Álvarez de Morales (Granada, Spain, 1996), pp. 147–64.

28 Abu Ali al-Shaykh al-Ra'is Ibn Sina, *Kitab al Qanoun fi al-Toubb [The Book of the Canon of Medicine]* (Rome, 1593), p. 248.

29 Martin Levey, 'Medieval Arabic Toxicology', *Transactions of the American Philosophical Society*, LVI (1966), pp. 1–130, quotation p. 27.

30 W. Derham, ed., *Philosophical Experiments and Observations of the Late Eminent Dr Robert Hooke* (London, 1726), p. 210.

31 Fred Rosner, ed., *Maimonides' Medical Writings: Moses Maimonides' Glossary of Drug Names* (Haifa, Israel, 1995), vol. VII, especially pp. 48–9, 274.

32 Lozano Cámara, 'Terminología'.

33 Ibid.

34 William W. Turner, *The Names of Herbes* [1548] (London, 1881), p. 22.

35 Orta Wherrell, 'Hemp-Seed and Hemp-Seed Oil', *Bulletin of Pharmacy*, XI (1897), pp. 340–42; William R. Guilfoyle, *Fibres from Plants, Indigenous and Introduced, Eligible for Industrial Culture and Experiment in Victoria* (Melbourne, VIC, 1894), p. 34; H. W. Dickinson, 'A Condensed History of Rope-Making', *Transactions of the Newcomen Society*, XXIII [1942–3] (1948), pp. 71–92.

36 William Roxburgh, 'Communication on the Culture, Properties, and Comparative Strength of Hemp, and Other Vegetable Fibres, the Growth of the East Indies', *Transactions of the Society Instituted at London, for the Encouragement of Arts, Manufactures, and Commerce*, XXII (1804), pp. 363–96.

37 Ellis W. Brewster, *125 Years of Rope-Making in Plymouth (1824–1949)* (New York, 1949), p. 35.

38 Anne L. Ash, 'Hemp-Production and Utilization', *Economic Botany*, II (1948), pp. 158–69; L. H. Dewey, 'Hemp', in *Yearbook of the United States Department of Agriculture, 1913* (Washington, DC, 1914), pp. 283–346.

39 Ernest Small and Arthur Cronquist, 'A Practical and Natural Taxonomy for *Cannabis*', *Taxon*, XXV (1976), pp. 405–35, quotation p. 405.

40 Hillig and Mahlberg, 'Chemotaxonomic Analysis'; Hillig, 'Genetic Evidence'; William A. Emboden, '*Cannabis*: A Polytypic Genus', *Economic Botany*, XXVIII (1974), pp. 304–10.

41 Hillig, 'Genetic Evidence'.

42 Small and Cronquist, 'Practical and Natural'.

43 Emboden, 'Correct Use'; Emboden, 'Polytypic Genus'; Schultes et al., 'Taxonomic Neglect'.

44 Andrew T. Weil, N. T. Zinberg and J. M. Nelsen, 'Clinical and Psychological Effects of Marihuana in Man', *Science*, CLXII (1968), pp. 1234–42, quotation p. 1235.

45 Emboden, 'Correct Use'; Small, 'American Law'.

46 Robert B. Strassler, ed., *The Landmark Herodotus: The Histories* (New York, 2007), book 4, chapter 74, quotation p. 311.

47 McPartland and Hillig, 'Early Iconography'.

48 Small and Cronquist, 'Practical and Natural'.
49 McPartland and Hillig, 'Early Iconography'.
50 Clarke, *Marijuana Botany*, pp. 157–8.
51 P. M. Zhukovsky, 'Hemp (*Cannabis* L.)', in *Cultivated Plants and Their Wild Relatives* (Leningrad, 1964), pp. 456–8.
52 Hillig, 'Genetic Evidence'.
53 McPartland and Hillig, 'Early Iconography'; Derham, *Philosophical Experiments*, p. 210.
54 Jean-Baptiste Lamarck, *Encyclopédie Méthodique: Botanique* (Paris and Liège, Belgium, 1783), vol. I, pt 2, p. 695.
55 Small and Cronquist, 'Practical and Natural'.
56 Starks, *Marijuana Chemistry*, p. 81; K. Szendrei, 'Cannabis as an Illicit Crop: Recent Developments in Cultivation and Product Quality', *United Nations Office on Drugs and Crime Bulletin on Narcotics* (1997), www.unodc.org.
57 Tom D. Whitson, ed., *Weeds of the West*, 5th edn (Newark, CA, 1996), p. 246.
58 Schultes and Hofmann, *Botany and Chemistry*; Hillig and Mahlberg, 'Chemotaxonomic Analysis'.
59 Jorge Cervantes, *Marijuana Horticulture* (Sacramento, CA, 2006), pp. 10–11.
60 Oner, *Cannabis Indica*; Oner, *Cannabis Sativa*.
61 Starks, *Marijuana Chemistry*; Hillig and Mahlberg, 'Chemotaxonomic Analysis'.
62 Ernest Small, 'On Toadstool Soup and Legal Species of Marihuana', *Plant Science Bulletin*, XXI (1975), pp. 34–8, quotations pp. 38, 34.
63 B. Fletcher, *Hemp Industries Association v. DEA*. Decision No. 03-71366 and No. 03-71603, Ninth Circuit United States Court of Appeals (San Francisco, CA, 2004).

2 Ancient *Cannabis*

1 Félix Forest and Mark W. Chase, 'Eurosid I', in *The Timetree of Life*, ed. S. B. Hedges and S. Kumar (Oxford, 2009), pp. 188–96.
2 A. Murakami, P. Darby, B. Javornik, M.S.S. Pais, E. Seigner, A. Lutz and P. Svoboda, 'Molecular Phylogeny of Wild Hops, *Humulus lupulus* L.', *Heredity*, XCVII (2006), pp. 66–74.
3 K. W. Hillig, 'Genetic Evidence for Speciation in *Cannabis* (Cannabaceae)', *Genetic Resources and Crop Evolution*, LII (2005), pp. 161–80; Richard Evans Schultes and Albert Hofmann, *The Botany and Chemistry of Hallucinogens*, 2nd edn (Springfield, IL, 1980); N. I. Vavilov, *Origin and Geography of Cultivated Plants* [1926] (Cambridge, 1992).
4 Robert C. Clarke, *Marijuana Botany* (Berkeley, CA, 1981), p. 123.
5 John Lydon, Alan H. Teramura and C. Benjamin Coffman, 'UV-B Radiation Effects on Photosynthesis, Growth and Cannabinoid Production of Two *Cannabis sativa* chemotypes', *Photochemistry and Photobiology*, XLVI (1987), pp. 201–6; David W. Pate, 'Possible Role of Ultraviolet Radiation in Evolution of *Cannabis* Chemotypes', *Economic Botany*, XXXVII (1983), pp. 396–405; David W. Pate, 'Chemical Ecology of *Cannabis*',

Journal of the International Hemp Association, II (1994), pp. 29, 32–7.

6 Pate, 'Chemical Ecology'.

7 W. Granoszewski, D. Demske, M. Nita, G. Heumann and A. A. Andreev, 'Vegetation and Climate Variability During the Last Interglacial Evidenced in the Pollen Record from Lake Baikal', *Global and Planetary Change*, XLVI (2005), pp. 187–98.

8 Peter K. Zeitler, Noye M. Johnson, Charles W. Naeser and Rashid A. K. Tahirkheli, 'Fission-Track Evidence for Quaternary Uplift of the Nanga Parbat Region, Pakistan', *Nature*, CCXCVIII (1982), pp. 255–7; Anne Dambricourt-Malassé, 'Relations between Climatic Changes and Prehistoric Human Migrations During Holocene between Gissar Range, Pamir, Hindu Kush and Kashmir: The Archaeological and Ecological Data', *Quaternary International*, CCXXIX (2011), pp. 123–31.

9 Lyudmila S. Shumilovskikh, Pavel Tarasov, Helge W. Arz, Dominik Fleitmann, Fabienne Marret, Norbert Nowaczyk, Birgit Plessen, Frank Schluetz and Hermann Behling, 'Vegetation and Environmental Dynamics in the Southern Black Sea Region since 18kyr BP Derived from the Marine Core 22-GC3', *Palaeogeography, Palaeoclimatology, Palaeoecology*, CCCXXXVII–CCCXXXVIII (2012), pp. 177–93; Robert C. Clarke and Mark David Merlin, *Cannabis: Evolution and Ethnobotany* (Berkeley, CA, 2013), p. 68.

10 Dambricourt-Malassé, 'Relations'.

11 Shehzadi Saima, Altaf A. Dasti, Farrukh Hussain, Sultan Mehmood Wazir and Saeed A. Malik, 'Floristic Composition along an 18-km Transect in Ayubia National Park District Abottabad, Pakistan', *Pakistani Journal of Botany*, XLI (2009), pp. 2115–27.

12 Claire Gaillard, Mukesh Singh and Anne Dambricourt-Malassé, 'Late Pleistocene to Early Holocene Lithic Industries in the Southern Fringes of the Himalaya', *Quaternary International*, CCXXIX (2011), pp. 112–22.

13 Ulrike Herzschuh, Pavel Tarasov, Bernd Wünnemann and Kai Hartmann, 'Holocene Vegetation and Climate of the Alashan Plateau, NW China, Reconstructed from Pollen Data', *Palaeogeography, Palaeoclimatology, Palaeoecology*, CCXI (2004), pp. 1–17; Hiroko Okazaki, Makiko Kobayashi, Arata Momohara, Sei-ichi Eguchi, Tozo Okamoto, Sei-ichi Yanagisawa, Susumu Okubo and Jota Kiyonaga, 'Early Holocene Coastal Environment Change Inferred from Deposits at Okinoshima Archeological Site, Boso Peninsula, Central Japan', *Quaternary International*, CCXXX (2011), pp. 87–94.

14 Cynthia A. Daley, Amber Abbott, Patrick S. Doyle, Glenn A. Nader and Stephanie Larson, 'A Review of Fatty Acid Profiles and Antioxidant Content in Grass-fed and Grain-fed Beef', *Nutrition Journal*, IX (2010), www.nutritionj.com.

15 J. C. Callaway, 'Hempseed as a Nutritional Resource: An Overview', *Euphytica*, CXL (2004), pp. 65–72.

16 Michael P. Fleming and Robert C. Clarke, 'Physical Evidence for the Antiquity of *Cannabis sativa* L. (Cannabaceae)', *Journal of the International Hemp Association*, V (1998), pp. 80–92.

17 Vavilov, *Origin*, p. 117.

18 Baltasar Cabezudo, Marta Recio, José María Sánchez-Laulhé, María del Mar Trigo, Francisco Javier Toro and Fausto Polvorinos, 'Atmospheric Transportation of Marihuana Pollen from North Africa to the Southwest of Europe', *Atmospheric Environment*, XXXI (1997), pp. 3323–8.

19 Pavel Tarasov, Guiyun Jin and Mayke Wagner, 'Mid-Holocene Environmental and Human Dynamics in Northeastern China Reconstructed from Pollen and Archaeological Data', *Palaeogeography, Palaeoclimatology, Palaeoecology*, CCXLI (2006), pp. 284–300.

20 Clarke and Merlin, *Cannabis*, p. 95.

21 Dieter Kuhn, *Science and Civilization in China: Chemistry and Chemical Technology: Textile Technology: Spinning and Reeling* (Cambridge, 1988), vol. V, pt 9, p. 15; Xin Jia, Guanghui Dong, Hu Li, Katherine Brunson, FaHu Chen, Minmin Ma, Hui Wang, Chengbang An and Keren Zhang, 'The Development of Agriculture and Its Impact on Cultural Expansion During the Late Neolithic in the Western Loess Plateau, China', *Holocene*, XXIII (2013), pp. 85–92.

22 Gary W. Crawford, 'Advances in Understanding Early Agriculture in Japan', *Current Anthropology*, LII (2011), pp. S331–S345.

23 Kuhn, *Spinning and Reeling*.

24 E. J. W. Barber, *Prehistoric Textiles* (Princeton, NJ, 1991).

25 Clarke and Merlin, *Cannabis*, p. 268 ff.; Kuhn, *Spinning and Reeling*, pp. 15–19.

26 H. T. Huang, *Science and Civilization in China: Fermentations and Food Science* (Cambridge, 2000), vol. VI, pt 5, p. 18.

27 Clarke and Merlin, *Cannabis*, pp. 95–7.

28 Joseph Needham and Gwei-Djen Lu, *Science and Civilization in China: Spagyrical Discovery and Invention: Magesteries of Gold and Immortality* (Cambridge, 1974), vol. V, pt 2, pp. 150–52; Hui-Lin Li, 'An Archaeological and Historical Account of *Cannabis* in China', *Economic Botany*, XXVIII (1974), pp. 437–48.

29 Xiaozhai Lu and Robert C. Clarke, 'The Cultivation and Use of Hemp (*Cannabis sativa* L.) in Ancient China', *Journal of the International Hemp Association*, II (1995), pp. 26–31; Robert C. Clarke, 'Traditional Fiber Hemp (Cannabis) Production, Processing, Yarn Making, and Weaving Strategies: Functional Constraints and Regional Responses. Part 1', *Journal of Industrial Hemp*, VII (2010), pp. 118–53.

30 Robert C. Clarke, 'Hemp (*Cannabis sativa* L.) Cultivation in the Tai'an District of Shandong Province, People's Republic of China', *Journal of the International Hemp Association*, II (1995), pp. 57, 60–65.

31 Huang, *Fermentations*, p. 29.

32 Li, 'Archaeological', p. 444.

33 Alimcan Inayet, 'East Turkistan as a Cradle of Civilizations', in *Hür Dogu Türkistan Sempozyumu* (Istanbul, 2010), pp. 273–88.

34 J. P. Mallory and Victor H. Mair, *The Tarim Mummies: Ancient China and the Mystery of the Earliest Peoples from the West* (London, 2000); Elizabeth W. Barber, *The Mummies of Ürümchi* (New York, 1999).

35 Ethan B. Russo, Hong-En Jiang, Xiao Li, Alan Sutton, Andrea Carboni, Francesca del Bianco, Giuseppe Mandolino, David J. Potter, You-Xing Zhao, Subir Bera, Yong-Bing Zhang, En-Guo Lü, David K. Ferguson, Francis Hueber, Liang-Cheng Zhao, Chang-Jiang Liu, Yu-Fei Wang and Cheng-Sen Li, 'Phytochemical and Genetic Analyses of Ancient Cannabis from Central Asia', *Journal of Experimental Botany*, LIX (2008), pp. 4171–82; Hong-En Jiang, Xiao Li, You-Xing Zhao, David K. Ferguson, Francis Hueber, Subir Bera, Yu-Fei Wang, Liang-Cheng Zhao, Chang-Jiang Liu and Cheng-Sen Li, 'A New Insight into *Cannabis sativa* (Cannabaceae) Utilization from 2500-Year-Old Yanghai Tombs, Xinjiang, China', *Journal of Ethnopharmacology*, CVIII (2006), pp. 414–22.

36 Ashutosh Mukherjee, Satyesh Chandra Roy, S. De Bera, Hong-En Jiang, Xiao Li, Cheng-Sen Li and Subir Bera, 'Results of Molecular Analysis of an Archaeological Hemp (*Cannabis sativa* L.) DNA Sample from North West China', *Genetic Resources and Crop Evolution*, LV (2008), pp. 481–5.

37 Mallory and Mair, *Tarim Mummies*; Russo et al., 'Phytochemical'.

38 John E. Hill, 'The Western Regions According to the Hou Hanshu', http://depts.washington.edu/silkroad (accessed 11 February 2014); John E. Hill, *Through the Jade Gate to Rome: A Study of the Silk Routes During the Later Han Dynasty* (Charleston, SC, 2009).

39 Huang, *Fermentations*; Alain P. A. Bonjean, 'Origins and Historical Diffusion of Major Native and Alien Cereals in China', in *Cereals in China*, ed. Z. He and A.P.A. Bonjean (Mexico City, 2010), pp. 1–14; Hong-En Jiang, Yong-Bing Zhang, Xiao Li, Yi-Feng Yao, David K. Ferguson, En-Guo Lü and Cheng-Sen Li, 'Evidence for Early Viticulture in China: Proof of a Grapevine (*Vitis vinifera* L., Vitaceae) in the Yanghai Tombs, Xinjiang', *Journal of Archaeological Science*, XXXVI (2009), pp. 1458–65.

40 Lu and Clarke, 'Cultivation and Use', not paginated.

41 Needham and Lu, *Magesteries of Gold*; Li, 'Archaeological'; Joseph Needham, Ping-Yü Ho, Gwei-Djen Lu and Nathan Sivin, *Science and Civilization in China: Spagyrical Discovery and Invention: Apparatus, Theory, and Gifts* (Cambridge, 1980), vol. V, pt 4; Joseph Needham, *Science and Civilization in China: History of Scientific Thought* (Cambridge, 1956), vol. II.

42 N. D. Mironov and S. M. Shirokogorov, 'Sramana and Shaman', *Journal of the North China Branch of the Royal Asiatic Society*, LV (1924), pp. 105–30.

43 Li, 'Archaeological'; Lu and Clarke, 'Cultivation and Use'.

44 Hui-Lin Li, 'The Origin and Use of *Cannabis* in Eastern Asia: Linguistic-Cultural Implications', *Economic Botany*, XXVIII (1974), pp. 293–301.

45 Berthold Laufer, *Sino-Iranica: Chinese Contributions to the History of Civilization in Ancient Iran* (Chicago, IL, 1919), vol. XV, no. 3, see pp. 288–9.

46 Huang, *Fermentations*, pp. 29–31; Laufer, *Sino-Iranica*, p. 289; Kuhn, *Spinning and Reeling*, p. 56.

47 Kuhn, *Spinning and Reeling*, pp. 57–8.

48 Tsien Tsuen-Hsuin, ed. Joseph Needham, *Science and Civilization in China*, vol. 5, pt 1, *Paper and Printing* (New York, 1985), pp. 54, 61.

49 Ibid., pp. 320, 331.

50 Michael R. Aldrich, 'Tantric Cannabis Use in India', *Journal of Psychoactive Drugs*, IX (1977), pp. 227–33.

51 Merlin, 'Archaeological Evidence'; Tsien, *Paper and Printing*, pp. 347, 356; Marie Alexandrine Martin, 'Ethnobotanical Aspects of *Cannabis* in Southeast Asia', in *Cannabis and Culture*, ed. V. Rubin (The Hague, The Netherlands, 1975), pp. 63–76.

52 Om Prakash, *Food and Drinks in Ancient India* (Delhi, 1961), pp. 61, 128; F. Max Müller, *Rig-Veda-Sanhita: Sacred Hymns of the Brahmans. Hymns to the Maruts or the Storm-Gods* (London, 1869), vol. I, book 2, hymn 4, verse 5.

53 William Dwight Whitney, *Atharva-Veda Samhita. First Half. Introduction. Books I to VII* (Cambridge, MA, 1905), book 11, hymn 6, verse 15.

54 G. Jan Meulenbeld, 'The Search for Clues to the Chronology of Sanskrit Medical Texts, as Illustrated by the History of *Bhanga* (*Cannabis sativa* Linn.)', *Studien zur Indologie und Iranistik*, XV (1989), pp. 59–70; Dominik Wujastyk, 'Cannabis in Traditional Indian Herbal Medicine', in *Ayurveda at the Crossroads of Care and Cure*, ed. A. Salema (Lisbon, 2002), pp. 45–73.

55 George Watt, *The Commercial Products of India* (London, 1908), pp. 251–2.

56 Prakash, *Food and Drinks*, p. 61.

57 Meulenbeld, 'The Search'; Wujastyk, 'Cannabis'.

58 Dambricourt-Malassé, 'Relations'; Gaillard et al., 'Late Pleistocene'; Claire Gaillard, A. Dambricourt-Malassé, J. Magraner, A. Maitrerobert, Taj Ali, J.-L. Voisin and Abdul Nasir, 'Discovery of Recent Lithic Industries with Archaic Features in the Hindu Kush Range (Chitral District, North Pakistan)', *Indo-Pacific Prehistory Association Bulletin*, XXII (2002), pp. 25–33.

59 David Stophlet Flattery and Martin Schwartz, *Haoma and Harmaline: The Botanical Identity of the Indo-Iranian Sacred Hallucinogen 'Soma'* (Berkeley, CA, 1989), pp. 121–9.

60 G. L. Possehl, 'The Middle Asian Interaction Sphere: Trade and Contact in the 3rd Millennium BC', *Expedition*, XLIX (2004), pp. 40–42.

61 Aline Emery-Barbier, 'L'homme et l'environnement en Egypte durant la période prédynastique', in *Man's Role in Shaping the Eastern Mediterranean Landscape*, ed. S. Bottema, G. Entjes-Nieborg and W. Van Zeist (Rotterdam, The Netherlands, 1990), pp. 319–26; Suzanne A. G. Leroy, 'Palynological Evidence of *Azolla nilotica* Dec. in Recent Holocene of the Eastern Nile Delta and Palaeo-environment', *Vegetation History and Archaeobotany*, I (1992), pp. 43–52.

62 Ethan B. Russo, 'History of *Cannabis* and its Preparations in Saga, Science, and Sobriquet', *Chemistry and Biodiversity*, IV (2007), pp. 1614–48.

63 Michael D. Frachetti and Lynne M. Rouse, 'Central Asia, the Steppe, and the Near East, 2500–1500 BC', in *A Companion to the Archaeology of the Ancient near East*, ed. D. T. Potts (Malden, MA, 2012), pp. 687–705.

64 Karl W. Hillig, 'A Combined Analysis of Agronomic Traits and Allozyme Allele Frequencies for 69 *Cannabis* Accessions', *Journal of Industrial Hemp*, X (2005), pp. 17–30; Karl W. Hillig, 'A Multivariate Analysis of Allozyme Variation in 93 *Cannabis* Accessions from the VIR Germplasm Collection', *Journal of Industrial Hemp*, IX (2005), pp. 5–22.

65 Hillig, 'Genetic Evidence'.

66 Meulenbeld, 'The Search'; Wujastyk, 'Cannabis'.

67 Jonathan Mark Kenoyer, *Ancient Cities of the Indus Valley Civilization*, 2nd edn (Karachi, Pakistan, 2010); Fredrik Talmage Hiebert, *Origins of the Bronze Age Oasis Civilization in Central Asia* (Cambridge, MA, 1994).

68 Brian E. Hemphill and J. P. Mallory, 'Horse-mounted Invaders from the Russo-Kazakh Steppe or Agricultural Colonists from Western Central Asia? A Craniometric Investigation of the Bronze Age Settlement of Xinjiang', *American Journal of Physical Anthropology*, CXXIV (2004), pp. 199–222.

69 Marco Madells, 'Investigating Agriculture and Environment in South Asia: Present and Future Contributions of Opal Phytoliths', in *Indus Ethnobiology: New Perspectives from the Field*, ed. S. A. Weber and W. R. Belcher (Lanham, MD, 2003), pp. 199–250.

70 Kenoyer, *Ancient Cities*; Iravatham Mahadevan, 'The Sacred Filter Standard Facing the Unicorn: More Evidence', *Annales Academiae Scientarum Fennicae. Series B*, CCLXXI (1993), pp. 434–45.

71 Hiebert, *Origins*; Victor Sarianidi, ed., *Margiana and Protozoroastrism* (Athens, 1998).

72 Mahadevan, 'Sacred Filter'; Victor Sarianidi, 'Margiana and Soma-Haoma', *Electronic Journal of Vedic Studies*, IX (2003), article 1d.

73 C. C. Bakels, 'The Contents of Ceramic Vessels in the Bactria-Margiana Archaeological Complex, Turkmenistan', *Electronic Journal of Vedic Studies*, IX (2003), article 1c.; N. R. Meyer-Melikyan and N. A. Avetov, 'Appendix 1: Analysis of Floral Remains in the Ceramic Vessel from the Gonur Temenos', in Sarianidi, *Margiana and Protozoroastrism*, pp. 176–7.

74 Mallory and Mair, *Tarim Mummies*, p. 307.

75 Flattery and Schwartz, *Haoma*; Harri Nyberg, 'The Problem of the Aryans and the Soma: The Botanical Evidence', in *The Indo-Aryans of Ancient South Asia: Language, Material Culture, and Ethnicity*, ed. G. Erdosy (Berlin, 1995), pp. 382–406.

76 Jiang et al., 'New Insight'; Hong-En Jiang, Xiao Li, David K. Ferguson, Yu-Fei Wang, Chang-Jiang Liu and Cheng-Sen Li, 'The Discovery of Capparis Spinosa L. (Capparidaceae) in the Yanghai Tombs (2800 Years B.P.), NW China, and Its Medicinal Implications', *Journal of Ethnopharmacology*, CXIII (2007), pp. 409–20.

77 Kazi Dawasamdup, *An English-Tibetan Dictionary* (Calcutta, 1919), p. 348.

78 Jeremy R. McMahan, 'From a Land in the West: An Examination of the Possibility of Persian Influence on the Tibetan Bon Religion', undergraduate honours thesis, College of William and Mary (Williamsburg, VA, 2010), p. 30.

79 G. Gnoli, 'Bang in Ancient Iran', in *Encyclopedia Iranica*, ed. E. Yarshater (London, 1989), vol. III, pp. 689–90.

80 M. S. Chauhan and M. F. Quamar, 'Pollen Records of Vegetation and Inferred Climate Change in Southwestern Madhya Pradesh during the Last ca. 3800 Years', *Journal of the Geological Society of India*, LXXX (2012), pp. 470–80.

81 Aldrich, 'Tantric Cannabis'.

82 John Wilson, *The Pársí Religion: As Contained in the Zand-Avastá* (Bombay, 1843), p. 81.

83 Abderrahmane Merzouki, F. ed-Derfoufi and Joaquín Molero Mesa, 'Hemp (*Cannabis sativa* L.) and Abortion', *Journal of Ethnobiology*, LXXIII (2000), pp. 501–503.

84 Joe Zias, Harley Stark, Jon Seligman, Rina Levy, Ella Werker, Aviva Breuer and Raphael Mechoulam, 'Early Medical Use of *Cannabis*', *Nature*, CCCLXIII (1993), p. 215.

85 Franz Rosenthal, *The Herb: Hashish versus Medieval Muslim Society* (Leiden, The Netherlands, 1971).

86 George Abraham Grierson, 'The Hemp Plant in Sanskrit and Hindi Literature', *The Indian Antiquary*, XXIII (1894), pp. 260–62; Ethan Russo, 'Cannabis in India: Ancient Lore and Modern Medicine', in *Cannabinoids as Therapeutics*, ed. R. Mechoulam (Geneva, 2005), pp. 1–22.

87 Stephen M. Rucina, Veronica M. Muiruri, Laura Downton and Rob Marchant, 'Late-Holocene Savanna Dynamics in the Amboseli Basin, Kenya', *Holocene*, XX (2010), pp. 667–77.

88 Etienne Zangato, 'Early Smoking Pipes in the North-western Central African Republic', *Africa: Rivista trimestrale di studi e documentazione dell'Istito italiano per l'Africa e l'Oriente*, LVI (2001), pp. 365–95; John Edward Philips, 'African Smoking and Pipes', *Journal of African History*, XXIV (1983), pp. 303–19; Alfred Dunhill, *The Pipe Book* [1924] (New York, 1969).

89 Nikolaas J. Van der Merwe, 'Cannabis Smoking in 13th–14th Century Ethiopia: Chemical Evidence', in *Cannabis and Culture*, ed. V. Rubin (The Hague, The Netherlands, 1975), pp. 77–80.

90 Robert C. Clarke and D. P. Watson, 'Botany of Natural Cannabis Medicines', in *Cannabis and Cannabinoids: Pharmacology, Toxicology and Therapeutic Potential*, ed. F. Grotenherman and E. Russo (Binghamton, NY, 2002), pp. 3–13.

91 Karl W. Hillig and Paul G. Mahlberg, 'A Chemotaxonomic Analysis of Cannabinoid Variation in *Cannabis* (Cannabaceae)', *American Journal of Botany*, XCI (2004), pp. 966–75.

92 Clarke and Merlin, *Cannabis*, p. 326.

93 Russo et al., 'Phytochemical'.

94 Meulenbeld, 'The Search'; Wujastyk, 'Cannabis'; Grierson, 'Hemp Plant'; Russo, 'Cannabis in India'.

95 Wujastyk, 'Cannabis'.

96 Whitney, *Atharva-Veda*, book XIX, hymns 34–5.

97 Clarke, *Marijuana Botany*; S. T. Oner, *Cannabis Sativa: The Essential Guide to the World's Finest Marijuana Strains* (San Francisco, CA, 2012); Jorge Cervantes, *Marijuana Horticulture* (Sacramento, CA, 2006).

98 Watt, *Commercial Products*, p. 249.

99 George Watt, *A Dictionary of the Economic Products of India. Cabbage to Cyperus* (Calcutta, 1889), vol. II, p. 104; Clarke and Merlin, *Cannabis*, p. 326.

100 Robert C. Clarke, *Hashish!*, 2nd edn (Los Angeles, CA, 2010).

101 Watt, *Commercial Products.*
102 Clarke, *Hashish!*
103 Rosenthal, *The Herb.*
104 Clarke, *Hashish!*
105 Clarke and Merlin, *Cannabis*, p. 68.
106 Barber, *Prehistoric Textiles*, pp. 16–17.
107 Ibid.
108 A. G. Sherratt, 'Cups that Cheered', in *Bell Beakers of the Western Mediterranean*, ed. W. H. Waldren and R. C. Kennard (Oxford, 1987), vol. XLVII, pt 2, pp. 81–114; A. G. Sherratt, 'Sacred and Profane Substances: The Ritual Use of Narcotics in Later Neolithic Europe', in *Sacred and Profane: Proceedings of a Conference on Archaeology, Ritual and Religion*, ed. P. Garwood, D. Jennings, R. Skeates and J. Toms (Oxford, 1991), vol. XXXII, pp. 50–64.
109 Mark D. Merlin, 'Archaeological Evidence for the Tradition of Psychoactive Plant Use in the Old World', *Economic Botany*, LVII (2003), pp. 295–323.
110 A. D. Godley, ed., *The Histories of Herodotus* (Cambridge, MA, 1920).
111 Fleming and Clarke, 'Physical Evidence'; Sergei I. Rudenko, *Frozen Tombs of Siberia: The Pazyryk Burials of Iron-Age Horsemen* [1953] (Berkeley, CA, 1970), p. 285; David W. Anthony, *The Horse, the Wheel, and Language: How Bronze-Age Riders from the Eurasian Steppes Shaped the Modern World* (Princeton, NJ, 2007), p. 362.
112 Clarke, *Hashish!*, p. 24; B. Derham, 'Archaeological and Ethnographic Toxins in Museum Collections', in *Impact of the Environment on Human Migration in Eurasia*, ed. E. M. Scott, A. Y. Alexseev and G. Zaitseva (Dordrecht, The Netherlands, 2003), pp. 185–97.
113 Victor Hehn, *Kulturpflanzen und Haustiere in Ihrem Übergang aus Asien nach Griechenland und Italien sowie in das Übrige Europa* (Berlin, 1870), p. 120.
114 Rudenko, *Frozen Tombs*, p. 285; Robert P. Walton, *Marihuana: America's New Drug Problem* (Philadelphia, PA, 1938), p. 8; Martin Booth, *Cannabis: A History* (New York, 2005), p. 29.
115 Derham, 'Archaeological and Ethnographic'.
116 Detlev Fehling, *Herodotus and his 'Sources': Citation, Invention, and Narrative Art* (Liverpool, 1989); O. Kimball Armayor, 'Did Herodotus ever go to the Black Sea?', *Harvard Studies in Classical Philology*, LXXXII (1978), pp. 45–62.
117 Robert B. Strassler, ed., *The Landmark Herodotus: The Histories* (New York, 2007), book IV, chapters 65 and 76.
118 M. Marcandier, *Traité du chanvre* (Paris, 1758), p. 7.
119 Timothy Taylor, 'Thracians, Scythians, and Dacians, 800 BC–AD 300', in *The Oxford Illustrated Prehistory of Europe*, ed. B. Cunliffe (Oxford, 1994), pp. 373–410.
120 Barber, *Prehistoric Textiles.*
121 Ibid.
122 Anonymous [G. C. Gilroy], *The History of Silk, Cotton, Linen, Wool, and Other Fibrous Substances* (New York, 1845), p. 389.

123 Robert James Forbes, *Studies in Ancient Technology*, 2nd edn (Leiden, The Netherlands, 1965), vol. IV, p. 39.

124 K. D. White, *Farm Equipment of the Roman World* (Cambridge, 1975), pp. 34–5.

125 Ibid., pp. 29–30.

126 John Peter Wild, *Textile Manufacturing in the Northern Roman Provinces* (London, 1970).

127 Oxford English Dictionary, 'Canvas / canvass, N.', in *Oxford English Dictionary Online Version* (Oxford, 2012).

128 Jan Bojer Vindheim, 'The History of Hemp in Norway', *Journal of Industrial Hemp*, VII (2002), pp. 89–103.

129 H. Godwin, 'Pollen-analytic Evidence for the Cultivation of *Cannabis* in England', *Review of Palaeobotany and Palynology*, 41 (1967), pp. 71–80, 137–8.

130 Lina Antonia Ruiz y Ruiz, 'A Tentative Portuguese Dictionary of Dated First Occurrences in Certain Documents Between 1351–1450', PhD dissertation, University of Pennsylvania (Philadelphia, 1964), p. 32; M. del Carmen Martínez, *Los nombres de tejidos en Castellano medieval* (Granada, Spain, 1989), p. 433.

131 Forbes, *Studies*, p. 61; White, *Farm Equipment*, pp. 29–30.

132 S. Riera, G. Wansard and R. Julià, '2000-year Environmental History of a Karstic Lake in the Mediterranean Pre-Pyrenees: The Estanya Lakes (Spain)', *Catena*, LV (2004), pp. 293–324.

133 Martínez, *Los Nombres*, pp. 433–5; Clarke and Merlin, *Cannabis*, p. 165; Leonor Freire Costa, *Naus e Galeões na ribeira de Lisboa* (Cascais, Portugal, 1997), p. 360; Julian Whitewright, 'Roman Rigging Material from the Red Sea Port of Myos Hormos', *International Journal of Nautical Archaeology*, XXXVI (2007), pp. 282–92.

134 William Mavor, ed., *Five Hundred Points of Good Husbandry . . . , by Thomas Tusser, Gentleman* [1580], new edn (London, 1812), p. 20.

135 Clarke, 'Traditional Fiber Hemp Part I'.

136 Walter Finsinger, Christian Bigler, Urs Kraehenbuehl, Andre F. Lotter and Brigitta Ammann, 'Human Impacts and Eutrophication Patterns during the Past Similar to 200 Years at Lago Grande Di Avigliana (N. Italy)', *Journal of Paleolimnology*, XXXVI (2006), pp. 55–67; Xiaoying Cheng, Shijie Li, Qing Shen and Jing Xue, 'Response of Cultural Lake Eutrophication to Hemp-retting in Quidenham Mere of England in Post-medieval', *Chinese Geographical Science*, XVII (2007), pp. 69–74.

137 Sula Benet, 'Early Diffusion and Folk Uses of Hemp', in *Cannabis and Culture*, ed. V. Rubin (The Hague, The Netherlands, 1975), pp. 39–49.

138 Alicja Zemanek, Bogdan Zemanek, Krystyna Harmata, Jacek Madeja and Piotr Klepacki, 'Selected Foreign Plants in Old Polish Botanical Literature, Customs and Art', in *Plants and Culture: Seeds of the Cultural Heritage of Europe*, ed. J.-P. Mortel and A. M. Mercuri (Bari, Italy, 2009), pp. 179–93.

139 Oleg V. Grigoriev, 'Application of Hempseed (*Cannabis sativa* L.) Oil in the Treatment of Ear, Nose, and Throat (ENT) Disorders', *Journal of Industrial Hemp*, VII (2002), pp. 5–15.

140 Adam Robert Lucas, 'Industrial Milling in the Ancient and Medieval Worlds', *Technology and Culture*, 46 (2005), pp. 1–30; Paolo Squatriti, *Working With Water in Medieval Europe: Technology and Resource-use* (Leiden, The Netherlands, 2000), p. 234.

141 Henri Pigeonneau, *Histoire du commerce de la France: Le seizième siècle – Henri IV – Richelieu* (Paris, 1889), vol. II, pp. 232, 338.

142 Leo Wiener, 'Economic History and Philology', *Quarterly Journal of Economics*, XXV (1911), pp. 239–78.

143 Frederic Chapin Lane, 'The Rope Factory and Hemp Trade of Venice in the Fifteenth and Sixteenth Centuries', *Journal of Economic and Business History*, IV (1932), pp. 830–47.

3 Hemp Travels the World

1 Stefano Fenoaltea, 'Slavery and Supervision in Comparative Perspective: A Model', *Journal of Economic History*, XLIV (1984), pp. 635–68.

2 Robert C. Clarke, 'Traditional Fiber Hemp (Cannabis) Production, Processing, Yarn Making, and Weaving Strategies: Functional Constraints and Regional Responses. Part I', *Journal of Industrial Hemp*, VII (2010), pp. 118–53.

3 Paolo Ranalli, ed., *Advances in Hemp Research* (New York, 1999), p. 71.

4 David P. West, 'Final Status Report', Hawai'i Industrial Hemp Research Project, online edn (Honolulu, HI, 2003).

5 Alfred W. Crosby, *The Columbian Exchange: Biological and Cultural Consequences of 1492* (Westport, CT, 1972).

6 Frederic Chapin Lane, 'The Rope Factory and Hemp Trade of Venice in the Fifteenth and Sixteenth Centuries', *Journal of Economic and Business History*, IV (1932), pp. 830–47, quotation p. 831.

7 Ibid.

8 Halil Inalcik and Donald Quataert, *An Economic and Social History of the Ottoman Empire, 1300–1914* (Cambridge, 1994), p. 465; Cengiz Toraman, Batuhan Güvemli and Fatih Bayramoglu, 'Imperial Shipyard (Tersane-I Amire) in the Ottoman Empire in the 17th Century: Management and Accounting', *Spanish Journal of Accounting History*, XIII (2010), pp. 191–226; Robert James Forbes, *Studies in Ancient Technology*, 2nd edn (Leiden, The Netherlands, 1965), vol. IV, p. 59.

9 Etienne P. M. de Meijer and L.J.M. van Soest, 'The CPRO *Cannabis* Germplasm Collection', *Euphytica*, LXII (1992), pp. 201–11.

10 Inalcik and Quataert, *Economic and Social History*, p. 38.

11 Ibid., p. 465; Toraman et al., 'Imperial Shipyard'.

12 Mehmet Genç, 'Ottoman Industry in the Eighteenth Century: General Framework, Characteristics and Main Trends', in *Manufacturing in the Ottoman Empire and Turkey: 1500–1950*, ed. D. Quataert (Albany, NY, 1994), pp. 59–86; Idris Bostan, *Ottoman Maritime Arsenals and Shipbuilding Technology in the 16th and 17th Centuries* (Manchester, 2007), p. 13; Jonathan A. Grant, 'Rethinking the Ottoman "decline": Military Technology Diffusion in the

Ottoman Empire, Fifteenth to Eighteenth Centuries', *Journal of World History*, X (1999), pp. 179–201.

13 Clarke, 'Traditional Fiber Hemp Part 1'; Peter von Schmidt, 'No. 18. Report on the Cultivation of Hemp', in *Message of the President of the United States to the Two Houses of Congress at the Commencement of the First Session of the Twenty-eighth Congress*, Office of President J. Tyler (Washington, DC, 1843), pp. 600–69; Erik Mueggler, 'The Poetics of Grief and the Price of Hemp in Southwest China', *Journal of Asian Studies*, XLVII (1998), pp. 979–1008; G. Schaefer, 'The Cultivation and Preparation of Flax; Hemp', *CIBA Review*, XLIX (1945), pp. 1773–95.

14 Ibid., p. 1783.

15 Girolamo Baruffaldi, *Il canapajo* (Bologna, Italy, 1741), pp. 15, 90.

16 M. Marcandier, *Traité du chanvre* (Paris, 1758), p. 38.

17 John M. McPartland, 'Byssinosis in Hemp Mill Workers', *Journal of Industrial Hemp*, VIII (2003), pp. 33–44.

18 A. Masclef, *Atlas des plantes de France utiles, nuisibles et ornamentales* (Paris, 1891), p. 244.

19 Geraldine L. Freeman, 'Allergic Skin Test Reactivity to Marijuana in the Southwest', *Western Journal of Medicine*, CXXXVIII (1983), pp. 829–31, Silvia Docampo, Marta Recio, M. Mar Trigo, Marta Melgar and Baltasar Cabezudo, 'Risk of Pollen Allergy in Nerja (Southern Spain): A Pollen Calendar', *Aerobiologia*, XXIII (2007), pp. 189–99; Sebastián P. Fernández, Cristina Wasowski, Leonardo M. Loscalzo, Renee E. Granger, Graham A. R. Johnston, Alejandro C. Paladini and Mariel Marder, 'Central Nervous System Depressant Action of Flavonoid Glycosides', *European Journal of Pharmacology*, DXXXIX (2006), pp. 168–76; Samir A. Ross, Mahmoud A. ElSouhy, Gazi N. N. Sultana, Zlatko Mehmedic, Chowdhury F. Hossain and Suman Chandra, 'Flavonoid Glycosides and Cannabinoids from the Pollen of *Cannabis sativa* L.', *Phytochemical Analysis*, XVI (2005), pp. 45–8.

20 Josip Faricic, Zeljka Siljkovic and Martin Glamuzin, 'Agrarian Changes in the Lower Neretvian Area from the Eighteenth to the Twentieth Century', *Agricultural History*, LXXVII (2005), pp. 193–220.

21 Janos Berenji and Milan Martinov, 'Hemp in Yugoslavia: Past, Present, and Future', in *Biorohstoff Hanf Technisch-Wissenschaftliches Symposium* (Cologne, Germany, 1997), p. 20.

22 Henri Pigeonneau, *Histoire du commerce de la France. Première partie: Depuis les origines jusqu'à la fin du XVe siècle* (Paris, 1885), p. 145.

23 Leonor Freire Costa, *Naus e galeões na ribeira de Lisboa* (Cascais, Portugal, 1997), p. 360.

24 Antonio García-Villaraco, Manuel Pardo de Santayana and Ramón Morales, 'Aportaciones a la Fitotoponimia de la Provincia de Ciudad Real', *Revista de Folklore*, XXXLVII (2011), pp. 4–23.

25 Ibid.

26 Isaac Campos, *Home Grown: Marijuana and the Origins of Mexico's War on Drugs* (Chapel Hill, NC, 2012).

27 Ramón M. Serrera Contreras, *Cultivo y manufactura de lino y cañamo en Nueva España (1777–1800)* (Seville, Spain, 1974); Jerry W. Cooney, 'A Colonial Naval Industry: The *Fabrica de Cables* of Paraguay', *Revista de Historia de América*, LXXXVII (1979), pp. 105–26.

28 Serrera Contreras, *Cultivo*.

29 Campos, *Home Grown*, p. 55.

30 Ibid., pp. 52–3.

31 Ibid., p. 56; Alfred W. Crosby, *America, Russia, Hemp, and Napoleon: American Trade with Russia and the Baltic, 1783–1812* (Columbus, OH, 1965), p. 15.

32 Serrera Contreras, *Cultivo*.

33 Enrique Pérez-Arbaláez, *Plantas útiles de Colombia*, 3rd edn (Bogotá, 1956), pp. 513–14.

34 Warren Dean, *With Broadax and Firebrand: The Destruction of the Brazilian Atlantic Forest* (Berkeley, CA, 1995), p. 131.

35 Ibid.; J. H. Galloway, 'Agricultural Reform and the Enlightenment in Late Colonial Brazil', *Agricultural History*, LIII (1979), pp. 763–79.

36 Francisco la Fonseca Henriquez, *Medicina Lusitana, e soccorro delphico a os clamores la natureza humana, para total profligação de seus males* (Amsterdam, 1710), p. 239.

37 César Augusto Marques, *Dicionário histórico-geografico la provincia do Maranhão* [1870] (Rio de Janeiro, Brazil, 1970), p. 517.

38 Carlos de Souza Moraes, *Feitoria do linho cânhamo* (Porto Alegre, Brazil, 1994).

39 Galloway, 'Agricultural Reform', p. 769; Andrew Grant, *History of Brazil* (London, 1809), p. 291; Marquis de Lavradio, 'Secret Instructions', in *The History of Brazil . . . , Volume 2* [1779], ed. J. Armitage (London, 1836), pp. 161–243, see pp. 227–8; John Mawe, *Travels in the Interior of Brazil* (London, 1812), p. 353.

40 Johann Baptist von Spix and Carl Friedrich Philippe von Martius, *Travels in Brazil, in the Years 1817–1820* (London, 1824), vol. II, p. 39.

41 Nicoláo Joaquim Moreira, 'Industria textil', *O auxiliador da industria nacional*, XLIII (1875), pp. 397–403, quotation p. 401.

42 Russell H. Bartley, *Imperial Russia and the Struggle for Latin American Independence, 1808–1828* (Austin, TX, 1978), p. 48.

43 Sanford A. Mosk, 'Subsidized Hemp Production in Spanish California', *Agricultural History*, XIII (1939), pp. 171–5.

44 E. Forster, 'History of Hemp in Chile', *Journal of the International Hemp Association*, III (1997), pp. 72–7.

45 Campos, *Home Grown*, p. 251.

46 Mosk, 'Subsidized'; William M. Mason, *Los Angeles under the Spanish Flag: Spain's New World* (Burbank, CA, 2004).

47 Mosk, 'Subsidized', p. 175.

48 Leslie Symons, *Russian Agriculture: A Geographic Survey* (New York, 1972).

49 Ziedonis Ligers, *Ethnographie Lettone* (Basel, Switzerland, 1954).

50 Crosby, *America, Russia, Hemp*.

51 James R. Gibson, *Imperial Russia in Frontier America: The Changing Geography of Supply in Russian America, 1784–1867* (New York, 1976).

52 Schmidt, 'Cultivation of Hemp', p. 631.

53 Ibid., p. 609.

54 Norman MacDonald, 'Hemp and Imperial Defence', *Canadian Historical Review*, XVII/4 (1936), pp. 385–98; Kenneth Andrews, *Trade, Plunder, and Settlement: Maritime Enterprise and the Genesis of the British Empire 1480–1630* (Cambridge, 1984), p. 76.

55 MacDonald, 'Imperial Defence', p. 386.

56 Crosby, *America, Russia, Hemp*.

57 E. Lipson, *The Economic History of England*, vol. III: *The Age of Mercantilism* (London, 1931), p. 185.

58 Serrera Contreras, *Cultivo*, pp. 251–2.

59 Marco Perron, 'La culture du chanvre d'après les données de l'APV', *Folklore Suisse*, LXXXIII (1993), pp. 125–32.

60 Anthony David Mills, *A Dictionary of English Place-Names*, 2nd edn (Oxford, 2011), p. 235.

61 E. Lipson, *The Economic History of England*, vol. II: *The Age of Mercantilism* (London, 1931), p. 109.

62 Lewis Tonna Dibdin, *Church Courts: An Historical Inquiry into the Status of the Ecclesiastical Courts* (London, 1882), vol. II, p. 98.

63 Lipson, *Age of Mercantilism III*, p. 429.

64 Ibid., pp. 21, 123.

65 Ibid.

66 James Munro and Almeric W. Fitzroy, *Acts of the Privy Council of England: Colonial Series, AD 1745–1766* (London, 1911), vol. IV, p. 632.

67 Lipson, *Age of Mercantilism III*; W. Tyson, *Rope: A History of the Hard Fibre Cordage Industry in the United Kingdom* (London, 1967).

68 Lewis Cecil Gray, *History of Agriculture in the Southern United States to 1860*, vol. I (Washington, DC, 1933), p. 25.

69 Anonymous, 'A Perfect Description of Virginia', in *Tracts and Other Papers, Relating Principally to the Origin, Settlement, and Progress of the Colonies in North America* [1649], ed. P. Force (Washington, DC, 1837), vol. II, p. 4.

70 Harry J. Carman, ed., *American Husbandry* [1775] (New York, 1939), p. 116.

71 Percy W. Bidwell and John I. Falconer, *History of Agriculture in the Northern United States, 1620–1860* (Washington, DC, 1925), p. 25.

72 Crosby, *America, Russia, Hemp*, p. 17.

73 Brent Moore, *A Study of the Past, the Present and the Possibilities of the Hemp Industry in Kentucky* (Lexington, KY, 1906), p. 9.

74 Eric Kerridge, *The Farmers of Old England* (Totowa, NJ, 1973); Rowland E. Prothero, *English Farming: Past and Present* (New York, 1912).

75 Jared Eliot, *Essays Upon Field-husbandry in New-England* (Boston, MA, 1760), p. 11.

76 MacDonald, 'Imperial Defence', p. 387; John Lambert, *Travels through Lower Canada and the United States* (London, 1810), vol. I, p. 465.

77 Eliot, *Essays*, p. 32.

78 Marquis de Lavradio, 'Secret Instructions', p. 228.

79 Charles Darwin, *On the Origin of Species by Means of Natural Selection, or the Preservation of Favoured Races in the Struggle for Life*, 1st edn (London, 1860), p. 360.

80 Charles Estienne and Jean Liebault, *L'agriculture, et maison rustique. Dernière edition* [1570] (Lyon, 1594), p. 202a.

81 Olivier de Serres, *Le Théâtre d'agriculture et mesnage des champs* (Paris, 1617), p. 319; Nathan Bailey, *Dictionarium rusticum, urbanicum and botanicum* (London, 1726), vol. I, see entry for 'Black-birds'; J. C. Hervieux de Chanteloup, *Nouveau traité des serins de canarie* (Paris, 1709), pp. 44–5.

82 Richard W. Johnson, 'Fort Snelling from its Foundation to the Present Time', *Collections of the Minnesota Historical Society*, VIII (1898), pp. 427–48.

83 Missouri State Board of Agriculture, *Third Annual Report of the State Board of Agriculture* (Jefferson City, MO, 1868), p. 186.

84 L. H. Dewey, 'Hemp', in *Yearbook of the United States Department of Agriculture, 1913* (Washington, DC, 1914), pp. 283–346; A. J. Pieters, 'Agricultural Seeds – Where Grown and How Handled', in *Yearbook of the United States Department of Agriculture, 1901*, ed. G. W. Hill (Washington, DC, 1902), pp. 233–56.

85 George M'Call Theal, *Compendium of the History and Geography of South Africa*, 3rd edn (London, 1878), p. 15; R. Montgomery Martin, *History of Southern Africa* (London, 1836), p. 257.

86 John Lawrence Jiggens, *Marijuana Australiana*, PhD dissertation, Queensland University of Technology (Brisbane, 2004), p. 36.

87 William Harcus, *South Australia: Its History, Resources, and Productions* (London, 1876), p. 226.

88 MacDonald, 'Imperial Defence', p. 387.

89 Gray, *History*, vol. I, p. 75.

90 Serrera Contreras, *Cultivo*, pp. 68, 75.

91 Gray, *History*, vol. I, p. 76.

92 Marcandier, *Traité*; de Serres, *Théâtre d'agriculture*, p. 665; Estienne and Liebault, *L'Agriculture*, p. 202a.

93 Ernest Small and David Marcus, 'Hemp: A New Crop with Uses for North America', in *Trends in New Crops and New Uses*, ed. J. Janick and A. Whipkey (Alexandria, VA, 2002), pp. 284–326.

94 C. Kresz (Ainé), *Le Pêcheur français* (Paris, 1818), p. 33.

95 Lipson, *Age of Mercantilism II*, p. 110; Lipson, *Age of Mercantilism III*, pp. 61, 162, 209.

96 Anonymous, *Les ordonnances royaux sur le faict et jurisdiction de la prévoste des marchans, eschevinage de la Ville de Paris* (Paris, 1556), p. 170.

97 Henri Pigeonneau, *Histoire du commerce de la France. Tome deuxième: Le seizième siècle – Henri IV – Richelieu* (Paris, 1889), p. 405.

98 von Schmidt, 'Cultivation of Hemp', p. 610; Marcandier, *Traité*, p. 46.

99 Moreira, 'Industria textil', p. 399.

100 Gray, *History*, vol. II, pp. 46–7, 181; James F. Hopkins, *A History of the Hemp Industry in Kentucky* (Lexington, KY, 1951), pp. 68–9.

101 K. L. Van Zant, T. Webb, III, G. M. Peterson and R. G. Baker, 'Increased Cannabis/Humulus Pollen, an Indicator of European Agriculture in Iowa', *Palynology*, III (1979), pp. 227–33.

102 Antoine Simon le Page du Pratz, *Histoire de la Louisiane* (Paris, 1758), p. 290.

103 Carman, *American Husbandry*, p. 117.

104 John C. Fitzpatrick, ed., *The Writings of George Washington* (Washington, DC, 1940), vol. XXXIII, pp. 233, 243, 266, 279, 288, 209, 469.

105 Anonymous, 'Monthly Commercial Report', *The Athenaeum*, V (1809), pp. 93–5; Anonymous, 'Home News; Falmouth, June 20', *The Universal Politician, and Periodical Reporter* (July and August 1796), p. 9.

106 Anonymous, 'Monthly Commercial Report', p. 24.

107 Fitzpatrick, *George Washington*, pp. 233, 243, 266, 279, 288, 209, 469.

108 Ibid., pp. 72, 265, 323.

109 Harbans L. Bhardwaj, Charles L. Webber III and Glenn S. Sakamoto, 'Cultivation of Kenaf and Sunn Hemp in the Mid-Atlantic United States', *Industrial Crops and Products*, XXII (2005), pp. 151–5.

110 Hopkins, *History*, pp. 11–12.

111 Moore, *Study of the Past*, p. 110.

112 Crosby, *America, Russia, Hemp*, pp. 47–50.

113 Gray, *History*, vol. II, p. 821; Hopkins, *History*, pp. 86–7.

114 Hopkins, *History*, p. 4.

115 Ibid., pp. 57–8.

116 Samuel L. Southard and John Rodgers, 'Report of the Secretary of the Navy', *American Farmer*, VI (1825), pp. 362–4.

117 Hopkins, *History*, p. 155; Charles Richards Dodge, *A Report on the Culture of Hemp and Jute in the United States* (Washington, DC, 1896), pp. 16–17.

118 Hopkins, *History*, p. 192.

119 Dewey, 'Hemp', p. 292.

120 Moore, *Study of the Past*, p. 61; Hopkins, *History*, p. 111.

121 Hopkins, *History*; Dewey, 'Hemp'; Moore, *Study of the Past*.

122 S. A. Clemens, 'Flax and Hemp', in *Third Annual Report*, Missouri State Board of Agriculture, ed. (Jefferson City, MO, 1868), pp. 155–91, see pp. 160, 183; Anonymous, 'Kentucky Hemp Returns', *New York Times* (14 March 1926), p. 5.

123 Clemens, 'Flax and Hemp', p. 186.

124 Moore, *Study of the Past*, p. 61.

125 Dewey, 'Hemp', p. 290.

126 Charles Richards Dodge, *A Report on the Culture of Flax, Hemp, Ramie, and Jute* (Washington, DC, 1890), p. 28.

127 Clemens, 'Flax and Hemp', p. 187; L. H. Dewey, 'The Hemp Industry in the United States', in *Yearbook of the United States Department of Agriculture, 1901* (Washington, DC, 1902), pp. 541–54, see p. 554; Hopkins, *History*, pp. 106–7; Dewey, 'Hemp', p. 303; Moore, *Study of the Past*, p. 73.

128 Dewey, 'The Hemp Industry', p. 553.

129 Dewey, 'Hemp', pp. 292–3; James H. Lanman, 'Commerce of the Mississippi', *Merchant's Magazine and Commercial Review*, IX (1843), pp. 154–61.

130 Hopkins, *History*; Dewey, 'Hemp'; Moore, *Study of the Past*; Small and Marcus, 'Hemp: A New Crop'; Sterling Evans, *Bound in Twine* (College Station, TX, 2007); B. B. Robinson, 'Hemp', USDA *Farmers' Bulletin*, No. 1935 (Washington, DC, 1943).

131 Dewey, 'Hemp'.

132 Lanman, 'Commerce'.

133 Dewey, 'Hemp', p. 339.

134 Moore, *Study of the Past*, p. 6.

135 Albert Hazen Wright, *Wisconsin's Hemp Industry* (Madison, WI, 1918), p. 13.

136 Evans, *Bound in Twine*, p. 30.

137 Howard T. Lewis, 'Distribution of Hard Fiber Cordage', *Publications of the Graduate School of Business Administration, Harvard University*, XVII/82 (1930), statistics on p. 9.

138 W. O. van der Knaap, J.F.N. van Leeuwen, A. Fankhauser and B. Ammann, 'Palynostratigraphy of the Last Centuries in Switzerland Based on 23 Lake and Mire Deposits: Chronostratigraphic Pollen Markers, Regional Patterns, and Local Histories', *Review of Palaeobotany and Palynology*, CVIII (2000), pp. 85–142; J. E. Schofield and M. P. Waller, 'A Pollen Analytical Record for Hemp Retting from Dungeness Foreland, UK', *Journal of Archaeological Science*, XXXII (2005), pp. 715–26; Peter Rasmussen and N. John Anderson, 'Natural and Anthropogenic Forcing of Aquatic Macrophyte Development in a Shallow Danish Lake During the Last 7000 Years', *Journal of Biogeography*, XXXII (2005), pp. 1993–2005; P. Lageras, 'Long-term History of Land-use and Vegetation at Femtingagolen – a Small Lake in the Smaland Uplands, Southern Sweden', *Vegetation History and Archaeobotany*, V (1996), pp. 215–28; H. Godwin, 'Pollen-analytic Evidence for the Cultivation of Cannabis in England', *Review of Palaeobotany and Palynology*, XLI (1967), pp. 71–80, 137–8.

139 Moore, *Study of the Past*, p. 63.

140 Robert C. Leslie, *Old Sea Wings, Ways, and Words, in the Days of Oak and Hemp* (London, 1890), p. 190.

141 Roswell Marsh, 'Hemp — Cannabis — Sativa [Flyer]"[Steubenville, OH]: Roswell Marsh, publisher, n.d. [1872] (held at the Center for Southwest Research, Zimmerman Library, University of New Mexico); Henri Lecomte, 'Les Textiles végétaux des colonies', *Annales de la science agronomique française et étrangère*, II (second series) (1896), pp. I–112, quotation p. III.

142 Mueggler, 'The Poetics', p. 987.

143 Francesca Bray, *Science and Civilization in China: Agriculture* (Cambridge, 1984), vol. VI, pt 2, pp. 535, 539.

144 Leslie Symons, *Russian Agriculture: A Geographic Survey* (New York, 1972), pp. 200–201.

145 Hopkins, *History*, p. 217.

146 Lewis, 'Distribution', p. 9.

147 Robinson, 'Hemp', p. 2.

148 Anonymous, 'Hemp Slows Up', *Business Week*, DCCXXXVIII (1943), p. 40.

149 Hopkins, *History*, pp. 212–13.

150 Renée Johnson, 'Hemp as an Agricultural Commodity', Congressional Research Service report (Washington, DC, 2013).

151 Hopkins, *History*, pp. 213–14.

152 G. Langdon White, Paul F. Griffin and Tom L. McKnight, *World Economic Geography* (Belmont, CA, 1964), p. 490.

153 Syndicat d'Initiatives de Villaines-la-Juhel et ses Environs, *Un Brin de causette . . . Le chanvre* (Villaines-la-Juhel, France, 1981), not paginated.
154 G. Bredemann, F. Schwanitz and R. von Sengbusch, 'Problems of Modern Hemp Breeding, with Particular Reference to the Breeding of Varieties of Hemp Containing Little or No Hashish', *UNODC Bulletin on Narcotics*, VIII (1956), pp. 31–5.

4 The Drug Goes Global

1 Igor Grant, J. Hampton Atkinson, Ben Gouaux and Barth Wilsey, 'Medical Marijuana: Clearing Away the Smoke', *Open Neurology Journal*, VI (2012), pp. 18–25; Dale Gieringer, Ed Rosenthal and Gregory T. Carter, *Marijuana Medical Handbook* (Oakland, CA, 2008).
2 Johannes Fabian, *Out of Our Minds: Reason and Madness in the Exploration of Central Africa* (Berkeley, CA, 2000), p. 163; Armand Corre and E. Lejanne, *Résumé de la matière médicale et toxicologique coloniale* (Paris, 1887), p. 71.
3 S. T. Oner, *Cannabis Sativa: The Essential Guide to the World's Finest Marijuana Strains* (San Francisco, CA, 2012); S. T. Oner, *Cannabis Indica: The Essential Guide to the World's Finest Marijuana Strains* (San Francisco, CA, 2011); Jorge Cervantes, *Marijuana Horticulture* (Sacramento, CA, 2006); Robert C. Clarke, *Marijuana Botany* (Berkeley, CA, 1981).
4 David J. Nutt, Leslie A. King and Lawrence D. Phillips, 'Drug Harms in the UK: A Multicriteria Decision Analysis', *The Lancet*, CCCLXXI (2010), pp. 1558–65.
5 Arpana Agrawal and Michael T. Lynskey, 'The Genetic Epidemiology of Cannabis Use, Abuse and Dependence', *Addiction*, CI (2006), pp. 801–12.
6 John M. McPartland and Geoffroy W. Guy, 'The Evolution of *Cannabis* and Coevolution with the Cannabinoid Receptor: A Hypothesis', in *The Medicinal Uses of Cannabis and Cannabinoids*, ed. G. W. Guy, B. A. Whittle and P. J. Robson (London, 2004), pp. 71–101; Ethan B. Russo, 'Clinical Endocannabinoid Deficiency (CECD): Can This Concept Explain Therapeutic Benefits of Cannabis in Migraine, Fibromyalgia, Irritable Bowel Syndrome and Other Treatment-resistant Conditions?', *Neuroendocrinology Letters*, XXV (2008), pp. 31–9.
7 Thomas Bowrey, *A Geographical Account of Countries Round the Bay of Bengal, 1669 to 1679* [1701] (Cambridge, 1905), p. 81.
8 Leslie L. Iversen, *The Science of Marijuana* (New York, 2000), pp. 229–31.
9 Howard S. Becker, 'History, Culture and Subjective Experience: An Exploration of the Social Bases of Drug Induced Experiences', *Journal of Health and Social Behavior*, VII (1967), pp. 163–76; Andrew T. Weil, N. T. Zinberg and J. M. Nelsen, 'Clinical and Psychological Effects of Marihuana in Man', *Science*, CLXII (1968), pp. 1234–42; Isaac Campos, *Home Grown: Marijuana and the Origins of Mexico's War on Drugs* (Chapel Hill, NC, 2012); James H. Mills, *Madness, Cannabis, and Colonialism: The 'Native-only' Lunatic Asylums of British India, 1857–1900* (New York, 2000).

10 John Huyghen van Linschoten, *The Voyage of John Huyghen Van Linschoten to the East Indies. From the Old English Translation of 1598* [1598] (London, 1885), vol. II, p. 125.

11 David T. Courtwright, *Forces of Habit: Drugs and the Making of the Modern World* (Cambridge, MA, 2001).

12 Cristoval Acosta, *Tractado de las Drogas, y Medicinas de la Indias Orientales* (Burgos, Spain, 1578), pp. 360–61.

13 Garcia de Orta, *Colloquies on the Simples and Drugs of India* [1563], 1895 translated edn (London, 1913), p. 56.

14 Van Linschoten, *Voyage*, p. 116.

15 Charles Fawcett, ed., *The Travels of the Abbé Carré in India and the near East 1672 to 1674* (London, 1947), vol. I, p. 227.

16 Fabian, *Out of Our Minds*; Brian M. du Toit, *Cannabis in Africa* (Rotterdam, 1980); Paul B. du Chaillu, *Explorations and Adventures in Equatorial Africa* (New York, 1861).

17 Peter Kolben, 'Histoire naturelle du Cap de Bonne-Esperance and des pays voisins', in *Histoire générale des voyages* [1713], ed. Abbé Prevost (The Hague, 1748), vol. VI, pp. 505–33; Antonio de Saldanha da Gama, *Memória sobre as colonias de Portugal: Situadas na Costa Occidental d'Afrique* (Paris, 1839), p. 73; João dos Santos, *Ethiopia Oriental* [1609] (Lisbon, 1891), vol. I, p. 88.

18 Ibid., p. 88.

19 John Edward Philips, 'African Smoking and Pipes', *Journal of African History*, XXIV (1983), pp. 303–19.

20 Etienne Zangato, 'Early Smoking Pipes in the North-western Central African Republic', *Africa: Rivista trimestrale di studi e documentazione dell'Istito italiano per l'Africa e l'Oriente*, LVI (2001), pp. 365–95; John Watt and Maria Breyer-Branwijk, *The Medical and Poisonous Plants of South Africa* (Edinburgh, 1932), pp. 156, 167.

21 John H. Parry, 'Ships and Seamen in the Age of Discovery', *Caribbean Quarterly*, II (1951–2), pp. 25–33; Dorothy Denneen Volo and James M. Volo, *Daily Life in the Age of Sail* (Westport, CT, 2002); Roger C. Smith, 'Vanguard of Empire: The Mariners of Exploration and Discovery', *Terrae Incognitae*, XVII (1985), pp. 15–27.

22 Alan W. Baxter, 'Portuguese and Creole Portuguese in the Pacific and Western Pacific Rim. Vol. 2', in *Atlas of Languages of Intercultural Communication in the Pacific, Asia, and the Americas*, ed. S. A. Wurm, P. Mühlhäuser and D. T. Tyron (Berlin, 1996), pp. 299–338.

23 Marcus Rediker, *The Slave Ship: A Human History* (New York, 2007); Emma Christopher, *Slave Ship Sailors and Their Captive Cargoes, 1730–1807* (New York, 2006); P. Linebaugh and M. Rediker, *The Many-headed Hydra: Sailors, Slaves, Commoners, and the Hidden History of the Revolutionary Atlantic* (Boston, MA, 2000).

24 Artur Teodoro de Matos, ed., *O Tombo de Dio* (Lisbon, 1999), folio 59v.

25 Robert Knox, *An Historical Relation of the Island Ceylon in the East-Indies* (London, 1681), p. 154.

26 Bowrey, *Geographical Account*, p. 281.

27 Kolben, 'Histoire Naturelle', p. 513.

28 Luiz Mott, 'A Maconha na História do Brasil', in *Diamba Sarabamba*,
    ed. A. Henman and O. Pessoa, Jr (São Paulo, Brazil, 1986), pp. 117–35.

29 Richard F. Burton, *Zanzibar; City, Island, and Coast* (London, 1872), vol. I,
    p. 247.

30 R. O. Clarke, 'Short Notice of the African Plant Diamba, Commonly
    Called Congo Tobacco', *Hooker's Journal of Botany*, III (1851), pp. 9–11,
    quotation p. 10.

31 Pablo Osvaldo Wolff, *Marihuana en la America Latina: La Amenaza que Constituye*
    (Buenos Aires, 1948), p. 37.

32 Mott, 'Maconha'; Bartholomé Juan Leonardo de Argensola, *The Discovery
    and Conquest of the Molucco and Philippine Islands* (London, 1708), p. 143.

33 Emmanuel Noumi, 'Treating Asthma with Medicinal Plants: An
    Ethnomedical Case Study from Baré-Bakem, Nkongsamba Region,
    Cameroon', *Syllabus Review*, I (2009), pp. 10–15; A. Engler and K. Prantl,
    *Die Natürlichen Pflanzenfamilien nebst Ihren Gattungen und Wichtigeren Arten
    Insbesondere den Nutzpflanzen* (Leipzig, Germany, 1889), vol. III, pt I; William
    H. Sanders and William Edwards Fay, *Vocabulary of the Umbundu Language*
    (Boston, MA, 1885); Padres Missionarios, *Diccionario Portuguez-Olunyaneka*
    (Huilla, Angola, 1896); António Francisco Ferreira da Silva Porto, *Viagens
    e Apontamentos de um Portuense em África* [1942] (Coimbra, Portugal, 1986);
    F. Creighton Wellman, 'Some Medicinal Plants of Angola, with
    Observations on Their Use by Natives of the Province', *American Medicine*,
    XI (1906), pp. 94–9; George Watt, *The Commercial Products of India* (London,
    1908), p. 249.

34 W. Derham, ed., *Philosophical Experiments and Observations of the Late Eminent
    Dr Robert Hooke* (London, 1726), p. 210.

35 Van Linschoten, *Voyage*, p. 116; de Argensola, *Discovery*, p. 143; Joseph Miller,
    Botanicum Officinale: Or, a Compendious Herbal (London, 1722), pp. 107–8;
    Louis Lémery, *A Treatise of All Sorts of Foods, Both Animal and Vegetable* (London,
    1745), p. 339.

36 Héli Chatelain and W. R. Summers, 'Bantu Notes and Vocabularies. No. I.
    The Language of the Bashi-Lange and Ba-Luba', *Journal of the American
    Geographical Society of New York*, XXV (1893), pp. 512–41, quotation pp. 519–20.

37 Ibid., pp. 519–20; Jan Vansina, 'Probing the Past of the Lower Kwilu
    Peoples', *Paideuma*, IXX/XX (1973/1974), pp. 332–64; Thomas Turner,
    '"Batetela", "Baluba", "Basonge": Ethnogenesis in Zaire', *Cahiers d'Études
    Africaines*, XXXIII (1993), pp. 587–612; Kjell Zetterström, 'Bena Riamba:
    Brothers of Hemp', *Studia Ethnographica Upsaliensia*, XXVI (1966), pp. 151–66.

38 William H. Sanders and William Edwards Fay, *Vocabulary of the Umbundu
    Language* (Boston, MA, 1885), p. 17; Padres Missionarios, *Diccionario*, p. 31;
    David Clement Scott, *A Cyclopaedic Dictionary of the Mang'anja Language Spoken
    in British Central Africa* (Edinburgh, 1892), p. 706; John Rebman, *Dictionary of
    the Kiniassa Language* (St Chrischona, Switzerland, 1877), p. 16; João Vicente
    Martins, *Crenças, Adivinhação e Medicina Tradicionais dos Tutchokwe do Nordeste de
    Angola* (Lisbon, 1993), p. 368.

39 Dr Flückiger, 'Pharmaceutische Reiseeindrucke [Part 1]', *Pharmaceutische Centralhalle für Deutschland*, VIII (1867), pp. 436–42.

40 Manoel Pio Corrêa, *Diccionario das Plantas Úteis do Brasil e das Exóticas Cultivadas* (Rio de Janeiro, Brazil, 1926), vol. I, p. 472.

41 Donald Pierson, *O homem no vale do São Francisco* (Rio de Janeiro, Brazil, 1972), vol. II, pp. 95–6; Richard Bucher, 'La Marihuana en el Folklore y la Cultura Popular Brasileña', *Revista Takiwasi*, II (1995), pp. 119–28; Mário Ypiranga Monteiro, 'Folclore da maconha', *Revista Brasileria de folclore*, VI (1966), pp. 285–300; Erasmo Dias, 'A Influência da maconha no folclore Maranhense', *Revista Maranhese de Cultura*, I (1974), p. 1; Jarbas Pernambuco, 'A Maconha em Pernambuco', in *Novos estudos Afro-Brasileiros: Trabalhos apresentados ao 1.º Congresso Afro-Brasileiro do Recife*, ed. A. Ramos (Rio de Janeiro, Brazil, 1937), vol. II, pp. 185–91.

42 Rediker, *Slave Ship*; Jerome S. Handler, 'The Middle Passage and the Material Culture of Captive Africans', *Slavery and Abolition*, XXX (2009), pp. 1–26; Andrew Pearson, Ben Jeffs, Annsofie Witkin and Helen MacQuarrie, *Infernal Traffic: Excavation of a Liberated African Graveyard in Rupert's Valley, St Helena* (Bootham, Yorkshire, 2011); Judith A. Carney and Richard Nicholas Rosomoff, *In the Shadow of Slavery: Africa's Botanical Legacy in the Atlantic World* (Berkeley, CA, 2009).

43 Judith A. Carney, 'Rice and Memory in the Age of Enslavement: Atlantic Passages to Suriname', *Slavery and Abolition*, XXVI (2005), pp. 325–47.

44 Chaillu, *Exploration*, p. 420.

45 Rediker, *Slave Ship*, pp. 58, 216, 238, 269, 328; Handler, 'Middle Passage'.

46 William Butterworth, *Three Years Adventures of a Minor in England, Africa, the West Indies, South-Carolina and Georgia*, 2nd edn (Leeds, 1831), p. 127.

47 Rediker, *Slave Ship*, p. 195; Handler, 'Middle Passage'.

48 Document in the British National Archives: Richard Hill to David Ewart, 25 June 1862, enclosed in No. 106, Edward Eyre to Duke of Newcastle, 8 November 1862, CO 137/368.

49 Luis da Câmara Cascudo, *Made in África (Pesquisas e notas)* (Rio de Janeiro, Brazil, 1965), pp. 179–80; José Rodrígues da Costa Doria, 'Os Fumadores de maconha; Effeitos males do vicio', in *Proceedings of the Second Pan American Scientific Congress*, ed. G. L. Swiggett (Washington, DC, 1917), Section VIII, Part I, pp. 151–61.

50 Clarke, 'Short Notice'; Doria, 'Os Fumadores', p. 151; Les Missionaires, *Dictionnaire Pongoué–Français* (Paris, 1881), p. 128; Ladisláu Netto, *Investigações históricas e scientíficas sobre o Museu Imperial e Nacional do Rio de Janeiro* (Rio de Janeiro, Brazil, 1870), p. 254; Augusto Carlos Teixeira de Aragão, *Breve Noticia Sobre o Descobrimento da América* (Lisbon, 1892), p. 37.

51 Renato Tomei, *Forbidden Fruits: The Secret Names of Plants in Caribbean Culture* (Rome, 2008); Gilberto Freyre, *O escravo nos anuncios de jornais brasileiros do seculo XIX*, 2nd edn (São Paulo, 1979), pp. 79–80.

52 Richard F. Burton, *Explorations of the Highlands of Brazil* (London, 1869), vol. II, p. 295.

53 Ibid., vol. I, p. 237; J. Descaisne and Louis Van Houtte, *Flore des serres et des jardins de l'Europe* (Gand, Belgium, 1861), p. 204; Carl Friedrich Philippe von Martius, *Systema materiae medicae vegetabilis brasiliensis* (Vienna, 1843), p. 121.

54 Gilberto Freyre, *Nordeste: Aspectos da influencia da canna sobre a vida e a Paizagem do nordeste do Brasil* (Rio de Janeiro, Brazil, 1937), p. 15.

55 Francisco Manuel Carlos de Mello Ficalho, *Plantas úteis da África Portuguesa* [1884], 2nd edn (Lisbon, 1947), p. 265.

56 Lopes Goncalves, *O Amazonas: Esboço historico, chorographico e estatistico até o Anno de 1903* (New York, 1904), p. 30; Vicente Chermont de Miranda, *Glossario Paraense: Ou, Colleção de vocabulos peculiares à Amazonia e especialemente á Ilha de Marajó* (Pará, Brazil, 1906), p. 35.

57 John Thornton and Linda M. Heywood, *Central Africans, Atlantic Creoles, and the Foundation of the Americas, 1585–1660* (New York, 2007).

58 Campos, *Home Grown*, p. 53.

59 Nicolás del Castillo Mathieu, 'El Léxico Negro–Africano de San Basilio de Palenque', *Thesaurus*, XXIX (1984), pp. 80–169.

60 Mott, 'Maconha,' p. 123.

61 Clarke, 'Short Notice'; I. C. Lang, 'Üeber das Arzneiwesen bei den Negern', *Repertorium für die Pharmacie*, LXXXII (1843), pp. 36–50; Descaisne and Van Houtte, *Flore*, p. 204; George M'Henry, 'An Account of the Liberated African Establishment at St Helena', *Simmond's Colonial Magazine*, V (1845), pp. 434–41, see p. 437; Johann Büttikofer, *Reisebilder aus Liberia* (Leiden, 1890), vol. II, p. 276; Ed Poisson, 'Itineraire suivi par les habitants de Bakel pour se rendre à Kaouroco . . .', *Bulletin de la Société de Géographie*, 4th series, XVII (1859), pp. 45–8, see p. 46; Anonymous [Richard F. Burton], *Wanderings in West Africa from Liverpool to Fernando Po* (London, 1863), vol. II, p. 225.

62 Campos, *Home Grown*; Frederick A. Ober, *Travels in Mexico*, revised edn (Boston, MA, 1887), p. 670.

63 Martin Booth, *Cannabis: A History* (New York, 2005), p. 156.

64 Joseph C. Miller, 'Retention, Reinvention, and Remembering: Restoring Identities through Enslavement in Africa and under Slavery in Brazil', in *Enslaving Connections: Changing Cultures of Africa and Brazil During the Era of Slavery*, ed. J. C. Curto and P. E. Lovejoy (New York, 2004), pp. 81–121.

65 Pearson et al., *Infernal Traffic*; Monica Schuler, 'Liberated Central Africans in Nineteenth-century Guyana', in *Central Africans and Cultural Transformations in the American Diaspora*, ed. L. M. Heywood (Cambridge, 2002), pp. 319–52; Monica Schuler, 'Alas, Alas, Kongo': A Social History of Indentured African Immigration into Jamaica, 1841–1865* (Baltimore, MD, and London, 1980); Sharla M. Fett, 'Middle Passages and Forced Migrations: Liberated Africans in Nineteenth-century U.S. Camps and Ships', *Slavery and Abolition*, XXXI (2010), pp. 75–98; Filipe Castro, 'Rigging the Pepper Wreck. Part 2 – Sails', *International Journal of Nautical Archaeology*, XXXVIII (2009), pp. 105–15.

66 Alexander Beatson, *Tracts Relative to the Island of St Helena* (London, 1816), p. 302.

67 M'Henry, 'An Account', quotation p. 437.

68 Clarke, 'Short Notice', p. 10; Büttikofer, *Reisebilder*, p. 276.

69 Pearson et al., *Infernal Traffic*.

70 Robert Thomas, *The Modern Practice of Physic* (London, 1802), vol. II, p. 100.

71 Schuler, 'Liberated', p. 342; Fett, 'Middle Passages', p. 86; Mary C. Karasch, *Slave Life in Rio de Janeiro, 1808–1850* (Princeton, NJ, 1987), p. 181.

72 Clarke, 'Short Notice', p. 11; M'Henry, 'An Account', p. 434.

73 Anonymous [Richard F. Burton], *Wanderings*, p. 222.

74 Clarke, 'Short Notice', p. 10.

75 Campos, *Home Grown*; Doria, 'Os Fumadores'; Du Toit, *Cannabis*; Monteiro, 'Folclore'; Pernambuco, 'Maconha'; Martins, *Crenças*; Louis Lewin, *Phantastica* (Berlin, 1924); Héli Chatelain, 'Angolan Customs', *Journal of American Folk-lore*, IX (1896), pp. 13–18; John M. Janzen, 'De l'ancienneté de l'usage des psychotropes en Afrique centrale', *Psychotropes*, I (1983), pp. 105–7.

76 Schuler, '*Alas, Alas, Kongo*'.

77 Document in the British National Archives: Richard Hill to David Ewart, 25 June 1862, enclosed in No. 106, Edward Eyre to Duke of Newcastle, 8 November 1862, CO 137/368.

78 J. F. Siler, W. L. Sheep, G. W. Cook, W. A. Smith, L. B. Bates and G. F. Clark, 'Mariajuana Smoking in Panama', *Military Surgeon*, LXXIII (1933), pp. 269–80.

79 Du Toit, *Cannabis*, p. 23.

80 Campos, *Home Grown*, p. 82.

81 Mott, 'Maconha', p. 130.

82 Christelle Taraud, 'Urbanisme, hygiénisme et prostitution à Casablanca dans les années 1920', *French Colonial History*, VII (2006), pp. 97–108; Christelle Taraud, 'Jouer avec la marginalité: Le cas des filles soumises "Indigènes" du Quartier Reéservé de Casablanca dans les Années 1920–1950', *CLIO. Histoire, femmes et societes [online]*, XVII (2003), DOI: 10.4000/clio.582; André-Paul Comor, 'Les plaisirs des Legionnaires au temps des colonies: L'alcool et les femmes', *Guerres mondiales et conflits contemporains*, II (2006), pp. 33–42.

83 James D. Griffith, Sharon Mitchell, Christian L. Hart, Lea T. Adams and Lucy L. Gu, 'Pornography Actresses: An Assessment of the Damaged Goods Hypothesis', *Journal of Sex Research* (2012), DOI:10.1080/00224499.2012.719168; Trevor Bennett, Katy Holloway and David Farrington, 'The Statistical Association between Drug Misuse and Crime: A Meta-Analysis', *Aggression and Violent Behavior*, XIII (2008), pp. 107–18.

84 Jason Kaplan, 'The Howard Stern Show for March 4, 2005', online at http://howardstern.com (accessed 11 September 2012); Sami Ali, *Le Haschisch en Égypte* (Paris, 1971), p. 95.

85 Driss Maghraoui, 'Knowledge, Gender, and Spatial Configuration in Colonial Casablanca', in *Revisiting the Colonial Past in Morocco*, ed. D. Maghraoui (New York, 2013), pp. 64–86.

86 Z. S. Strother, 'Display of the Body Hottentot', in *Africans on Stage: Studies in Ethnological Show Business*, ed. B. Lindfors (Bloomington, IN, 1999), pp. 1–61.

87 Kolben, 'Histoire naturelle', p. 513.

88 David Gordon, 'From Rituals of Rapture to Dependence: The Political Economy of Khoikhoi Narcotic Consumption, *c.* 1487–1870', *South African Historical Journal*, XXXV (1996), pp. 62–88.

89 Bilby, 'Holy Herb'.

90 David Northrup, *Indentured Labor in the Age of Imperialism, 1834–1922* (Cambridge, 1995).

91 Vera Rubin and Lambros Comitas, *Ganja in Jamaica: The Effects of Marijuana Use* (New York, 1975); Ansley Hamid, *The Ganja Complex: Rastafari and Marijuana* (Lanham, MD, 2002).

92 Bilby, 'Holy Herb'.

93 Siddharth Chandra and Aaron Swoboda, 'Are Spatial Variables Important? The Case for Multiple Drugs in British Bengal', in *Geography and Drug Addiction*, ed. Y. F. Thomas, D. Richardson and I. Cheung (New York, 2008), pp. 221–42.

94 Indian Hemp Drugs Commission, *Report of the Indian Hemp Drugs Commission, 1893–1894* [1894], reprint edn (Silver Spring, MD, 1969).

95 Derham, *Philosophical Experiments*, p. 210; Indian Immigrants (Wragg) Commission, 'Report', in *Documents of Indentured Labour, Natal 1851–1917*, ed. Y. S. Meer (Durban, South Africa, 1887), pp. 246–633, see p. 256.

96 Bowrey, *Geographical Account*, p. 79.

97 R. J. Wilkinson, *A Malay–English Dictionary* (Hong Kong, 1901), p. 577; Georg Eberhard Rumpf, *Herbarium Amboinense* (Amsterdam, 1747), vol. V, p. 209.

98 Ernest E. Heimbach, *White Meo–English Dictionary* (Ithaca, NY, 1969), p. 193.

99 Corre and Lejanne, *Résumé*, p. 24.

100 Rumpf, *Herbarium*, p. 210; D. Prain, *Report on the Cultivation and Use of Gánjá* (Calcutta, India, 1893), p. 1.

101 Bowrey, *Geographical Account*, p. 79.

102 George Abraham Grierson, 'The Hemp Plant in Sanskrit and Hindi Literature', *The Indian Antiquary*, XXIII (1894), pp. 260–62.

103 Chandra and Swoboda, 'Spatial Variables'.

104 'Quem Quizar Comprar . . .', *Jornal do commercio* (11 November 1828), p. 3; 'Manoel Francisco Pedroso . . .', *Jornal do commercio* (21 February 1847), p. 3.

105 Poisson, 'Itineraire', p. 46.

106 Burton, *Zanzibar*, vol. I, p. 381.

107 'Intended Sale of Goods for Warehouse Rent', *Daily Chronicle* (Georgetown, Guyana) (24 September 1886), p. 1.

108 M. Lartigue, 'La Lagune de Fernand-Vaz et le delta de l'Ogo-Wé', *Archives de médecine navale*, XIV (1870), pp. 163–91; Carlos de Almeida, 'Generos Coloniaes [Advertisement]', in *Novo almanach de Lembranças Luso Brazileiro para o anno de 1884*, ed. A. X. Rodrigues Cordeiro (Lisbon, 1883), p. 189; Charles Ivens, 'L'Angola Méridional', *Société d'études coloniales* (Belgium), V (1898), pp. 233–69; A. Moller, 'Einige Medizinische Pflanzen von S. Thomé', *Berichte der Deutschen Pharmaceutischen Gesellschaft*, VII (1898), pp. 491–501.

109 Graeme Henderson, 'The Wreck of the Ex-slaver *James Matthews*', *International Journal of Historical Archaeology*, XII (2008), pp. 39–52.

110 Campos, *Home Grown*; John G. Bourke, 'The American Congo', *Scribner's Magazine*, XV (1894), pp. 590–610.

111 James H. Mills, *Cannabis Nation: Control and Consumption in Britain, 1928–2008* (Oxford, 2012), pp. 18ff.

112 Emmanuel Akyeampong, 'Diaspora and Drug Trafficking in West Africa: A Case Sudy of Ghana', *African Affairs*, CIV (2005), pp. 429–47; Meyer Berger, 'About New York', *New York Times* (8 February 1940), p. 20.

113 Dale H. Gieringer, 'The Forgotten Origins of Cannabis Prohibition in California', *Contemporary Drug Problems*, XXVI (1999), pp. 237–88.

114 'Local Hashish-Eaters', *The San Francisco Call*, LXXXXVIII (24 June 1895), p. 7.

115 Abderrahmane Merzouki and Joaquín Molero Mesa, 'Concerning Kif, a *Cannabis sativa* L. Preparation Smoked in the Rif Mountains of Northern Morocco', *Journal of Ethnopharmacology*, LXXXI (2002), pp. 403–6; Tod H. Mikuriya, 'Kif Cultivation in the Rif Mountains', *Economic Botany*, XXI (1967), pp. 231–4.

116 G. M. Carstairs, 'Daru and Bhang: Cultural Factors in the Choice of Intoxicant', *Quarterly Journal of Studies on Alcohol*, XV (1954), pp. 220–37; Risto Pekka Pennanen, 'Melancholic Airs of the Orient: Bosnian Sevdalinka Music as an Orientalist and National Symbol', in *Music and Emotions*, ed. R. P. Pennanen (Helsinki, 2010), pp. 76–90.

117 Isidore Dukerley, 'Note sur les différences que présente avec le chanvre ordinaire et la variété de cette espèce connue en Algérie sous les noms de *Kif* et de *Tekrouri*', *Bulletin de la Société Botanique de France*, III (1866), pp. 401–6; M. H. Fisquet, *Histoire de l'Algérie* (Paris, 1842), p. 209; M. Larue du Barry, 'Note sur l'usage du chanvre en Algérie', *Journal de chimie médicale, de pharmacie et de toxicologie* (January 1845), pp. 31–4.

118 Roger Joseph, 'The Economic Significance of *Cannabis sativa* in the Moroccan Rif', *Economic Botany*, XXVII (1973), pp. 235–40.

119 Gregory Mann, 'Citizenship after Empire: Recognizing "French" West Africans in Sudan', in *De la Colonie à l'etat-nation: Constructions identitaires au Maghreb*, ed. P.-N. Denieu (Paris, 2013), pp. 119–32.

120 Philips, 'African Smoking'; Zangato, 'Early Smoking'.

121 Dukerley, 'Note', p. 406.

122 Ernest L. Abel, *Marihuana: The First Twelve Thousand Years* (New York, 1980); Larry Sloman, *Reefer Madness: The History of Marijuana in America* (Indianapolis, IN, 1979).

123 Milton Mezzrow and Bernard Wolfe, *Really the Blues* (New York, 1946), p. 213.

124 Bourke, 'American Congo', pp. 596–7; 'Stronger Than Opium', *The Prospector* (Tombstone, AZ) (15 September 1897), p. 2.

125 Gieringer, 'Forgotten Origins', p. 254.

126 'T. Puente and Son [Advertisement]', *El Regidor* (San Antonio, TX) (23 June 1910), p. 8; 'Sale of Mariahuana is Forbidden in City', *The Evening*

CANNABIS

Herald (Albuquerque, NM) (11 September 1917), p. 4.

127 'Marihuana May Be Grown Here; Terrible Drug Hits Kansas and Is Much Worse than Heroin', Santa Fe New Mexican (3 November 1925), p. 6.

128 State Narcotic Committee, 'The Trend of Drug Addiction in California', in Appendix to the Journals of the Senate and Assembly of the Forty-ninth Session of the Legislature of the State of California, Legislature of the State of California (Sacramento, CA, 1932), vol. V, document 9, p. 17.

129 James B. Slaughter, 'Marijuana Prohibition in the United States: History and Analysis of a Failed Policy', Columbia Journal of Law and Social Problems, XXI (1987–1988), pp. 417–40.

130 Antonio Castilho, ed., Exposition Universelle d'Anvers. Exposition Coloniale du Portugal. Catalogue Officiel (Antwerp, Belgium, 1885), pp. 109, 117, 171; A. Sébire, Les Plantes utiles du Sénégal: Plantes indigènes –plantes exotiques (Paris, 1899), p. 163.

131 Sloman, Reefer Madness, p. 117; W. W. Stockberger, 'Drug Plants under Cultivation', USDA Farmers' Bulletin No. 663 (Washington, DC, 1915), p. 19; 'First Medicinal Drug Plant Farm in the World', The Tucumcari [NM] News (17 June 1915), p. 3; '[A Medicinal Drug Plant Farm]', The Lancet, CXIII (1915), p. 610; 'Use for Deadly Weed', The Florida Star (Jacksonville, FL) (16 October 1908), p. 3; 'Cultivating Drugs', The Watchman and Southron (Sumter, SC) (13 April 1904), p. 1.

132 Siler et al., 'Mariajuana Smoking', p. 270.

133 Ibid., p. 271.

134 R. N. Mack and W. M. Lonsdale, 'Eradicating Invasive Plants: Hard-won Lessons for Islands', in Turning the Tide: The Eradication of Invasive Species, ed. C. R. Veitch and M. N. Clout (Gland, Switzerland, 2002), pp. 164–72, see p. 165.

135 'Bird Seed', Vick's Illustrated Monthly Magazine, XIV (1891), p. 130.

136 'Imported Hemp Seed', The Mt Sterling [KY] Advocate (4 April 1916), p. 3; L. H. Dewey, 'Hemp', in Yearbook of the United States Department of Agriculture, 1913 (Washington, DC, 1914), pp. 283–346.

137 Sloman, Reefer Madness, p. 73.

138 Michael Starks, Marijuana Chemistry, 2nd edn (Berkeley, CA, 1990), p. 81.

139 John Lawrence Jiggens, Marijuana Australiana, PhD dissertation, Queensland University of Technology (Brisbane, 2004), p. 36; 'Weed which is Noxious: Hashish Found', The Mail (Adelaide, NSW) (27 August 1938), p. 24.

140 'Hashish Grown near Border: Rumour Investigated', The Courier-mail (Brisbane, QLD), (22 June 1938), p. 1.

141 Ibid..

142 United States Bureau of Narcotics, Traffic in Opium and Other Dangerous Drugs for the Year Ended December 31, 1934 (Washington, DC, 1935), p. 31.

143 'Profitable Sidelines to Dairying', Northern Star (Lismore, NSW) (22 June 1938), p. 3.

144 Jiggens, Marijuana, p. 33 ff.

145 Lewin, Phantastica, p. 102.

226

146 James H. Mills, *Cannabis Britannica: Empire, Trade, Prohibition, 1800–1928* (Oxford, 2003); Mills, *Cannabis Nation*.

147 François Rabelais, *Gargantua et Pantagruel* [1546] (Paris, 1913), vol. II, p. 121.

148 Henri de Monfried, *La Croisière du hachich* (Paris, 1933); Henri de Monfried, *La Cargaison enchantée: Charas* (Paris, 1962).

149 European Monitoring Centre for Drugs and Drug Addiction, *Cannabis Production and Markets in Europe* (Luxembourg, 2012).

150 Joel H. Kaplan, 'Marijuana and Drug Abuse in Vietnam', *Annals of the New York Academy of Sciences*, CXCI (1971), pp. 261–9; Franklin D. Jones, 'Sanctioned Use of Drugs in Combat', in *Psychiatry: The State of the Art*, ed. P. Pichot, P. Berner, R. Wolf and K. Thau (New York, 1985), pp. 489–94.

151 Campos, *Home Grown*, pp. 162–3.

152 Mark Harrison, 'The British Army and the Problem of Venereal Disease in France and Egypt During the First World War', *Medical History*, XXXIX (1995), pp. 133–58.

153 Joseph, 'Economic Significance'.

154 Eli Marcovitz and Henry J. Meyers, 'The Marijuana Addict in the Army', *War Medicine*, VI (1944), pp. 382–91.

155 Akyeampong, 'Diaspora', p. 434.

156 Kaplan, 'Marijuana'.

157 Ibid.; Roger A. Roffman and Ely Sapol, 'Marijuana in Vietnam: A Survey of Use among Army Enlisted Men in the Two Southern Corps', *International Journal of Addiction*, V (1970), pp. 1–42.

158 Robert H. Scales, *Certain Victory: The US Army in the Gulf War* (Washington, DC, 1994), p. 6.

159 Lamont Lindstrom, ed., *Drugs in Western Pacific Societies* (Lanham, MD, 1987), pp. 38, 219.

160 FoxNews.com, '"Synthetic" Marijuana Use Becoming Problem for U.S. Military', online at www.foxnews.com (accessed 24 July 2013).

161 Alcinda Honwana, *Child Soldiers in Africa* (Philadelphia, PA, 2006), pp. 59, 66, 95.

162 Patrick Peretti-Watel, François Beck and Stéphane Legleye, 'Beyond the U-Curve: The Relationship between Sport and Alcohol, Cigarette and Cannabis Use in Adolescents', *Addiction*, XCVII (2002), pp. 707–16.

163 Dave Meggysey, *Out of Their League* (Berkeley, CA, 1970).

164 Deron Snyder, 'Rehab Only Concern for Mathieu', *Albuquerque* [NM] *Journal* (21 August 2012), p. D6; Zodiac News Service, 'Three-quarters of the National Football League Would Be in Jail if the Marijuana Laws were Enforced', *Ann Arbor* [NM] *Sun* (27 October–9 November 1972), p. 17.

165 Mills, *Cannabis Britannica*, pp. 165–6.

166 Rubin and Comitas, *Ganja in Jamaica*; Mills, *Cannabis Nation*; Hamid, *Ganja Complex*; Timothy White, *Catch a Fire: The Life of Bob Marley* (New York, 1983).

167 U.S. Drug Enforcement Administration, 'A Tradition of Excellence: A History of the DEA', online at www.justice.gov (accessed 5 July 2013).

168 'Green Grows the Grass', *Tucson* [AZ] *Daily Citizen* (9 June 1972), pp. 1–2;

'Police Find Marijuana Farm', *The Daily Review* (Hayward, CA) (9 June 1972), pp. 1–2.

169 Cervantes, *Marijuana Horticulture*, p. 11; Michael Pollan, *The Botany of Desire: A Plant's Eye View of the World* (New York, 2001), pp. 131–2.

170 United Nations Office on Drugs and Crime (UNODC), *World Drug Report 2013* (Vienna and New York, 2013).

171 U.S. Customs and Border Patrol, 'U.S. Border Patrol Fiscal Year 2011 Profile', online at www.cbp.gov (accessed 12 September 2012); US Drug Enforcement Administration, *B. C. Bud: Growth of the Canadian Marijuana Trade* (Washington, DC, 2000); Barry Brown, 'Canadian Pot Holds Dubious Distinction', *Washington Times* (31 August 1998), p. A11.

172 Mikuriya, 'Kif Cultivation'; UNODC, *Report 2013*.

173 UNODC, *Report 2013*; UNODC, *Afghanistan: Survey of Commercial Cannabis Cultivation and Production 2012* (Kabul and Vienna, 2013).

174 Anonymous, 'The Maynard W. Quimby Medicinal Plant Garden', online at www.pharmacy.olemiss.edu (accessed 12 September 2012); U.S. Drug Enforcement Administration, 'Manufacturer of Controlled Substances; Notice of Registration; National Center for Natural Products Reseach-NIDA Project (Doc. 2012-5441)', *Federal Register*, 77 FR 13633 (2012), pp. 13633–4.

175 U.S. Food and Drug Administration, 'National Center for Natural Products Research, University of Mississippi; Single Source Cooperative Agreement; Catalog of Federal Domestic Assistance Number 93-103; Request for Application (Doc. E6-14109)', *Federal Register*, 71 FR 50434 (2006), pp. 50434–5; U.S. Food and Drug Administration, 'Cooperative Agreement with the University of Mississippi's National Center for Natural Products Research (U01) to Develop and Disseminate Botanical Natural Product Research with an Emphasis on Public Safety (Doc. 2011-8521)', *Federal Register*, 76 FR 19996 (2011), pp. 19996–7.

176 Jeffrey A. Miron, 'The Budgetary Implications of Drug Prohibition', Report of the Harvard University Department of Economics and the Criminal Justice Policy Foundation (Cambridge, MA, 2010).

5 Things to Make With and For *Cannabis*

1 James Lane Allen, *The Reign of Law: A Tale of the Kentucky Hemp Fields* (New York, 1900), p. 11.

2 Ibid., p. 12; A. Masclef, *Atlas des plantes de France utiles, nuisibles et ornamentales* (Paris, 1891), p. 244.

3 Robert C. Clarke, 'Traditional Fibre Hemp (Cannabis) Production, Processing, Yarn Making, and Weaving Strategies: Functional Constraints and Regional Responses. Part 1', *Journal of Industrial Hemp*, VII (2010), pp. 118–53.

4 William Mavor, ed., *Five Hundred Points of Good Husbandry . . ., by Thomas Tusser, Gentleman* [1580], new edn (London, 1812), p. 153.

5 Olivier de Serres, *Le théâtre d'agriculture et mesnage des champs* (Paris, 1617), pp. 665–6.

6   A. J. Pieters, 'Agricultural Seeds: Where Grown and How Handled', in
    Yearbook of the United States Department of Agriculture, 1901, ed. G. W. Hill
    (Washington, DC, 1902), pp. 233–56, quotation p. 250.

7   B. B. Robinson, 'Hemp', *USDA Farmers' Bulletin*, no. 1935 (Washington, DC,
    1943), p. 15.

8   Mavor, *Five Hundred*, p. 110; de Serres, *Théâtre*, p. 667; James Durno, 'A
    Statement of the Mode of Cultivating Flax and Hemp, in Russia, Prussia,
    and Poland', in *Retrospect of Philosophical, Mechanical, Chemical, and Agricultural
    Discoveries* (London, 1809), vol. IV, pp. 344–6; G. Schaefer, 'The Cultivation
    and Preparation of Flax; Hemp', *CIBA Review*, XLIX (1945), pp. 1773–95.

9   Alicja Zemanek, Bogdan Zemanek, Krystyna Harmata, Jacek Madeja and
    Piotr Klepacki, 'Selected Foreign Plants in Old Polish Botanical
    Literature, Customs and Art', in *Plants and Culture: Seeds of the Cultural Heritage
    of Europe*, ed. J.-P. Mortel and A. M. Mercuri, (Bari, Italy, 2009), pp. 179–93.

10 Bruno Ryves, John Barwick and George Wharton, *Mercurius Rusticus: Or, the
    Countries Complaint of the Barbarous Outrages Committed by the Secretaries* (London,
    1685), p. 40.

11 Clarke, 'Traditional Fibre Hemp Part 1'; Robert C. Clarke, 'Traditional
    Fibre Hemp (Cannabis) Production, Processing, Yarn Making, and
    Weaving Strategies – Functional Constraints and Regional Responses.
    Part 2', *Journal of Industrial Hemp*, VII (2010), pp. 229–50.

12 Joseph Wright, ed., *The English Dialect Dictionary. A–C* (London, 1898),
    vol. I, p. 374.

13 James Orchard Halliwell, *A Dictionary of Archaic and Provincial Words: J–Z*,
    3rd edn (London, 1847), vol. II, p. 645.

14 Robert H. Mair, *Debrett's Peerage, Baronetage, Knightage, and Companionage*
    (London, 1882), p. 276.

15 Joannes Amos Comenius, Theodore Simon and Stephanus Curcellaeus,
    Janua Linguarum Reserata (Amsterdam, 1665), p. 129; César-Pierre Richelet,
    Dictionnaire François (Geneva, 1680), p. 95.

16 De Serres, *Théâtre*, p. 666; Académie Française, *Le Dictionnaire de l'Académie
    Françoise. M–Z* (Paris, 1694), vol. II, p. 167; Girolamo Baruffaldi, *Il Canapajo*
    (Bologna, Italy, 1741), p. 43; M. Marcandier, *Traité du chanvre* (Paris, 1758),
    pp. 70–71.

17 Clarke, 'Traditional Fibre Hemp Part 1'.

18 Marcandier, *Traité*, p. 82; Robert Wissett, *On the Cultivation and Preparation of
    Hemp* (London, 1804), see p. 213 ff.; Ziedonis Ligers, *Ethnographie Lettone*
    (Basel, Switzerland, 1954), p. 352; Peter von Schmidt, 'No. 18. Report on
    the Cultivation of Hemp', in *Message of the President of the United States to the
    Two Houses of Congress at the Commencement of the First Session of the Twenty-eighth
    Congress*, Office of President J. Tyler (Washington, DC, 1843), pp. 600–69,
    see pp. 625–7.

19 Dieter Kuhn, *Science and Civilization in China: Chemistry and Chemical Technology:
    Textile Technology: Spinning and Reeling* (Cambridge, 1988), vol. V, pt 9, p. 246;
    H. W. Dickinson, 'A Condensed History of Rope-making', *Transactions of
    the Newcomen Society*, XXIII (1948 [1942–3]), pp. 71–92.

20 Henry Wadsworth Longfellow, *The Poetical Works of Henry Wadsworth Longfellow* (London, 1877), p. 324.

21 Dickinson, 'Condensed History'.

22 Peter Sharp, *Flax, Tow, and Jute Spinning: A Handbook*, 4th edn (Dundee, 1907), p. 28.

23 Albert Hazen Wright, *Wisconsin's Hemp Industry* (Madison, WI, 1918).

24 Robinson, 'Hemp'.

25 'New Billion-Dollar Crop', *Popular Mechanics*, LXIX (1938), pp. 238–9, 144A.

26 Marcandier, *Traité*, p. iv.

27 Michael L. Ryder, 'Parchment – Its History, Manufacture and Composition', *Journal of the Society of Archivists*, II (1960), pp. 391–9.

28 The Thomas Jefferson Foundation, 'Declaration of Independence Paper', online at www.monticello.org (accessed 31 July 2013).

29 Patrick Leech, '"Who Says Manchester Says Cotton": Textile Terminology in the Oxford English Dictionary (1000–1960)', *inTRAlinea*, II (1999), online at www.intralinea.org.

30 George S. Cole, *A Complete Dictionary of Dry Goods* (Chicago, IL, 1892), pp. 310–11.

31 Joseph Needham, *Science and Civilization in China: Civil Engineering and Nautics* (Cambridge, 1971), vol. IV, pt 3, pp. 161, 185, 191, 664.

32 Charles Tomlinson, *Cyclopaedia of Useful Arts, Mechanical and Chemical, Manufactures, Mining, and Engineering* (London, 1852), vol. I, p. 405; Eusebius Renaudot, *Ancient Accounts of India and China by Two Mohammedan Travellers* (London, 1733), p. 89, and notes pp. 9, 10, 75.

33 Société de Naturalistes, *Flore Économique des plantes qui croissent aux environs de Paris* (Paris, 1796), p. 119.

34 Renaudot, *Ancient Accounts*, p. 48.

35 Mary Philadelphia Merrifield, *Original Treatises, Dating from the XIIth to XVIIIth Centuries, on the Arts of Painting* (London, 1849), vol. I, pp. 3–4, 312–15; Charles Lock Eastlake, *Materials for a History of Oil Painting* (London, 1847), pp. 130, 133, 279, 305, 325, 343–4.

36 William Rhind, *A History of the Vegetable Kingdom* (London, 1841), p. 145.

37 Rudolf Benedikt and Julius Lewkowitsch, *Chemical Analysis of Oils, Fats, Waxes and of the Commercial Products Derived Therefrom*, 2nd edn (London, 1895), p. 280; Francesca Bray, *Science and Civilization in China: Agriculture* (Cambridge, 1984), vol. VI, pt 2, p. 519; John Mowbray Trotter, *Western Turkestán* (Calcutta, 1882), p. 521; Jacques Savary des Bruslons and Philemon Louis Savary, *Dictionnaire Universel de Commerce* (Paris, 1723), vol. II, p. 716; George M. Beringer, 'Sapo Mollis and Linimentum Saponis Mollis', *American Druggist and Pharmaceutical Record*, XLIV (1904), pp. 200–201.

38 Trotter, *Western Turkestán*, pp. 59–60.

39 D. Prain, *Report on the Cultivation and Use of Gánjá* (Calcutta, 1893), p. 1.

40 Robert C. Clarke and Mark David Merlin, *Cannabis: Evolution and Ethnobotany* (Berkeley, CA, 2013), p. 205.

41 Zemanek et al., 'Selected Foreign Plants'.

42 R.E.F. Smith and David Christian, *Bread and Salt: A Social and Economic History of Food and Drink in Russia* (Cambridge, 1984), p. 5.

43 Ligers, *Ethnographie*, pp. 359–60.

44 P. W. Bomli, *La femme dans l'espagne du siècle d'or* (The Hague, 1950), p. 148; J. C. Hervieux de Chanteloup, *Nouveau traité des serins de canarie* (Paris, 1709), pp. 69–70; M. Barruel, 'Considérations hygiéniques sur le lait vendu à Paris comme substance alimentaire', *Annales d'hygiène publique et de médecine légale*, I (1829), pp. 404–19.

45 'Pinch-Hitters for Defense', *Popular Mechanics*, LXXVI (1941), pp. 1–3, 201–9.

46 Bray, *Agriculture*, p. 475.

47 R. J. Bouquet, 'Cannabis', UNODC *Bulletin on Narcotics*, IV (1950), pp. 14–30; Henry Yule and A. C. Burnell, *Hobson-Jobson: A Glossary of Colloquial Anglo-Indian Words and Phrases* (London, 1903).

48 Hakim Bey and Abel Zug, eds, *Orgies of the Hemp Eaters: Cuisine, Slang, Literature and Ritual of Cannabis Culture* (Brooklyn, NY, 2004).

49 Franz Rosenthal, *The Herb: Hashish Versus Medieval Muslim Society* (Leiden, The Netherlands, 1971), pp. 56 ff.; 'The Surprising Extinction of the Charas Traffic', *Bulletin on Narcotics*, V (1953), pp. 1–7; R. N. Chopra and G. S. Chopra, 'Present Position of Hemp Drug Addiction in India', *British Journal of Inebriety*, XXXVIII (1940), pp. 71–4; Christian Rätsch, *Marijuana Medicine: A World Tour of the Healing and Visionary Powers of Cannabis* (Rochester, VT, 2001), p. 51.

50 Michael Starks, *Marijuana Chemistry*, 2nd edn (Berkeley, CA, 1990), p. 109.

51 Vera Rubin and Lambros Comitas, *Ganja in Jamaica: The Effects of Marijuana Use* (New York, 1975); Kenneth Bilby, 'The Holy Herb: Notes on the Background of Cannabis in Jamaica', *Caribbean Quarterly*, monograph (1985), pp. 82–95.

52 Arno Hazekamp, *Cannabis; Extracting the Medicine*, PhD dissertation, Universiteit Leiden (Leiden, The Netherlands, 2007).

53 'The Growth of Inebriety among Women', *The Sunday Appeal* (Memphis, Tennessee) (22 August 1869), p. 1.

54 Phineas Taylor Barnum, *The Humbugs of the World* (New York, 1866), pp. 177–8.

55 John Edward Philips, 'African Smoking and Pipes', *Journal of African History*, XXIV (1983), pp. 303–19, quotation pp. 314–15.

56 Berthold Laufer, 'The Introduction of Tobacco into Africa', in *Tobacco and Its Use in Africa. Anthropology Leaflet 29*, ed. B. Laufer, W. D. Hambly and R. Linton (Chicago, IL, 1930), pp. 2–15.

57 Philips, 'African Smoking'; Brian M. du Toit, *Cannabis in Africa* (Rotterdam, 1980); C.J.G. Bourhill, *The Smoking of Dagga (Indian Hemp) among the Native Races of South Africa and the Resultant Evils*, PhD dissertation, University of Edinburgh (Edinburgh, 1913).

58 William V. Erickson, Paul K. Jarvie and Fred L. Miller, *Water Pipe or Bong*, U.S. Patent No. 827,691 (Washington, DC, 1980).

59 Philips, 'African Smoking'; Edward J. Keall, 'One Man's Mead is Another Man's Persian: One Man's Coconut is Another Man's Grenade', *Muqarnas*,

x (1993), pp. 275–85; Henry Balfour, 'Earth Smoking-pipes from South Africa and Central Asia', *Man*, xxii (1922), pp. 65–9; Alfred Dunhill, *The Pipe Book* [1924] (New York, 1969).

60 Jeremy Green, 'Southeast Asian Ceramic Smoking Pipes', *International Journal of Nautical Archaeology*, xv (1986), pp. 167–9.

61 Keall, 'One Man's Mead'; Edward J. Keall, 'Smokers' Pipes and the Fine Pottery Tradition of Hays', *Proceedings of the Seminar for Arabian Studies*, xxii (1992), pp. 29–46.

62 Keall, 'One Man's Mead'.

63 Yule and Burnell, *Hobson-Jobson*, p. 428.

64 Joseph Westermeyer, 'Sex Differences in Drug and Alcohol Use among Ethnic Groups in Laos, 1965–1975', *American Journal of Drug and Alcohol Abuse*, xiv (1988), pp. 443–61.

65 'Biggest Seizure of "Pot" Is Made', *Lebanon* [PA] *Daily News* (5 January 1973), pp. 1, 13.

66 Juliet P. Lee and Sean Kirkpatrick, 'Social Meanings of Marijuana Use for Southeast Asian Youth', *Journal of Ethnicity and Substance Abuse*, iv (2005), pp. 135–52.

67 Erickson et al., *Water Pipe*.

68 Richard Edward Dennett, *Notes on the Folklore of the Fjort (French Congo)* (London, 1898), p. 154.

69 Johann Büttikofer, *Reisebilder aus Liberia* (Leiden, 1890), vol. ii, p. 277.

70 Alfredo Carvalho, 'Diario da viagem do Capitão João Blaer aos Palmares em 1645', *Revista do Instituto Arqueológico, Histórico e Geográfico Pernambucano*, x (1902), pp. 87–96, see p. 93.

71 Bilby, 'Holy Herb'; Du Toit, *Cannabis*; Mário Ypiranga Monteiro, 'Folclore da Maconha', *Revista Brasileira de Folclore*, vi (1966), pp. 285–300; Lopes Goncalves, *O Amazonas: Esboço histórico, chorographico e estatístico até o anno de 1903* (New York, 1904), p. 30.

72 Du Toit, *Cannabis*; Bourhill, *Smoking*; Jarbas Pernambuco, 'A Maconha em Pernambuco', in *Novos Estudos Afro-Brasileiros*, ed. A. Ramos (Rio de Janeiro, Brazil, 1937), vol. ii, pp. 185–91.

73 Nicolás del Castillo Mathieu, 'Bantuismos en el Español de Colombia', in *América negra: Expedicion humana a la zaga de la América oculta*, ed. A. Martán Bonilla, E. Felicité-Maurice and S. Friedemann (Bogotá, Colombia, 1995), pp. 73–94, see p. 79; Edward A. Alpers, '"Moçambiques" in Brazil: Another Dimension of the African Diaspora in the Atlantic World', in *Africa and the Americas: Interconnections During the Slave Trade*, ed. J. C. Curto and R. Soulodre-LaFrance (New York, 2005), pp. 43–69, see p. 52.

74 David Clement Scott, *A Cyclopaedic Dictionary of the Mang'anja Language Spoken in British Central Africa* (Edinburgh, 1892), p. 206.

75 Eric Axelson, *Portuguese in South-east Africa 1488–1600* (Johannesburg, 1973).

76 P.E.H. Hair, 'Portuguese Contacts with the Bantu Languages of the Transkei, Natal and Southern Mozambique 1497–1650', *African Studies*, xxxix (1980), pp. 3–46, quotation p. 14.

77 Thurstan Shaw, 'Early Smoking Pipes: In Africa, Europe, and America', *The Journal of the Royal Anthropological Institute of Great Britain and Ireland*, XC (1960), pp. 272–305, quotation p. 281.

78 Domingos Pereira Bracamonte, *Banquete que Apolo Hizo a los embaxadores del rey de Portugal Don Ivan Quarto* (Lisbon, 1642), p. 112.

79 Joam Curvo Semmedo, *Polyanthea Medicinal* (Lisbon, 1697), pp. 166, 205; Joam Vigier, *Thesouro apollineo, galenico, chimico, chirurgico, pharmaceutico, ou compendio de remedios* (Lisbon, 1714), p. 480; Francisco da Fonseca Henriquez, *Medicina lusitana, e soccorro delphico a os clamores da natureza humana, para total profligação de seus males* (Amsterdam, 1710), pp. 346, 416, 439, 457; Abraham Alewin and Joannes Cole, *Vocabulario das duas lenguas, Portugueza e Flamenga* (Amsterdam, 1718), p. 179.

80 Abdolali Mohagheghzadeh, Pouya Faridi, Mohammadreza Shams-Ardakani and Younes Ghasemi, 'Medicinal Smokes', *Journal of Ethnopharmacology*, CVIII (2006), pp. 161–84; Marcello Pennacchio, Lara Jefferson and Kayri Havens, *Uses and Abuses of Plant-Derived Smoke: Its Ethnobotany as Hallucinogen, Perfume, Incense, and Medicine* (New York, 2010).

81 Frédéric Mistral, *Lou Tresor dóu felibrige, ou Dictionnaire Provençal–Français* (Aix-en-Provence, France, 1878), vol. I, p. 409; Pedro de Mugica, *Dialectos Castellanos: Montañés, Vizcaíno, Aragonés* (Berlin, 1892), vol. I, p. 59; Alcée Fortier, 'The Acadians of Louisiana and Their Dialect', *Proceedings of the Modern Language Association*, VI (1891), pp. 64–94, see p. 87.

82 Richard F. Burton, *Two Trips to Gorilla Land and the Cataracts of the Congo* (London, 1876), vol. II, p. 30; J. B. Douville, *Voyage au Congo et dans l'interieur de l'Afrique Equinoxiale, fait dans les années 1828, 1829, et 1830* (Paris, 1832), vol. I, p. 167; Dennett, *Notes*, p. 154; Padres Missionarios, *Diccionario Portuguez-Olunyaneka* (Huilla, Angola, 1896), p. 28; W. Holman Bentley, *Appendix to the Dictionary and Grammar of the Kongo Language* [1887] (London, 1895), p. 160; Les Missionaires, *Dictionnaire Pongoué–Français* (Paris, 1881), p. 191; Luis da Câmara Cascudo, *Made in Africa (Pesquisas e Notas)* (Rio de Janeiro, Brazil, 1965), pp. 179–80.

83 Philips, 'African Smoking'; Shaw, 'Early Smoking Pipes'.

84 Oxford English Dictionary, 'Pipe, N. 1', in *Oxford English Dictionary Online Version* (Oxford, 2006).

85 Shaw, 'Early Smoking Pipes', pp. 279–80.

86 Mark Davies, 'Corpus del Español: 100 Million Words, 1200s–1900s', online at www.corpusdelespanol.org (accessed 19 December 2012).

87 Daniel Granada, *Vocabulario Rioplatense razonada* (Montevideo, 1890), p. 306.

88 Rafael Padilla, *España Actual* (Madrid, 1908), p. 8.

89 Mario Martínez Ruiz and Gabriel Rubio Valladolid, *Manual de drogodependencias para enfermería* (Madrid, 2002), p. 160.

90 William E. Carter, *Cannabis in Costa Rica: A Study of Chronic Marijuana Use* (Philadelphia, PA, 1980), p. 214.

91 Yule and Burnell, *Hobson-Jobson*, p. 195.

92 Roger Joseph, 'The Economic Significance of *Cannabis sativa* in the Moroccan Rif', *Economic Botany*, XXVII (1973), pp. 235–40.

93 Jerome S. Handler, 'Aspects of the Atlantic Slave Trade: Smoking Pipes, Tobacco, and the Middle Passage', *African Diaspora Archaeology Network Newsletter* (June 2008), online at www.diaspora.illinois.edu.

94 Syndicat d'Initiatives de Villaines-la-Juhel et ses Environs, *Un brin de causette . . . le chanvre* (Villaines-la-Juhel, France, 1981), not paginated.

95 David T. Courtwright, *Forces of Habit: Drugs and the Making of the Modern World* (Cambridge, MA, 2001), p. 106.

96 Thomas Hawkes Tanner, *The Practice of Medicine*, 6th American edn (Philadelphia, PA, 1874), p. 475.

97 Jeanette M. Tetrault, Kristina Crothers, Brent A. Moore, Reena Mehra, John Concato and David A. Fiellin, 'Effects of Marijuana Smoking on Pulmonary Function and Respiratory Complications: A Systematic Review', *Archives of Internal Medicine*, CLXVII (2007), pp. 221–8.

98 '[Short Announcements]', *New Zealand Times* (20 November 1895), p. 3.

99 Louis von Cotzhausen, 'Gleanings from the German Journals', *American Journal of Pharmacy*, LII (1880), pp. 469–73, quotation p. 471.

100 Edward P. Krenzelok, 'Aspects of *Datura* Poisoning and Treatment', *Clinical Toxicology*, XLVIII (2010), pp. 104–10.

101 E. Lebaigue, 'Cigarettes Indiennes au Cannabis indica', *Répertoire de pharmacie*, IX (1881), pp. 162–3.

102 Eduard Hahn and J. Holfert, *Spezialitäten und Geheimmittel: Ihre Herkunft und Zusammensetzung* (Berlin, 1906), p. 41.

103 Léopold Baron de Neuman and Adolphe de Plason, eds, *Recueil des traités et conventions conclus par l'Autriche* (Vienna, 1891), vol. XIX, p. 543.

104 Ministère de l'industrie et du travail (Belgium), *Recueil officiel des marques de fabrique et de commerce déposées en Belgique* (Brussels, 1886), vol. III, pp. 98–9.

105 John Lawrence Jiggens, *Marijuana Australiana*, PhD dissertation, Queensland University of Technology (Brisbane, 2004), p. 28.

106 'A Hardship on the Afflicted [Paid Article]', *The Star* (Lyttleton, NZ) (17 September 1898), p. 7.

107 U.S. Senate, *Compilation of Reports of Committee on Foreign Relations, United States Senate, 1789–1901* (Washington, DC, 1901), vol. V, p. 386; C. S. Fairchild, 'Proprietary and Medicinal Preparations: Duty On', in *Synopsis of Decisions of the Treasury Department on the Construction of the Tariff, Navigation, and Other Laws*, ed. U.S. Department of the Treasury (Washington, DC, 1886), pp. 126–9.

108 '[Price Lists]', *The Pharmaceutical Era*, XXV (1901), pp. 1–131, see pp. 11, 60.

109 Rowan Robinson, *The Great Book of Hemp* (Rochester, VT, 1996), p. 47.

110 Tod H. Mikuriya, 'Marijuana in Medicine: Past, Present, and Future', *California Medicine*, CX (1969), pp. 34–40.

111 Anonymous, 'Bromidia', in *Annual Reprint of the Reports of the Council on Pharmacy and Chemistry*, ed. American Medical Association (Chicago, IL, 1915), pp. 15–20; Anonymous, 'Neurosine, Germiletum, Dioviburnia, and Palpebrine', in ibid., pp. 86–95.

112 G. Cresswell Burns, 'Neurosine Poisoning', *Journal of the American Medical Association*, XCVI (1931), pp. 1225–6.

113 James H. Mills, *Cannabis Nation: Control and Consumption in Britain, 1928–2008* (Oxford, 2012), p. 12.

114 Fitz Hugh Ludlow, *The Hasheesh Eater: Being Passages from the Life of a Pythagorean* (New York, 1857), p. 34.

115 Marcus Clarke, 'Cannabis Indica (a Psychological Experiment)', in *The Marcus Clarke Memorial Volume*, ed. H. MacKinnon (Melbourne, VIC, 1884), pp. 194–209.

116 'An Ordinance Relating to Dangerous Drugs', *Northern Territory Times* (Darwin, NT) (27 July 1928), p. 6; Editors, 'Hemp and Opium Poppy Noxious Weeds', *Sunday Mail* (Brisbane, QLD) (28 August 1938), p. 4.

117 James H. Mills, *Cannabis Britannica: Empire, Trade, and Prohibition, 1800–1928* (Oxford, 2003); Indian Hemp Drugs Commission, *Report of the Indian Hemp Drugs Commission, 1893–1894* [1894], reprint edn (Silver Spring, MD, 1969).

118 Robert C. Clarke, *Hashish!*, 2nd edn (Los Angeles, 2010), pp. 72, 75.

119 United Nations Office on Drugs and Crime, *Afghanistan Survey of Commercial Cannabis Cultivation and Production 2012* (Kabul and Vienna, 2013), p. 16.

120 'The Surprising Extinction'; Yongming Zhou, *Anti-drug Crusades in Twentieth Century China: Nationalism, History, and State-Building* (Boston, MA, 1999).

121 'The Surprising Extinction'.

122 Henry M. Grey, *In Moorish Captivity* (London, 1899), p. 241; Bouquet, 'Cannabis'.

123 Isaac Campos, *Home Grown: Marijuana and the Origins of Mexico's War on Drugs* (Chapel Hill, NC, 2012), p. 80; Antonio Castilho, ed., *Exposition universelle d'Anvers. Exposition coloniale du Portugal. Catalogue officiel* (Antwerp, Belgium, 1885), pp. 109, 117, 171.

124 Henry Morton Stanley, *The Congo and the Founding of Its Free State: A Story of Work and Exploration* (New York, 1885), vol. II, p. 354.

125 Mónica Ferreirinha, *Breve história do BNU*, online edn (Lisbon, 2009), p. 36.

126 United Nations Office on Drugs and Crime, *World Drug Report 2013* (Vienna and New York, 2013).

127 InfoGroup, 'Pot and Business Newsletter', online at http://lp.infogroup.com (accessed 11 September 2012).

128 SIC code 512227 on InfoGroup, 'ReferenceUSA [Online Database]', online at www.referenceUSA.com (accessed 11 September 2012).

129 InfoGroup, 'Referenceusa [Online Database]'.

130 Jeffrey A. Miron, *The Budgetary Implications of Drug Prohibition*, online edn (Cambridge, 2010); Melinda Beck and Stephen Gayle, 'Homegrown Grass', *Newsweek* (30 October 1978), p. 35; CNBC.com, 'How Big Is the Marijuana Market?', online at www.cnbc.com (accessed 12 September 2012).

131 Jon Gettman, 'Marijuana Production in the United States (2006)', *The Bulletin of Cannabis Reform*, 11 (2006), online at www.drugscience.org.

132 CNBC.com, 'How Big'; Rachel Emma Silverman and Rachel Dodes, 'High Expectations: Marketers Hope for Buzz on 4/20', *Wall Street Journal* (20 April 2012), p. A1.

133 Stephan Piotrowski and Michael Carus, 'Natural Fibres in Technical Applications: Market and Trends', in *Industrial Applications of Natural Fibres:*

Structure, Properties and Technical Applications, ed. J. Müssig (Chichester, 2010), pp. 73–88; Food and Agriculture Organization of the United Nations (FAO), 'FAOstat Database', online at http://faostat.fao.org (accessed 12 July 2013).

134 Piotrowski and Carus, 'Natural Fibres'; Agriculture and Agri-food Canada, 'Canadian Hemp: Nature's Wonder Fibre' [press release], online edition (Ottawa, n.d. [2011]).

135 USDA Economic Research Service, *Industrial Hemp in the United States: Status and Market Potential* (Washington, DC, 2000); Renée Johnson, *Hemp as an Agricultural Commodity* (Washington, DC, 2013), p. 8.

136 Associated Press, 'Drunken Driver Who Hit a Car, Gets 122 Days', *Albuquerque [NM] Journal* (19 January 1930), p. 1.

137 National Park Service, 'Battling Marijuana Farms in America's National Parks' [press release], online edn (Washington, DC, 2008); Lisa Morehouse, 'The Environmental Cost of Growing Pot' [radio news programme], *Weekend Edition Sunday*, National Public Radio [Washington, DC] (27 June 2010).

138 Mountain West Research, *What Businesses Make Sense for Humboldt County?* (Phoenix, AZ, 1989); Peter Hecht, 'California's Emerald Triangle Pot Market is Hitting Bottom', *Sacramento [CA] Bee* (5 May 2012), online at www.sacbee.com.

139 Tom Blickman, Jorge Atilo Silva Iulianelli, Luiz Paulo Guanabara and Paulo Cesar Pontes Fraga, *A Pointless War: Drugs and Violence in Brazil*, Drugs and Conflict Debate Papers No. 11 (Amsterdam, 2004), p. 4.

140 Martin Booth, *Cannabis: A History* (New York, 2005), pp. 304, 308.

141 J. Pronczuk de Garbino, 'Epidemiology of Paraquat Poisoning', in *Paraquat Poisoning: Mechanisms, Prevention, Treatment*, ed. C. Bismuth and A. H. Hall (New York, 1995), pp. 37–51; J. Routt Reigart and James R. Roberts, *Recognition and Management of Pesticide Poisonings*, 5th edn (Washington, DC, 1999), p. 109.

142 Julian Bloomer, 'Using a Political Ecology Framework to Examine Extra-Legal Livelihood Strategies: A Lesotho-Based Case Study of Cultivation of and Trade in Cannabis', *Journal of Political Ecology*, XVI (2008), pp. 49–69; Craig Paterson, *Prohibition and Resistance: A Socio-political Exploration of the Changing Dynamics of the Southern African Cannabis Trade, c. 1850–the Present*, Master's thesis, Rhodes University (Johannesburg, South Africa, 2009); Thembela Kepe, 'Cannabis Sativa and Rural Livelihoods in South Africa: Politics of Cultivation, Trade and Value in Pondoland', *Development Southern Africa*, XX (2003), pp. 605–15.

143 'Manoel Francisco Pedroso . . .', *Jornal do commercio* (21 February 1847), p. 3.

144 Clarke, *Hashish!*, p. xiv.

145 United Nations Office on Drugs and Crime, *World Drug Report 2013* (Vienna and New York, 2013); Ikramul Haq, 'Pak-Afghan Drug Trade in Historical Perspective', *Asian Survey*, XXXVI (1996), pp. 945–63.

146 Clarke, *Hashish!*; Jorge Cervantes, *Marijuana Horticulture: The Indoor/Outdoor Medical Grower's Bible* (Sacramento, CA, 2006).

147 Clarke, *Hashish!*; Michael Starks, *Marijuana Chemistry*, 2nd edn (Berkeley, CA, 1990).

6 Symbolism Starring *Cannabis*

1 Lesley Head and Jennifer Atchison, 'Cultural Ecology: Emerging Human–plant Geographies', *Progress in Human Geography*, XXXIII (2009), pp. 236–45; Chris S. Duvall, 'On the Origin of the Tree *Spondias mombin* in Africa', *Journal of Historical Geography*, XXXII (2006), pp. 249–66; Chris S. Duvall, 'Symbols, Not Data: Rare Trees and Vegetation History in Mali', *Geographical Journal*, CLXIX (2003), pp. 295–312.

2 Matthew Hall, *Plants as Persons: A Philosophical Botany* (Albany, NY, 2011); Michael Pollan, *The Botany of Desire: A Plant's Eye View of the World* (New York, 2001).

3 Joseph Needham and Lu Gwei-Djen, *Science and Civilization in China: Spagyrical Discovery and Invention: Magesteries of Gold and Immortality* (Cambridge, 1974), vol. V, pt 2, p. 152; Patricia Bjaaland Welch, *Chinese Art: A Guide to Motifs and Visual Imagery* (North Clarenden, VT, 2008), p. 205.

4 Léon Gozlan, *Aventures merveilleuses et touchantes du Prince Chènevis et de sa jeune soeur* (Paris, 1846), p. 9.

5 Robert James Devine, *The Moloch of Marijuana* (Findlay, OH, 1943).

6 Harry Shapiro, *Waiting for the Man: The Story of Drugs and Popular Music* (London, 1999), p. 26.

7 Franz Rosenthal, *The Herb: Hashish Versus Medieval Muslim Society* (Leiden, The Netherlands, 1971).

8 James Orchard Halliwell, *A Dictionary of Archaic and Provincial Words*, 3rd edn (London, 1855), vol. II, p. 573.

9 John Taylor, *The Praise of Hemp-seed* (London, 1620), pp. 19, 14, 15.

10 Charles Pigott, *A Political Dictionary: Explaining the True Meaning of Words* [1795] (London, n.d.), p. 56.

11 Claudius Galen, *De Alimentorum Facultatibus, Libri Tres* (Lyon, 1547), p. 84.

12 Edward Saïd, *Orientalism: Western Conceptions of the Orient* (London, 1978); Nicolás Wey Gómez, *The Tropics of Empire: Why Columbus Sailed South to the Indies* (Cambridge, MA, 2008); Lucy Jarosz, 'Constructing the Dark Continent: Metaphor as Geographic Representation of Africa', *Geografiska Annaler: Series B, Human Geography*, LXXIV (1992), pp. 105–15; David Arnold, *The Tropics and the Traveling Gaze* (Seattle, WA, 2006); Derek Gregory, 'Between the Book and the Lamp: Imaginative Geographies of Egypt', *Transactions of the Institute of British Geographers*, XX (1995), pp. 29–57; J. Pouchepadass, ed., *Colonisations et environnement* (Paris, 1993).

13 James H. Mills, *Cannabis Britannica: Empire, Trade, and Prohibition, 1800–1928* (Oxford, 2003).

14 W. Derham, ed., *Philosophical Experiments and Observations of the Late Eminent Dr Robert Hooke* (London, 1726), p. 210.

15 Constantine Samuel Rafinesque, *The World, or Instability: A Poem* (Philadelphia, PA, and London, 1836), pp. 107–8.

16 Ernest L. Abel, *Marihuana: The First Twelve Thousand Years* (New York, 1980), pp. 113–14.

17 Denis Lebey-de Batilly, *L'orígine des anciens Assassins-Porte-Couteaux* ([Paris?], 1603); Antoine Isaac Silvestre de Sacy, 'Mémoire sur le dynastie des Assassins et sur l'origine de leur nom', *Le Moniteur universel*, XLI (1809), pp. 828–30.

18 Raghib Sarhan, 'Hashish and Assassins', *Al-Kulliyah*, XVII (1972), pp. 1–21, as cited in Kevin M. McCarthy, 'The Origin of Assassin', *American Speech*, XLVIII (1973), pp. 77–83.

19 Isaac Campos, *Home Grown: Marijuana and the Origins of Mexico's War on Drugs* (Chapel Hill, NC, 2012), pp. 11–13; McCarthy, 'The Origin'; Farhad Daftary, 'The "Order of the Assassins:" J. Von Hammer and the Orientalist Misrepresentations of the Nizari Ismailis', *Iranian Studies*, XXXIX (2006), pp. 71–81; Don Casto, III, 'Marijuana and the Assassins, an Etymological Investigation', *British Journal of Addiction*, LXV (1970), pp. 219–25; Dominique Colas, *Civil Society and Fanaticism: Conjoined Histories* (Stanford, CA, 1997), p. 92 ff.

20 Casto, 'Marijuana and the Assassins', p. 224.

21 Rosenthal, *The Herb*, p. 91.

22 Ibid., p. 91.

23 De Sacy, 'Mémoire'.

24 H. J. Anslinger and Courtney Ryley Cooper, 'Marijuana, Assassin of Youth', *American Magazine*, CXXIV/1 (July 1937).

25 Sarhan, 'Hashish and Assassins', as cited in McCarthy, 'The Origin', p. 1.

26 Richard F. Burton, *The Book of the Thousand Nights and a Night* (London, 1886), vol. III, p. 93.

27 Richard F. Burton, *Scinde; or, the Unhappy Valley* (London, 1851), vol. II, pp. 234–5.

28 William Winwood Reade, *The African Sketch-book* (London, 1873), vol. II, pp. 343–4.

29 'Character of the Mexican Proper and Improper', *The Sun* (New York) (17 May 1914), p. 7.

30 Victor Hehn, *Kulturpflanzen und Haustiere in Ihrem Übergang aus Asien nach Griechenland und Italien sowie in das Übrige Europa* (Berlin, 1870), p. 157.

31 Graham Huggan and Helen Tiffin, *Postcolonial Ecocriticism: Literature, Animals, Environment* (London, 2010).

32 D. C. Rankin, 'Atrocities in the Kongo Free State', *The Independent*, LII (1900), pp. 304–6, quotation p. 305.

33 John G. Bourke, 'The American Congo', *Scribner's Magazine*, XV (1894), pp. 590–610, quotations pp. 594–5, 606.

34 Ibid., p. 594.

35 David W. Pate, 'Possible Role of Ultraviolet Radiation in Evolution of *Cannabis* Chemotypes', *Economic Botany*, XXXVII (1983), pp. 396–405, quotation p. 397.

36 Ernest Small and Arthur Cronquist, 'A Practical and Natural Taxonomy for *Cannabis*', *Taxon*, XXV (1976), pp. 405–35, quotation p. 416.

37 Reade, *African Sketch-Book*, p. 343.

38 Campos, *Home Grown*; Abel, *Marihuana*; Larry Sloman, *Reefer Madness: The History of Marijuana in America* (Indianapolis, IN, 1979).

39 James C. Munch, 'Marihuana and Crime', *UNODC Bulletin on Narcotics*, XVIII (1950), pp. 15–22.

40 Júlio César Adiala, *O Problema da maconha no Brasil: Ensaio sobre racismo e drogas* (Rio de Janeiro, Brazil, 1986).

41 Martin A. Lee, *Smoke Signals: A Social History of Marijuana – Medical, Recreational, and Scientific* (New York, 2012), pp. 13–14.

42 Oskar Lenz, *Timbuktu. Reise durch Marokko, die Sahara und den Sudan* (Leipzig, 1892), vol. I, p. 207.

43 Dick Hobson, 'A Hunting Trip to Mozambique in 1868', *Geographical Journal*, CLXIX (1983), pp. 202–10, quotation p. 208.

44 Henry Morton Stanley, *Through the Dark Continent* (London, 1878), vol. I, p. 68.

45 Henry Morton Stanley, *The Congo and the Founding of Its Free State: A Story of Work and Exploration* (New York, 1885), vol. II, p. 345.

46 D. J. Harvey, 'Stability of Cannabinoids in Dried Samples of Cannabis Dating from around 1896–1905', *Journal of Ethnopharmacology*, XXVIII (1990), pp. 117–28, see p. 120.

47 M. H. Fisquet, *Histoire de l'Algérie* (Paris, 1842), p. 300; John Reynell Morell, *Algeria: The Topography and History, Political, Social, and Natural, of French Africa* (London, 1854), quotation p. 108.

48 M. Larue du Barry, 'Note sur l'usage du chanvre en Algérie', *Journal de chimie médicale, de pharmacie et de toxicologie* (January 1845), pp. 31–4, quotation p. 31.

49 Morell, *Algeria*, pp. 108–9.

50 Marcus Clarke, 'Cannabis Indica (a Psychological Experiment)', in *The Marcus Clarke Memorial Volume*, ed. H. MacKinnon, ed. (Melbourne, VIC, 1884), pp. 194–209, quotation p. 196.

51 Morell, *Algeria*, p. 108.

52 Christelle Taraud, 'Urbanisme, hygiénisme et prostitution à Casablanca dans les années 1920', *French Colonial History*, VII (2006), pp. 97–108; Christelle Taraud, 'Jouer avec le marginalité: Le cas des filles soumises "indigenes" du Quartier Reserve de Casablanca dans les années 1920–1950', *CLIO. Histoire, femmes et societes [online]*, XVII (2003), DOI: 10.4000/clio.582; André-Paul Comor, 'Les plaisirs des Legionnaires au temps des colonies: L'alcool et les femmes', *Guerres mondiales et conflits contemporains*, II (2006), pp. 33–42.

53 Carol Sherman, Andrew Smith and Erik Tanner, *Highlights: An Illustrated History of Cannabis* (Berkeley, CA, 2002).

54 Campos, *Home Grown*; Mills, *Cannabis Britannica*; James H. Mills, *Madness, Cannabis, and Colonialism: The Native-only Lunatic Asylums of British India, 1857–1900* (New York, 2000); David T. Courtwright, *Forces of Habit: Drugs and the Making of the Modern World* (Cambridge, MA, 2001).

55 'War on Marihuana Smoking', *The Sun* (New York) (26 May 1907), p. 1.

56 The Trove online database, National Library of Australia: http://trove.nla.gov.au/newspaper (accessed 25 July 2013).

57 Mills, *Cannabis Britannica*; Mills, *Madness, Cannabis*.

58 C.J.G. Bourhill, *The Smoking of Dagga (Indian Hemp) among the Native Races of South Africa and the Resultant Evils*, PhD dissertation, University of Edinburgh (Edinburgh, 1913); José Rodrígues da Costa Doria, 'Os fumadores de maconha: Effeitos males do vicio', in *Proceedings of the Second Pan American Scientific Congress*, ed. G. L. Swiggett (Washington, DC, 1917), vol. VIII, pt I, pp. 151–61; Serviço Naçional de Educação Sanitária, ed., *Maconha: Coletânea de trabalhos Brasileiros*, 2nd edn (Rio de Janeiro, Brazil, 1958).

59 J. F. Siler, W. L. Sheep, G. W. Cook, W. A. Smith, L. B. Bates and G. F. Clark, 'Mariajuana Smoking in Panama', *Military Surgeon*, LXXIII (1933), pp. 269–80, quotation p. 279.

60 Lawrence Kolb, 'Marihuana', *Federal Probation*, II (1938), pp. 22–5, quotations pp. 22, 23.

61 R. J. Wilkinson, *A Malay–English Dictionary* (Hong Kong, 1901); Anonymous, 'Running Amuck', in *A Dictionary of Psychological Medicine*, ed. D. H. Tuke (London, 1892), vol. II, pp. 1097–8.

62 De Sacy, 'Mémoire', p. 830.

63 'Mania of the Malay', *Daily Yellowstone Journal* (Miles City, MT) (31 January 1885), p. 3.

64 Campos, *Home Grown*, p. 7 ff.

65 J. D. Reichard, 'The Marihuana Problem', *Journal of the American Medical Association*, CXXV (1944), pp. 594–5.

66 Rebecca Kuepper, Jim van Os, Roselind Lieb, Hans-Ulrich Wittchen, Michael Höfler and Cécile Henquet, 'Continued Cannabis Use and Risk of Incidence and Persistence of Psychotic Symptoms: 10 Year Follow-up Cohort Study', *British Medical Journal*, CCCXLII (2011), p. d738; David M. Semple, Andrew M. McIntosh and Stephen M. Lawrie, 'Cannabis as a Risk Factor for Psychosis: A Review', *Journal of Psychopharmacology*, XIX (2005), pp. 187–94; Haroon Rashid Chaudry, Howard B. Moss and Tahir Suliman, 'Cannabis Psychosis Following Bhang Ingestion', *Addiction*, LXXXVI (1991), pp. 1075–81; Wayne Hall and Louisa Degenhardt, 'Prevalence and Correlates of Cannabis Use in Developed and Developing Countries', *Current Opinion in Psychiatry*, XX (2007), pp. 393–7.

67 Jim van Os, M. Bak, M. Hanssen, R. V. Bijl, R. de Graaf and H. Verdoux, 'Cannabis Use and Psychosis: A Longitudinal Population-based Study', *American Journal of Epidemiology*, CLVI (2002), pp. 319–27.

68 J. Moreau, *Du hachisch et de l'aliénation mentale* (Paris, 1845).

69 K. C. Quek and J. S. Cheah, 'Poisoning Due to Ingestion of the Seeds of Kechubong (*Datura fastuosa*) for Its Ganja-like Effect in Singapore', *Journal of Tropical Medicine and Hygiene*, LXXVII (1974), pp. 111–12.

70 Wilkinson, *Malay–English Dictionary*, p. 506.

71 'Marihuana May Be Grown Here; Terrible Drug Hits Kansas and Is Much Worse Than Heroin', *Santa Fe New Mexican* (3 November 1925), p. 6.

72 Mia Touw, 'The Religious and Medicinal Uses of *Cannabis* in China, India and Tibet', *Journal of Psychoactive Drugs*, XIII (1981); D. Prain, *Report on the Cultivation and Use of Gánjá* (Calcutta, India, 1893), p. 1.

73 E. Lebaigue, 'Cigarettes Indiennes au Cannabis Indica', *Répertoire de pharmacie*, IX (1881), pp. 162–3; Eduard Hahn and J. Holfert, *Spezialitäten und Geheimmittel: Ihre Herkunft und Zusammensetzung* (Berlin, 1906), p. 41.

74 John Fryer, *A New Account of East India and Persia. Being Nine Years' Travels, 1672–1681* (London, 1698), p. 32.

75 Quek and Cheah, 'Poisoning'; A. Djibo and S. Brah Bouzou, 'Intoxication Aiguë au "Sobi-Lobi" (Datura)', *Bulletin de la société de pathologie exotique*, XCIII (2000), pp. 294–7; D. Diker, D. Markovitz, M. Rothman and U. Sendovski, 'Coma as a Presenting Sign of Datura Stramonium Seed Tea Poisoning', *European Journal of Internal Medicine*, XVIII (2007), pp. 336–8.

76 Asma Bouziri, Asma Hamdi, Aida Borgi, Sarra Bel Hadj, Zohra Fitouri, Khaled Menif and Ben Jaballah Nejla, '*Datura stramonium* L. Poisoning in a Geophagous Child: A Case Report', *International Journal of Emergency Medicine*, IV (2011), online at www.intjem.com, accessed 1 August 2013; Edward P. Krenzelok, 'Aspects of *Datura* Poisoning and Treatment', *Clinical Toxicology*, XLV (2010), pp. 104–10.

77 Anonymous, '[Review of] Voyage au Congo, et dans l'Interieur de l'Afrique Equinoxiale . . . by J. B. Douville . . . Paris, 1832', *Nautical Journal*, I (1832), pp. 194–203, quotation p. 202.

78 J. B. Douville, *Voyage au Congo et dans l'interieur de l'Afrique Equinoxiale, fait dans les années 1828, 1829, et 1830* (Paris, 1832), vol. I; Chantal Edel, ed., *Un Voyage au Congo, 1827–1828: Les tribulations d'un aventurier en Afrique équinoxiale* (Paris, 1991).

79 Burton, *Scinde*, pp. 122–3.

80 Ibid., pp. 123, 125, 150.

81 Gilberto Freyre, *Nordeste: Aspectos da influencia da canna sobre a vida e a paizagem do nordeste do Brasil* (Rio de Janeiro, Brazil, 1937), p. 15; Victor Frond, *Brazil pittoresco* (Rio de Janeiro, Brazil, 1859), vol. III, p. 42; Anonymous, 'Relação de uma Viagem a Serra dos Orgãos', *Revista trimensal de história e geographia*, III (1841), pp. 76–95, see p. 86.

82 S.-J. Honnorat, *Dictionnaire Provençal–Français, ou dictionnaire de la langue d'Oc: P–Z* (Digne, France, 1847), vol. II, pt 3, p. 889.

83 Manuel Alvarez Nazario, *El Habla campesina del País: Orígenes y desarrollo del Español en Puerto Rico* (Río Piedras, Puerto Rico, 1990), p. 357.

84 Estéban Pichardo, *Diccionario provincial Casi-Razonado de voces Cubanas*, 3rd edn (Havana, 1862), p. 38, 244.

85 Don Eduardo de Echegaray, *Diccionario general etimológico de le lengua Española* (Madrid, 1898), p. 26.

86 Stefano Fenoaltea, 'Slavery and Supervision in Comparative Perspective: A Model', *Journal of Economic History*, XLIV (1984), pp. 635–68.

87 Rhea L. Dornbush and Alfred M. Freedman, eds, *Chronic Cannabis Use: A Special Issue of the Annals of the New York Academy of Sciences* (1976), vol. CCLXXXII, pp. 1–430; Norman Q. Brill, Evelyn Crumpton, Ira M. Frank, Joel S. Hochman, Peter Lomax, William H. McGlothlin and Louis Jolyon West, 'The Marijuana Problem', *Annals of Internal Medicine*, LXXIII (1970), pp. 449–65.

88 A. S. Reece, 'Chronic Toxicology of Cannabis', *Clinical Toxicology (Philadelphia)*, XLVII (2009), pp. 517–24; Harold Kalant, 'Adverse Effects of Cannabis on Health: An Update of the Literature since 1996', *Progress in Neuro-Psychpharmacology and Biological Psychiatry*, XXVIII (2004), pp. 849–63.

89 Office of National Drug Control Policy, *The Economic Costs of Drug Abuse, 1992–2002* (Washington, DC, 2004).

90 Lambros Comitas, 'Cannabis and Work in Jamaica: A Refutation of the Amotivational Syndrome', *Annals of the New York Academy of Science*, CCLXXXII (1976), pp. 24–32; Melanie Creagan Dreher, *Working Men and Ganja: Marihuana Use in Rural Jamaica* (Philadelphia, PA, 1982).

91 Leslie L. Iversen, *The Science of Marijuana* (New York, 2000), pp. 92–7.

92 Doria, 'Os fumadores', p. 151; Carl Friedrich Philippe von Martius, *Systema Materiae Medicae Vegetabilis Brasilieisis* (Vienna, 1843) p. 121.

93 Campos, *Home Grown*; Mills, *Cannabis Nation*; 'The New Customs Law. Legal Quays and Bonded Warehouses. Importation of Ganje, and C.', *Daily Chronicle* (Georgetown, Guyana) (10 March 1885), p. 3; C. W. Brebner, *New Handbook for the Indian Ocean, Arabian Sea and Bay of Bengal* (Mumbai, 1898), p. 22; Indian Immigrants (Wragg) Commission, 'Report 1980', in *Documents of Indentured Labour, Natal 1851–1917*, ed. Y. S. Meer (Durban, South Africa, 1887), pp. 246–633, see pp. 256–7; Joachim John Monteiro, *Angola and the River Congo* (London, 1875), vol. II, p. 257; Michael R. Aldrich, *A Brief Legal History of Marihuana* [1973] (Phoenix, AZ, 1974), not paginated [pp. 15–16]; Richard J. Bonnie and Charles H. Whitebread, *The Marihuana Conviction: A History of Marihuana Prohibition in the United States* (Charlottesville, VA, 1974), p. 43.

94 Bourhill, '*The Smoking*', p. 57; Siler et al., 'Mariajuana', p. 273.

95 Siler et al., 'Mariajuana'; 'Military Police Start War against Mariahuana Users', *Evening Herald* (Albuquerque, NM) (6 September 1917), p. 3.

96 Samuel Chew, 'Profit of a Hemp Crop', *Silk Culturist and Farmer's Manual*, I (1836), pp. 76–7, quotation p. 76.

97 James F. Hopkins, *A History of the Hemp Industry in Kentucky* (Lexington, KY, 1951), p. 4.

98 James Lane Allen, *The Reign of Law: A Tale of the Kentucky Hemp Fields* (New York, 1900).

99 L. H. Dewey, 'Hemp', in *Yearbook of the United States Department of Agriculture, 1913* (Washington, DC, 1914), pp. 283–346, quotation p. 293.

100 'Kentucky Hemp Returns', *New York Times* (14 March 1926), p. 5.

101 Samuel Hartlib, *A Treatise Concerning the Husbandry and Natural History of England* [1742], 2nd edn (London, n.d.), p. 40.

102 Edmund Quincy, *A Treatise of Hemp-Husbandry* (Boston, MA, 1765), p. 5.

103 Edward Antil, 'Observations on the Raising and Dressing of Hemp', *Transactions of the American Philosophical Society*, I (1769–71), pp. 198–204, quotation p. 198.

104 William Cobbett, 'India Hemp', *Cobbett's Political Register*, XIII (1808), pp. 175.

105 Antil, 'Observations', p. 198.

106 Hugh Jones, *The Present State of Virginia* [1724] (New York, 1895), p. 122.

107 Henry Mayhew and John Binny, *The Criminal Prisons of London and Scenes of Prison Life* [1862] (New York, 1968), p. 313.

108 Hopkins, *History*, p. 137.

109 Sterling Evans, *Bound in Twine: The History and Ecology of the Henequen–Wheat Complex for Mexico and the American and Canadian Plains, 1880–1950* (College Station, TX, 2007).

110 Evans, *Bound*; 'New Billion-Dollar Crop', *Popular Mechanics*, LXIX (1938), pp. 238–9, p. 144A.

111 Hopkins, *History*, p. 213.

112 Renée Johnson, *Hemp as an Agricultural Commodity*, online edition (Washington, DC, 2013).

113 William A. Emboden, 'The Genus *Cannabis* and the Correct Use of Taxonomic Categories', *Journal of Psychoactive Drugs*, XIII (1981), pp. 15–21.

114 Hemp Industries Association, online at www.thehia.org (accessed 4 July 2013).

115 Anslinger and Cooper, 'Assassin of Youth'.

116 Gabriel G. Nahas, *Marihuana: Deceptive Weed* (New York, 1973).

117 Andrew Golub and Bruce D. Johnson, 'The Misuse of the "Gateway Theory" in U.S. Policy on Drug Abuse Control: A Secondary Analysis of the Muddled Deduction', *International Journal of Drug Policy*, XIII (2002), pp. 5–19; Ralph E. Tarter, Michael Vanyukov, Levent Kirisci, Maureen Reynolds and Duncan B. Clark, 'Predictors of Marijuana Use in Adolescents before and after Licit Drug Use: Examination of the Gateway Hypothesis', *American Journal of Psychiatry*, CLXIII (2006), pp. 2134–40.

118 U.S. Drug Enforcement Administration, 'A Tradition of Excellence: A History of the DEA', online at www.justice.gov (accessed 5 July 2013).

119 Ashley Fantz, 'The Mexico Drug War: Bodies for Billions', CNN.com, online at http://edition.cnn.com (accessed 24 July 2012).

120 Jamie Dettmer, 'Is the War on Drugs Over?', macleans.ca, online at www.macleans.ca (accessed 24 July 2012).

121 'War on Marihuana Smoking'.

122 'Military Police Start War'.

123 Devine, *Moloch*.

124 U.S. Drug Enforcement Administration, 'Tradition'.

125 Paul Armentano, 'Marijuana Arrests Driving America's So-called "Drug War", Latest FBI Data Shows', NORML.org, online at http://blog.norml.org (accessed 18 September 2012).

126 Adiala, *Problema*.

127 Jamie Fellner, 'Race, Drugs, and Law Enforcement in the United States', *Stanford Law and Policy Review*, XX (2009), pp. 257–92; Substance Abuse and Mental Health Services Administration (SAMHSA), *Results from the 2010 National Survey on Drug Use and Health: Summary of National Findings*, online edn (Rockville, MD, 2011).

128 Ira Glasser, 'American Drug Laws: The New Jim Crow', *Albany Law Review*, LXIII (1999), pp. 703–15.

129 Jamie Fellner, *Decades of Disparity: Drug Arrests and Race in the United States*, online edition (New York, 2009), p. 1.

130 Anthony Henman, 'War on Drugs is War on People', *The Ecologist*, X (1980), pp. 282–9; Tom Blickman, Jorge Atilo Silva Iulianelli, Luiz Paulo Guanabara and Paulo Cesar Pontes Fraga, *A Pointless War: Drugs and Violence in Brazil*, Drugs and Conflict Debate Papers, no. 11 (Amsterdam, 2004).

131 Henman, 'War on Drugs'; Erika Macedo Moreira, *A Criminalização dos Trabalhadores Rurais no Polígono da Maconha*, PhD dissertation, Universidade Federal Fluminense (Rio de Janeiro, Brazil, 2007); Kent Mathewson, 'Drugs, Moral Geographies, and Indigenous Peoples: Some Initial Mappings and Central Issues', in *Dangerous Harvests: Drug Plants and Indigenous Peoples*, ed. M. K. Steinberg, J. J. Hobbs and K. Mathewson (New York, 2004), pp. 11–23; Edward E. Telles, *Race in Another America: The Significance of Skin Color in Brazil* (Princeton, NJ, 2004), pp. 166–9.

132 Jorge Cervantes, *Marijuana Outdoors: Guerrilla Growing* (Sacramento, CA, 2000).

133 Lee, *Smoke Signals*; John McCabe, *Marijuana and Hemp: History, Uses, Laws, and Controversy* (Santa Monica, CA, 2010).

134 Juan Carlos Ramírez-Pimienta, 'Del Corrido de narcotráfico al narcocorrido: Orígenes y desarrollo del canto a los traficantes', *Studies in Latin American Popular Culture*, XXIII (2004), pp. 21–41; Mark Cameron Edberg, *El Narcotraficante: Narcocorridos and the Construction of a Cultural Persona on the U.S.-Mexican Border* (Austin, TX, 2004).

135 N.W.A., 'Gangsta, Gangsta', on *Straight Outta Compton* (Los Angeles, 1988).

136 Jonathan Mark Kenoyer, *Ancient Cities of the Indus Valley Civilization*, 2nd edn (Karachi, Pakistan, 2010), p. 182.

137 Thomas Bowrey, *A Geographical Account of Countries Round the Bay of Bengal, 1669 to 1679* [1701] (Cambridge, 1905), p. 80.

138 Rosenthal, *The Herb*.

139 Theodore M. Godlaski, 'Shiva, Lord of Bhang', *Substance Use and Misuse*, XLVII (2012), pp. 1067–72; Ajai Mansingh and Laxmi Mansingh, 'Hindu Influences on Rastafarianism', *Caribbean Quarterly*, monograph (1985), pp. 96–115.

140 Touw, 'Religious and Medicinal', pp. 23–34; Christian Rätsch, *Marijuana Medicine: A World Tour of the Healing and Visionary Powers of Cannabis* (Rochester, VT, 2001), Michael R. Aldrich, 'Tantric Cannabis Use in India', *Journal of Psychoactive Drugs*, IX (1977), pp. 227–33.

141 Henman, 'War on Drugs'.

142 John M. Janzen, 'De l'ancienneté de l'usage des psychotropes en Afrique Centrale', *Psychotropes*, I (1983), pp. 105–7.

143 Kenneth Bilby, 'The Holy Herb: Notes on the Background of Cannabis in Jamaica', *Caribbean Quarterly*, monograph (1985), pp. 82–95.

144 Lee, *Smoke Signals*, p. 13; Georges Balandier, *Le Vie Quotidienne au Royaume de Kongo du XVIe au XVIIIe siècle* (Monaco, 1965), p. 155; Martin Booth, *Cannabis: A History* (New York, 2005), p. 157.

145 Tim Boekhout van Solinge, 'Ganja in Jamaica', *Amsterdams Drug Tijdschrift*, 11 (December 1996), pp. 11–14; Ajai Mansingh and Laxmi Mansingh, 'Hindu

Influences on Rastafarianism', *Caribbean Quarterly*, monograph (1985), pp. 96–115; Ansley Hamid, *The Ganja Complex: Rastafari and Marijuana* (Lanham, MD, 2002).

146 Moreau, *Du hachisch*, pp. 4–5.

147 Charles Baudelaire, *Les Paradis artificiels: Opium et haschisch* (Paris, 1860).

148 Peter Blecha, *Taboo Tunes: A History of Banned Bands and Censored Songs* (San Francisco, CA, 2004); Christopher M. Lawrence, 'Miserable Banditti: The Pot-Head Outlaws of Rural Greece', *Dialectical Anthropology*, XXXV (2011), pp. 33–47; Gail Holst-Warhaft, 'Resisting Translation: Slang and Subversion in the Rebetika', *Journal of Modern Greek Studies*, VIII (1990), pp. 183–96.

149 Milton Mezzrow and Bernard Wolfe, *Really the Blues* (New York, 1946), p. 213 ff.; Meyer Berger, 'Tea for a Viper', *New Yorker* (12 March 1938), pp. 36–48.

150 Holst-Warhaft, 'Resisting Translation', p. 190.

151 William S. Burroughs, *Naked Lunch* [1959] (New York, 2009), pp. 221, 224; Jack Kerouac, *The Dharma Bums* (New York, 1958), pp. 127, 159.

152 Allen Ginsberg, 'The Great Marijuana Hoax', *The Atlantic Monthly*, CCXVIII (1966), pp. 104–12, quotation p. 104.

153 Timothy Leary, 'The Politics, Ethics, and Meaning of Marijuana', in *The Marijuana Papers*, ed. D. Solomon (New York, 1966), pp. 82–90.

154 Timothy Leary, 'The Dealer is the New Robin Hood', *International Times* (London), I (1970), p. 20.

155 Joseph G. Weis, 'Styles of Middle-class Adolescent Drug Use', *The Pacific Sociological Review*, XVII (1974), pp. 251–85.

156 George Andrews and Simon Vinkenoog, eds, *The Book of Grass: An Anthology on Indian Hemp* (New York, 1967).

157 Ginsberg, 'Marijuana Hoax', p. 106.

158 Leary, 'The Dealer', p. 20.

159 Trent Cunningham, *Psychedelic Orientalism: Representation of India and the Music of the Beatles*, Master's thesis, University of Pittsburgh (Pittsburgh, PA, 2011); Robert C. Fuller, 'Drugs and the Baby Boomers' Quest for Metaphysical Illumination', *Nova Religio: The Journal of Alternative and Emergent Religions*, III (1999), pp. 100–18.

160 'Bust Measurements', *The Marijuana Review*, I/II (1969), pp. 20–21.

161 Lee, *Smoke Signals*.

162 Richard Glen Boire, *Marijuana Law*, 2nd edn (Berkeley, CA, 1996).

163 Devine, *Moloch*; Anslinger and Cooper, 'Assassin of Youth'; Kolb, 'Marihuana'.

164 Henri de Monfreid, *La Crosière du hachich* (Paris, 1933).

165 Leary, 'The Dealer'.

166 Hot97.com, '50 Cent Never Smoked a Day of His Life and Light Drinker', online at www.worldstarhiphop.com (accessed 11 September 2012).

167 Regina Austin, '"The Black Community", Its Lawbreakers, and a Politics of Identification', *Southern California Law Review*, LXV (1991–2), pp. 1769–1817; Jenna Bowley, *Robin Hood or Villain: The Social Constructions of*

Pablo Escobar, undergraduate honours thesis, University of Maine (Farmington, 2013).

168 'Gingrich on Drug Dealers', *New York Times* (15 July 1995), p. A9.

169 Tim Malyon and Anthony Henman, 'No Marihuana: Plenty of Hemp', *New Scientist*, LXXXVIII (1980), pp. 433–5.

170 McCabe, *Marijuana and Hemp*.

171 Christopher S. Wren, 'Bird Food is a Casualty of the War on Drugs', *New York Times* (3 October 1999), p. 20.

172 David P. West, *Final Status Report, Hawai'i Industrial Hemp Research Project* (Honolulu, HI, 2003).

173 B. Fletcher, *Hemp Industries Association v. DEA*, Decisions No. 03-71366, No. 03-71603, Ninth Circuit United States Court of Appeals (San Francisco, CA, 2004).

174 Lee, *Smoke Signals*; Richard Knox, 'Medicinal Marijuana: A Patient-Driven Phenomenon', National Public Radio, online at www.npr.org (accessed 14 September 2012).

175 California Department of Public Health, 'Proposition 215: Text of Proposed Law', online at www.cdph.ca.gov (accessed 14 September 2012).

176 M. Wolfe, 'Pot for Parents', *New York Times* (8 September 2012), p. A21.

177 Ray Martinez, *The Truth About Marijuana: America's Snake Oil* (Dartford, CT, 2012); Letters to the Editor, 'This is Your Dad on Pot: Not so Groovy', *New York Times* (11 September 2012), p. A22; U.S. Drug Enforcement Administration, 'The DEA Position on Marijuana', online at www.justice.gov (accessed 11 September 2012).

7 How Do You Know *Cannabis*?

1 J. M. Blaut, 'Some Principles of Ethnogeography', in *Philosophy in Geography*, ed. S. Gale and G. Olsson (Dordrecht, The Netherlands, 1979), pp. 1–7; Chris S. Duvall, 'Ferricrete, Forests, and Temporal Scale in the Production of Colonial Science in Africa', in *Knowing Nature: Conversations between Political Ecology and Science Studies*, ed. M. J. Goldman, P. Nadasdy and M. D. Turner (Chicago, IL, 2011), pp. 113–27; Sheila Jasanoff, 'Ordering Knowledge, Ordering Society', in *States of Knowledge: The Co-production of Science and Social Order*, ed. S. Jasanoff (London, 2004), pp. 13–45.

2 James M. Blaut, 'Geographic Models of Imperialism', *Antipode*, II (1970), pp. 65–85.

3 Erich Goode, 'Marijuana and the Politics of Reality', *Journal of Health and Social Behavior*, X (1969), pp. 83–94; John F. Decker, 'The Official Report of the National Commission Studying Marihuana: More Misunderstanding', *University of San Francisco Law Review*, VIII (1973–4), pp. 1–28.

4 John McCabe, *Marijuana and Hemp: History, Uses, Laws, and Controversy* (Santa Monica, CA, 2010), p. 2.

5 Leslie L. Iversen, *The Science of Marijuana* (New York, 2000), p. ix.

6 U.S. Food and Drug Administration, *Inter-agency Advisory Regarding Claims that Smoked Marijuana is a Medicine*, online edn (Washington, DC, 2006).

7 Gervase Markham and William Lawson, *A Way to Get Wealth: Containing Six Principal Vocations, or Callings, in Which Every Good Husband or House-wife May Lawfully Imploy Themselves* (London, 1676); John McCabe, *Hemp: What the World Needs Now* (Santa Monica, CA, 2010).

8 Murray Galt Motter and Martin I. Wilbert, 'III. Comments on Official Articles. Cannabis Indica', in *Digest of Comments on the Pharmacopoeia of the United States of America and on the National Formulary*, ed. M. G. Motter and M. I. Wilbert (Washington, DC, 1912), pp. 369–71.

9 John Barrow, *An Account of Travels into the Interior of Southern Africa in the Years 1797 and 1798* (London, 1801), p. 408.

10 Antonio de Saldanha da Gama, *Memoria Sobre as Colonias de Portugal: Situadas na Costa Occidental d'Afrique* (Paris, 1839), p. 73.

11 William Roxburgh, 'Communication on the Culture, Properties, and Comparative Strength of Hemp, and Other Vegetable Fibres, the Growth of the East Indies', *Transactions of the Society Instituted at London, for the Encouragement of Arts, Manufactures, and Commerce*, XXII (1804), pp. 363–96.

12 'New Billion-Dollar Crop', *Popular Mechanics*, LXIX (1938), pp. 238–9, 144A; C. G. Lloyd, 'Inquiries Answered. (691) Cannabis Indica', *American Gardening*, XV (1894), pp. 309–11.

13 J. D. Reichard, 'The Marihuana Problem', *Journal of the American Medical Association*, CXXV (1944), pp. 594–5.

14 Isidore Dukerley, 'Note sur les différences que présente avec le chanvre ordinaire et la variété de cette espèce connue en Algérie sous les noms de *kif* et de *tekrouri*', *Bulletin de la Société Botanique de France*, III (1866), pp. 401–6, quotation pp. 402–3.

15 Indian Hemp Drugs Commission, *Report of the Indian Hemp Drugs Commission, 1893–1894* [1894], reprint edn (Silver Spring, MD, 1969).

16 B. H. Vogelzang, C. Scutaru, S. Mache, K. Vitzthum, B. Kusma, K. Mutawakel, D. A. Groneberg and D. Quarcoo, 'Cannabis Publication Analysis Using Density-equalising Mapping and Research Output Benchmarking', *South African Journal of Psychiatry*, XVI (2010), pp. 131–7.

17 David Vlahov, Sandro Galea, Heidi Resnick, Jennifer Ahern, Joseph A. Boscarino, Michael Bucuvalas, Joel Gold and Dean Kilpatrick, 'Increased Use of Cigarettes, Alcohol, and Marijuana among Manhattan, New York Residents after the September 11th Terrorist Attacks', *American Journal of Epidemiology*, CLV (2002), pp. 988–96.

18 Weston La Barre, 'Anthropological Views of Cannabis', *Reviews in Anthropology*, IV (1977), pp. 237–50, quotation p. 237; Harry William Hutchinson, 'Patterns of Marihuana Use in Brazil', in *Cannabis and Culture*, ed. V. Rubin (The Hague, The Netherlands, 1975), pp. 173–83, quotation p. 176; David T. Courtwright, 'Review of *The Cult of Pharmacology*, Richard Degrandpre (2006)', *Addiction*, CII (2007), p. 107.

19 John M. McPartland and Karl W. Hillig, 'Early Iconography of *Cannabis sativa* and *Cannabis indica*', *Journal of Industrial Hemp*, XIII (2008), pp. 189–203.

20 Larry Sloman, *Reefer Madness: The History of Marijuana in America* (Indianapolis, IN, 1979), p. 52 ff.; Robert James Devine, *The Moloch of*

Maríjuana (Findlay, OH, 1943); James C. Munch, 'Marihuana and Crime', *UNODC Bulletin on Narcotics*, XVIII (1950), pp. 15–22; 'Dangerous Drug Plant', *The Advocate* (Burnie, TAS) (26 April 1938), p. 2.

21 Gabriel G. Nahas, Kenneth M. Sutin, David J. Harvey and Stig Agurell, eds, *Maríhuana and Medicine* (Totowa, NJ, 1999); Ray Martinez, *The Truth About Maríjuana: America's Snake Oil* (Dartford, CT, 2012); U.S. Food and Drug Administration, *Inter-agency Advisory Regarding Claims that Smoked Marijuana is a Medicine*, online edn (Washington, DC, 2006).

22 Dale Gieringer, Ed Rosenthal and Gregory T. Carter, *Maríjuana Medical Handbook* (Oakland, CA, 2008).

23 Rowan Robinson, *The Great Book of Hemp* (Rochester, VT, 1996), pp. 135, 229, 235.

24 The Tribal Messenger, 'Pot and Presidents', *Green Egg*, VIII/71 (1975), p. 20; 'Pot and Presidents', *The Weekly Tribal Messenger* (Albuquerque, NM), III/11 (1972), p. 11.

25 Ron Young, *Make the Most of the India Hemp Seed and Sow it Everywhere* (San Francisco, CA, n.d. [1973]). (Poster held in the Yanker Collection, U.S. Library of Congress Prints and Photographs Division.)

26 Barack Obama, *Dreams from My Father: A Story of Race and Inheritance* (New York, 1995), p. 93; Gwen Ifill, 'Clinton Admits Experiment with Marijuana in 1960s', *New York Times* (30 March 1992), p. A15; David D. Kirkpatrick, 'In Secretly Taped Conversations, Glimpses of the Future President', *New York Times* (20 February 2005), pp. 1, 26.

27 J. Russell Reynolds, 'Therapeutical Uses and Toxic Effects of Cannabis Indica', *The Lancet*, I (1890), pp. 637–8.

28 Virginia Berridge, 'Queen Victoria's Cannabis Use: Or, How History Does and Does Not Get Used in Drug Policy Making', *Addiction Research and Theory*, XI (2003), pp. 213–15.

29 Jack Herer, *The Emperor Wears No Clothes*, 11th edn (Van Nuys, CA, 1998), p. 89.

30 John Rebman, *Dictionary of the Kiniassa Language* (St Chrischona, Switzerland, 1877), p. 134; C.J.G. Bourhill, *The Smoking of Dagga (Indian Hemp) among the Native Races of South Africa and the Resultant Evils*, PhD dissertation, University of Edinburgh (Edinburgh, 1913), pp. 16–18.

31 Meyer Berger, 'Tea for a Viper', *New Yorker* (12 March 1938), pp. 36–48.

32 S. T. Oner, *Cannabis sativa: The Essential Guide to the World's Finest Maríjuana Strains* (San Francisco, CA, 2012), p. xi.

33 Jorge Cervantes, *Maríjuana Horticulture* (Sacramento, CA, 2006), p. xxiii.

34 George Abraham Grierson, 'The Hemp Plant in Sanskrit and Hindi Literature', *The Indian Antiquary*, XXIII (1894), pp. 260–62; Dominik Wujastyk, 'Cannabis in Traditional Indian Herbal Medicine', in *Ayurveda at the Crossroads of Care and Cure*, ed. A. Salema (Lisbon, 2002), pp. 45–73; Franz Rosenthal, *The Herb: Hashish Versus Medieval Muslim Society* (Leiden, The Netherlands, 1971); Indalecio Lozano Cámara, 'Terminología Científica Árabe del Cáñamo', in *Ciencias naturaleza en al-Andalus*, ed. C. Álvarez de Morales (Granada, Spain, 1996), pp. 147–64.

35 Dale H. Gieringer, 'The Forgotten Origins of Cannabis Prohibition in California', *Contemporary Drug Problems*, XXVI (1999), pp. 237–88.

36 Vincent Joseph Monteleone, *Criminal Slang: The Vernacular of the Underworld Lingo* (Boston, MA, 1949).

37 Renato Tomei, *Forbidden Fruits: The Secret Names of Plants in Caribbean Culture* (Rome, 2008).

38 I. Willis Russell and Mary Gray Porter, 'Among the New Words', *American Speech*, LVII (1982), pp. 270–76.

39 Rachel Emma Silverman and Rachel Dodes, 'High Expectations: Marketers Hope for Buzz on 4/20', *Wall Street Journal* (20 April 2012), p. A1; Maria Alicia Gaura, 'Stoner Chic Traces Origin to San Rafael', *San Francisco Chronicle* (20 April 2000), p. A6.

40 U.S. Food and Drug Administration, *Inter-agency Advisory*.

41 Editors, '30 Firemen Gassed in Narcotic Blaze', *The Sun* (New York) (18 February 1919), p. 14.

42 David P. West, *Final Status Report, Hawai'i Industrial Hemp Research Project* (Honolulu, HI, 2003); John F. Decker, 'The Official Report'.

43 Stanley Einstein, 'Proofiness Infopinion Truthiness: "Drug Treatment," "Alcohol Treatment"', *Substance Use and Misuse*, XLVII (2012), pp. 343–6.

44 Emily Heil, 'Hemp Flag to Fly High over Capitol Building', *Washington Post* (2 July 2013), online at www.washingtonpost.com (accessed 29 July 2013).

45 George Henry Preble, *History of the Flag of the United States of America* (Albany, NY, 1872), p. 192 ff.; Marc Leepson, *Flag: An American Biography* (New York, 2005), pp. 71, 125.

46 Tench Coxe, *A View of the United States of America* (Philadelphia, PA, 1794), p. 274; George Schley, 'Southern Planters! Encourage Your Own Manufactures!! [Advertisement]', *The Mississippi Planter and Mechanic*, I (1857), p. [251]; Victor Selden Clark, *History of Manufactures in the United States, 1607–1860* (Washington, DC, 1916), p. 110.

47 Jan E. G. van Dam and Harriëtte L. Bos, *The Environmental Impact of Fibre Crops in Industrial Applications* (Rome, 2004).

48 Hayo van der Werf, 'Hemp Facts and Hemp Fiction', *Journal of the International Hemp Association*, I (1994), pp. 58; Ricardo da Silva Vieira, Paulo Canaveira, Ana de Samões and Tiago Domingos, 'Industrial Hemp or Eucalyptus Paper? An Environmental Comparison Using Life Cycle Assessment', *International Journal of Life Cycle Assessment*, XV (2010), pp. 368–75; Ernest Small and David Marcus, 'Hemp: A New Crop with Uses for North America', in *Trends in New Crops and New Uses*, ed. J. Janick and A. Whipkey (Alexandria, VA, 2002), pp. 284–326.

49 McCabe, *Marijuana and Hemp*, p. 223.

50 T. Randall Fortenberry and Michael Bennett, 'Opportunities for Commercial Hemp Production', *Applied Economic Perspectives and Policy*, XXVI (2004), pp. 97–117.

51 David T. Courtwright, *Forces of Habit: Drugs and the Making of the Modern World* (Cambridge, MA, 2001), p. 206.

52 Ibid.

53 Martina Melis and Marie Nougier, *IDPC Briefing Paper: Drug Policy and Development: How Action against Illicit Drugs Impacts on the Millennium Development Goals*, online edn (London, 2010).

54 Brian D. Earp, Brendan Dill, Jennifer L. Harris, Joshua A. Ackerman and John A. Bargh, 'No Sign of Quitting: Incidental Exposure to "No-smoking" Signs Ironically Boosts Cigarette-approach Tendencies in Smokers', *Journal of Applied Social Psychology* (in press).

55 Molly Charles, Dave Bewley-Taylor and Amanda Neidpath, *Drug Policy in India: Compounding Harm?*, Beckley Foundation Drug Policy Programme Briefing Paper 10 (Oxford, 2005).

56 Bourhill, *The Smoking*, p. 9.

Further Reading

Abel, Ernest L., *Marihuana: The First Twelve Thousand Years* (New York, 1980)

Campos, Isaac, *Home Grown: Marijuana and the Origins of Mexico's War on Drugs* (Chapel Hill, NC, 2012)

Cervantes, Jorge, *Marijuana Horticulture* (Sacramento, CA, 2006)

Clarke, Robert C., *Marijuana Botany* (Berkeley, CA, 1981)

—, *Hashish!*, 2nd edn (Los Angeles, 2010)

Clarke, Robert C., and Mark David Merlin, *Cannabis: Evolution and Ethnobotany* (Berkeley, CA, 2013)

Courtwright, David T., *Forces of Habit: Drugs and the Making of the Modern World* (Cambridge, MA, 2001)

Dreher, Melanie, *Working Men and Ganja: Marihuana Use in Rural Jamaica* (Philadelphia, 1982)

Du Toit, Brian M., *Cannabis in Africa* (Rotterdam, 1980)

Gieringer, Dale, Ed Rosenthal and Gregory T. Carter, *Marijuana Medical Handbook* (Oakland, CA, 2008)

Herman, Anthony, and O. Pessoa Jr, eds, *Diamba Sarabamba* (São Paulo, 1986)

Indian Hemp Drugs Commission, *Report of the Indian Hemp Drugs Commission, 1893–1894* [1894], reprint edn (Silver Spring, MD, 1969)

Iversen, Leslie L., *The Science of Marijuana* (New York, 2000)

Lee, Martin A., *Smoke Signals: A Social History of Marijuana – Medical, Recreational, and Scientific* (New York, 2012)

Mills, James H., *Madness, Cannabis, and Colonialism: The 'Native-only' Lunatic Asylums of British India, 1857–1900* (New York, 2000)

—, *Cannabis Britannica: Empire, Trade, and Prohibition, 1800–1928* (Oxford, 2003)

—, *Cannabis Nation: Control and Consumption in Britain, 1928–2008* (Oxford, 2012)

Oner, S. T., *Cannabis Sativa: The Essential Guide to the World's Finest Marijuana Strains* (San Francisco, CA, 2012)

Ranalli, Paolo, ed., *Advances in Hemp Research* (New York, 1999)

Sloman, Larry, *Reefer Madness: The History of Marijuana in America* (Indianapolis, IN, 1979)

Associations and Websites

ANTIQUE CANNABIS BOOK
www.antiquecannabisbook.com

ASSOCIACIÓN MEXICANA DE ESTUDIOS SOBRE CANNABIS
www.ameca.org.mex

CANNABIS COLLEGE, AMSTERDAM, THE NETHERLANDS
www.cannabiscollege.com

CANNABIS CULTURE MAGAZINE (CANADA)
www.cannabisculture.com

CANNABIS INTERNET ACTIVIST – THE CANNABIS INFORMATION SITE (UK)
www.ukcia.org

CANNABIS LAW REFORM, UK POLITICAL PARTY
www.clear-uk.org

CHRIS CONRAD, *CANNABIS* EXPERT
www.chrisconrad.com

THE DAGGA COUPLE (SOUTH AFRICA)
www.daggacouple.co.za

DRUG FREE AMERICA FOUNDATION, MARIJUANA FAQS
www.dfaf.org/qa/marijuana

DRUG TEXT, LIBRARY OF ELECTRONIC DOCUMENTS
www.drugtext.org

HANF MUSEUM (GERMANY)
www.hanfmuseum.de

HASH, MARIJUANA, AND HEMP MUSEUM (THE NETHERLANDS)
www.hashmuseum.com

THE HEMP INDUSTRIES ASSOCIATION (U.S.)
www.thehia.org

HEMP INFO (SWITZERLAND)
www.chanvre-info.ch

HEMP MAGAZINE (U.S.)
www.hempmagazine.com

HEMP MUSEUM (U.S.)
www.hempmuseum.us

THE HERB MUSEUM (CANADA)
www.herbmuseum.ca

HIGH TIMES MAGAZINE (U.S.)
www.hightimes.com

INTERNATIONAL HEMP ASSOCIATION (THE NETHERLANDS)
www.internationalhempassociation.org

IQELA LENTSANGO: THE DAGGA PARTY OF SOUTH AFRICA
www.daggaparty.co.za

MARIJUANA PARTY OF CANADA
www.marijuanaparty.ca

MARIJUANA POLICY PROJECT (U.S.)
www.mpp.org

NATIONAL ORGANIZATION FOR THE REFORM OF MARIJUANA LAWS (U.S.)
www.norml.org

PHOTOGRAPHS OF RUSSIAN HEMP FARMERS IN 2011
www.englishrussia.com/2011/11/11/russian-hemp-growers

PHOTOGRAPHS OF SOUTH ASIAN *SADHUS* SMOKING *GANJA*
www.sadhus.org

SCHAFFER LIBRARY OF DRUG POLICY, LIBRARY OF ELECTRONIC
DOCUMENTS
www.druglibrary.org/schaffer

STRAIN HUNTERS DOCUMENTARIES
www.strainhunters.com

UNITED NATIONS OFFICE ON DRUGS AND CRIME, WORLD DRUG REPORT
www.unodc.org/wdr/en/cannabis

U.S. DRUG ENFORCEMENT ADMINISTRATION CANNABIS ERADICATION
PROGRAM (U.S.)
www.justice.gov/dea/ops/cannabis

VAULTS OF EROWID, LIBRARY OF ELECTRONIC DOCUMENTS
www.erowid.org/plants/cannabis/cannabis

Acknowledgements

I must thank several people for enabling the completion of this book. First, William Maxwell, Jonathan Nelson and Maureen Meyer professionally assisted with research and cartography. Joel Gruley provided feedback on early material, Florence Das translated Bangla for me and Emma Trentman translated Arabic. I wish them continued success in their careers. Second, the Department of Geography and Environmental Studies, the College of Arts and Sciences and the University Libraries at the University of New Mexico (UNM) supported my research and writing. I look forward to continued collaboration. Third, I benefited from discussions with colleagues in my home department and at professional meetings organized by: the Association of American Geographers (2012 and 2013), and its Southwest Division (2012); Harvard University's Center for Geographic Analysis (2012); the International Consortium of Environmental History Organizations (2014); UNM's International Studies Institute (2012); and the University of Wisconsin's African Studies Program (2012). I anticipate further fruitful discussions. Fourth, candid discussions with students (especially M. S.), friends (especially T. S. and R. Z.) and many strangers and acquaintances have expanded my perspectives on *Cannabis*. Finally, I thank family in Wyoming, Colorado, New Mexico, Queensland and Palau (for now) for all manner of support – especially J., H. and R., who are each and all the best. This book is dedicated to my grandparents.

Photo Acknowledgements

The author and the publishers wish to express their thanks to the below sources of illustrative material and /or permission to reproduce it.

Aleks/Wikimedia Commons: p. 143; image © and courtesy of www.americanart classics.com: p. 192; courtesy anonymous: p. 90; author's collection: pp. 13 (grace à S.C.), 14, 19, 34, 37, 45, 50, 52, 54, 55, 58, 64, 65, 68, 69, 70, 73, 76, 77, 80, 82, 83, 84, 86, 87, 95, 96, 97, 106, 109, 110 (thanks to A.D.), 111, 112, 113, 114, 116, 117, 122, 123, 124, 125, 129, 130, 131, 132, 133, 135, 136, 141, 147, 148, 152, 157, 161, 163, 166, 169, 172, 174, 175, 178, 182, 183, 185, 188, 190, 191; BananaPatrol/ Wikimedia Commons: p. 11; Barbetorte/Wikimedia Commons: p. 120; © Trustees of the British Museum: pp. 62, 93, 102; D-Kuru/Wikimedia Commons: p. 50; Fatbuu1000/Wikimedia Commons: p. 150; image © and courtesy of Freer Gallery of Art, Smithsonian Institution, Washington, DC, Gift of Charles Lang Freer, F1917.115: p. 33; images © and courtesy of the President and Fellows of Harvard College: pp. 36, 164; images courtesy of the Library of Congress: pp. 41, 48; Khalid Mahmood/Wikimedia Commons: p. 40; Lewenstein and Nina-No/Wikimedia Commons: p. 16; images © and courtesy of NORML: pp. 180, 187; images courtesy of Peter H. Raven Library, Missouri Botanical Garden, St Louis, Missouri: pp. 6, 20, 23, 24, 28, 29, 44; image courtesy of the U.S. Drug Enforcement Agency: p. 168; Zoboar/Wikimedia Commons: p. 140.

Cartography: pp. 31, 94 (Jonathan K. Nelson and Chris Duvall), p. 137 (Chris Duvall).

Index

abacá (*Musa textilis*) 18, 83, 86
addiction 91
admixtures to drug *Cannabis* 159–60
Afghanistan 115, 118, 139, 144, *168*
African tobacco 100
agriculture
    environmental constraints 60, 78
    hemp, historic 33–4, *34*, 53, 60, 73–5,
    119–23, *120*, *122*, *163*
    hemp, recent 141–2, *143*, 190–92, 194
    indoor marijuana 116–18, 139–41,
    140, 142
    outdoor marijuana 47, 100, 142–3,
    157, 186
Alaska 68–9
alcoholic beverages 49, 99, 108, 115, 163,
    170, 173
Algeria 103, *109*, *135*, 157
American hemp 80
amotivational syndrome 162–3
Angola
arrival of *Cannabis* 97–8
    colonial agricultural trials 109, 181
    colonial anti-drug policies 163
    colonial drug commerce 107, 139
    drug use in 103
    slave and other labourers 100, 107, *155*
Angolan tobacco 100
Anslinger, Harry 168, 185–6
Arabic medicine 17–18, 40, 45, 56
Armstrong, Louis 146, 156
Australia
    arrival of *Cannabis* 75, 182

Hunter Valley infestation 111
recreational use of medicinal
    products 136, *137*, 138
recognition of feral marijuana
    110–11
smoke-in protest *169*
Argentina 67, *68*
Assassin tale 149–53, 159, 172
asthma 135, 138
Atharva Veda (religious text) 39, 43,
    47
Austria 81–2
Austro-Hungarian Empire 65, 136
Avicenna 16

Baartman, Saartje *102*, 104
Bactria-Margiana Archaeological
    Complex (BMAC) 42
Bahamas 102
Baltic, region 56, 68, 71, 79, 184
Bangladesh *106*
Barnum, P. T. 127
Baudelaire, Charles 173
Beatles, The 174
Belarus 68
belladonna (*Atropa belladonna*) 17, 135–6,
    159–60
Bena-Diamba movement 98, 172
Benin 103, 107
bhang
    beverage *41*, 43, 94, 96, 105–6, 127,
    160
    cultural origins 40–46

birds, and hempseed dispersal 31, 74–5, 109–10, *178*
Black Sea 30, 51–2, 62
Blackwell, Elizabeth
 Cannabis mas 23
 Cannabis foemina 24
Bologna 61, 63
Bonaparte, Napoleon 70, 112
Bowrey, Thomas 96, 105, 171
Brazil
 arrival of *Cannabis* 66–7, 97
 drug commerce 107, 144
 drug production 142
 Native Americans in 100, 171
 portrayals of drug use *112, 161*
 slaves and other labourers 102–3, 130, 162
 terminology of *Cannabis* in 99–100
 War on Drugs in 169–70
 breaking hemp *54*, 56, 70, 80, 121–22, *122, 123, 190*
British 69–75
Bulgaria 30, 49, 53
Burton, Richard 153, 162

cachexia 103
California 67, 69, 83, 107–9, 140, 142, 188
Canada 88, 115, 118
Canapajo, Il (book) 63–4
Cannabaceae 11–12
cannabinoids 12, 89
'cannabis', definition 12
'*Cannabis*', definition 10
'Cannabis indica', pharmaceutical 22, 135, 138
Cannabis, putative species 12, 22, 81
Caribbean, region 186–8
Caspian Sea 39, 41
Central Africa, region 14–15, 46, 89, 97–103, 130, 156, 162, 171–2
Central America, region 100, 104, 108, 142, 158, 162, 169
Central Asia, region 15, 22, 27–30, 35, 41, 51–2, 127, 151
Chalupova, Zuzana, *Konoplyjie 65*

charas
 associated with indica folk species 89
 cultural origins 46–8
 definition 46
 see also hashish
Chile 67, 141
China
 anti-drug policies 139, 183, *183*
 arrival of *Cannabis* 30
 development of *Cannabis* culture 32–9, *33, 34, 36,* 41
 low opinions of hemp fabric 32, 85
 recent hemp production 141
 Xinjiang region *see* Tarim Basin
Christianity 146, 164–5, 170
Cigares de Joy 135
cigarettes 134–8
Clarke, Marcus 138
Club des Haschischins 172
cocaine 144, 160
Colombia 66, 143, 169–70, 175
colonialism 104, *135,* 156–7, 179
Colorado 118, 140
Congo basin 94, 100, 103
Congo, Republic of *130*
Congo, Democratic Republic of 139, 154, 156
Congo tobacco 100
'Congo', ethnonym 99, 101, 103
cordage 30–31, 49, 53
Costa Rica 134, 169
cotton (*Gossypium arboreum*) 37, 75, 78–9, 85, 122, 190
crime 166–70
Croatia 64
Cuba 96, 102, 162

dagga 95, 96, *96,* 101, 104, 143, 164, 193
Datura species 17, 46, 95, 129, 135–6, 159–60
Δ9-tetrahydrocannabinol *see* THC
diamba see liamba
Dioscorides 15, *16,* 22, 184
ditchweed 23, 110, 118
dogbane (*Apocynum cannabinum*) 18, 78–9

drug commerce
  advertisements for 107, 109, 127,
    135–6, *137*
  black markets 107–9, 111–12, 118,
    144, 169, 186
  legal markets 112, 138–40, 144, 156
  taxes generated by 96, 137–40,
    141
  total value, U.S. 141
drug dealers 175
drug use
  athletes and 115
  in middle class 92, 115–16, 138, 144,
    172
  labour and 101–2, 104–5, 155–6,
    160–64
  morality of 48–9, 157–8, 179–80
  newspaper accounts of 153–5,
    158–60, 164, 169–70, 173, 185, 189
  prisoners and 104, 107–8, 173
  sailors and 92–7, 99, 103, 105, 107
  sex workers and 92, 104, 157, *157*
  slaves and 92, 98–104
  soldiers and 92, *97*, 104, 107, 109, *114*,
    114–15, 157, 164

East Africa, region 46, 93–4, 107, 156,
    162
edible drugs 16–17, 48, 126–7, 172
effects of drug *Cannabis*,
  pharmacological 89–91, 159
effects of drug *Cannabis*, stereotypical
  aphrodisiac 153, 157
  degeneration 151, 168
  insanity 99, 158
  sloth 160–63, *161*
  spirituality 193
  violence 151, 153–4, 158–60, 168
Egypt 40, 48, 112, 115, 158
El Salvador 169
endocannabinoid system 89, 90
Ephedra 42–3
esparto (*Stipa tenacissima*) 49, 53, 65
Estonia 68, 126
Ethiopia 46
European sailors 91–3, 95, 99, *132*
evolutionary ecology 27–32

Ferghana Valley 36
flax (*Linum usitatissimum*)
  arrival in Britain 73
  arrival in China 36
  compared with *Cannabis* 63
  fibre interchangeable with hemp *69*,
    71, *73*, 76, 78, 124
  in Tarim Basin 35
  origins of fibre use in Europe 52–3
  succeeds while hemp declines 85,
    122, 124
  uses 65, 125
Ford, Henry 126
420 (four twenty), name for marijuana
    188, *188*, *192*
France
  arrival of *Cannabis* 49
  decline of *Cannabis* 85
  drug use in *13*, 112, 172
  hemp commerce 57, 65
  hemp processing equipment *52*, 56,
    143
  hemp production 75–8, *76*, *77*, *84*, *87*,
    88, 141
  indica hemp in 82, *82*
  place names 70
  Roman Gaul 53
  trade policies 76–7
Freyre, Gilberto 100

Gabon 99, 107
Galen 15–17, 48, 92, 184
Gambia 107
ganja
  compared with hashish 43, 46,
    106
  cultural origins 46–8
  definition 46
  practices of use *90*, 106, 126–7, 129
  production techniques 46–8, 144
  gateway hypothesis 168
Germany 49, 56, 168
Ghana 107
Ginsberg, Allen 173–4
Great Book of Hemp, The (book) 185
Greece 52–3, 62
Greek medicine 15–17, 40, 56

Grimault's Indian cigarettes 135–8, *137*, *172*
Guatemala 138, 169
Guyana 102, 107, 163

hackberries (*Celtis* species) 12
Hamilton, Edward, *Cannabis* 6
hanging, death by 124, *125*, 147–8, *147*
Hanseatic League 56, 68–9
harakeke (*Phormium tenax*) 18, 75, 83
Harappan civilization 42
hashish
    as Orientalist motif 149
    commerce 112, 139
    compared with *ganja* 43, 46, 106
    definition 46, 48–9
    hasheesh candy 127, *137*
    hash oil 144
    misconceptions 17, 189
    production techniques 46–8, 138–9, 144
Hawaii 111
'hemp', definition 19, 23
'Hemp for Victory', U.S. government programme 87
hemp
    in poorhouses 71, 165
    in prisons *164*, 165, *166*
    inducements for production 71–2, 86–7
    labour and 60, 62–4, 68, 72, 80–81, 164–6
    mechanization and 85, 122–3, 141
    patriotism and 60–61, 165–6, 191–2
    plastic made from 126
    production techniques 33–4, 54–6, 88, 119–23
    renaissance of 88, 141, 168, 176
    slaves and 80–81, 164–5
    youth and 115–16
hempseed *50*, *51*, 74
    as birdseed 73–6, 110, 119
    as fishbait 76
    as food 30, 34, 56, 88, 125–6, 141

as fuel source 125, 190–91, *191*
    in soap 125
    milk 126
    oil 34, 76, 88, 125, 141
henbane (*Hyoscyamus niger*) 17, 136, 159–60
henequen (*Agave* species) 67, 83
Herodotus 15, 21, 50–53
heroin 144, 193
Himalaya mountains 27, 30, 38–9
Hindu Kush mountains 29, 39, 41–2, 47
Hinduism 39, 43, 171
Hippie Hash Trail 144
Hmong *37*
Hogarth, William, *The Harlot Beats Hemp in Bridewell Prison* 164
homespun industries 74, 78, 85
Honduras 169
Hooke, Robert 22, 149
hop species (*Humulus*) 11–12, 27
Huguenots 76
Hungary 88, 120, 141

Iceland 54
Illinois 82, *83*, 109
India
    arrival of *Cannabis* 43
    anti-drug policies 192–3
    colonial agricultural trials 18, 182
    colonial drug commerce 107, 111, 138–9
    colonial psychiatry in 158
    drug use in *45*, 46, 92, *93*, *97*, 134, *171*, 192–3
Indian Hemp Drugs Commission 184
Indian hemp
    meaning dogbane 18, 78
    meaning *Cannabis indica* 17–18, 22, 79
    meaning jute 18, 78
indica (folk species) 23–5, 47, 89
indica (genetic species), definition 20–22, 28–30
indica hemp
    in Central Asia 125
    in East Asia 32–4, 35–8, 85

in Europe and North America 81–2, 182, 192
in Hawaii 176
Indonesia 97
Indra, Hindu deity 47, 171
Iran 43, 48, 53, 128, 144
Ireland 76
Islam 48–9, 107, 146–7, 157, 159, 171
Italy
    arrival of *Cannabis* 30
    hemp commerce 62
    hemp culture transported to Serbia 65
    hemp production *18*, *54*, *56*, *64*, 88, 141

Jamaica 99, 102–4, 130, 163, 172
Japan 32–3, 88, *174*
Just Say No!, U.S. anti-drugs campaign 171
jute (*Corchorus* species) 18, 78–9, 122, 189–90

Kansas 109
Kentucky 79–83, *80*, 109–10, 164–5, 183, *190*
Kentucky hemp 82
Kenya 46
kif 107–8, *109*, *152*, *157*, 157
Knox, Robert, sailor 96, 148
Köhler, F. E., *Cannabis sativa* 28
Korea 32–3, 38, 88, 126, 141

Latvia 68, 126
Leary, Timothy 173–5
Lesotho 143
Lesser Antilles 102
Levant, region 16, 47–8, 97, 108, 129
liamba *10*, 15, 98, 100–101, *112*, 153, *155*
Liberia 102–3, 130
Linnaeus, Carolus 25
Lithuania 56
locoweed, name for marijuana 108, 186
Longfellow, Henry Wadsworth 122
Louisiana 75, 78
Losch, Friedrich, *Hanf* *45*
Ludlow, Fitz Hugh 138

McCartney, Paul *174*
maconha 100–101
Madagascar 89, 97
Maghreb region 107–8
Magu, Chinese hemp goddess *33*, 146
Malaysia 97, 158–9
Manila hemp *see* abacá
'marijuana', etymology 14–15, 100
marijuana boom (1960s) 109, 111, 115–16, 144, 173–5, 188
Marley, Bob 172
Mary Jane, name for marijuana 146
Massachusetts *141*
Mauritius 163
medical marijuana 109, 118, 135, 138, 175–6, 188, 192
Mediterranean, region 18, 52–3, 61, 65, 108, 112
Mexico
    arrival of *Cannabis* 66–8, 100
    drug commerce 139, 143
    drug production 143
    drug use in 104, 158
    stereotypes about 109, 154
    term *marihuana* in 14, 101
    War on Drugs in 169–70
    midwifery 43–5
Millspaugh, C. F., *Cannabis* 29
Minnesota 74
Mississippi 118
Missouri 81–3
Moldova 53
Moloch of Marijuana, The (book) 146, *167*
Monfried, Henri de 175
Montana 159
Moreau, Jacques-Joseph 172–3
Morocco 31, 45, 103, 118, 139, 144, *152*, 157
morphine 173
Mozambique 96–7, 156, 163
mulberry family (Moraceae) 12
music referencing drug *Cannabis* 108, 116, 170–73, 180–81
Myanmar 47

naval stores *59*, 60, 73, 165
Nebraska 165

Nepal 144
Netherlands, The 65, 69, 78
nettle (*Urtica dioica*) 49
nettle family (Urticaceae) 12, 27
New Mexico 68, 109, 142, 185
New York City 107, 110, 184, 186
New Zealand 75, 135–6
New Zealand hemp *see* harakeke
Nigeria 103, 107
Nixon, Richard 116, 170
North Africa, region 53, 114, 134, 139,
    157–8, 162
North America, region 18, 23, 31,
    72–83, 110, 134, 164–5, 174, 186
Northern Territory, Australia 138
Norway 54
Nova Scotia 75

oakum 123, 165
Obama, Barack 185
Ontario 74
opium
    commerce in 96, 139
    confused with drug *Cannabis* 149
    poppy (*Papaver somnifera*) 42, 49, 118,
        144
    prepared drug 153, 160
    used with drug *Cannabis* 105, 129,
        136, 159
Oregon 12
Orientalism 148–54, 168, 173–4
Ottoman Empire 62, 62, 64–5

Panama 103, 109, 158, 164
Pakistan 30, 40, 139, 162
paper 37–8, 76, 88
paper, for rolling cigarettes 123–4, 134,
    136
paraquat 143
patent medicines 138
PCP 160
Pennsylvania 72
Pên-ts'ao Chíng (book) 35
Peru 66
pharmacology *see* effects of drug
    Cannabis
pita (*Agave* species) 67

place names 65, 70
Playboy (magazine) 186, 187
Poland 56, 68, 88, 126
pollen 29–31, 49, 55, 64, 78, 83
Portugal 54, 56, 65–7
Praise of Hemp-seed, The (book) 147
Prince Chènevis, fictional character 146
prohibition and other controls
    against drug *Cannabis* 115, 118, 163–4
    against hemp 75, 168, 176
    against medical marijuana 45, 136, 138
    against paraphernalia 175
    for legalization of drug *Cannabis* 118,
        140, 169
    for legalization of hemp *Cannabis* 176
    for medical marijuana 176
    International Opium Convention
        (1925) 115
    law enforcement 139–43, 166, 168,
        169–70
prohibition 13, 83, 166, 175, 179–80,
    183, 189–90, 192–3
protests against prohibition 116, 118, 169,
    175–6
Puerto Rico 162

Québec 75
Queensland 111

Rabelais, François 112
race and racism 148, 154–6, 164–5, 170
ramie (*Boehmeria nivea*) 32, 37, 85
Rastafarianism 172
Reagan, Ronald 171, 175
Reign of Law, The (book) 164–5
retting hemp 54–6, 54, 63–4, 65, 70,
    80–81, 82, 191
Romania 51, 53, 88
Roman Empire 53–4, 54
rope
    economic importance 18, 32
    made of hemp 32, 36, 67
    manufacturing 19, 69–70, 72, 74, 77,
        81, 122, 123
    maritime quality 54, 63, 66, 124–5
    not made of hemp 35, 53–4, 86, 124–5
    uses 53, 84, 124, 125, 147, 147–8,

Rousseau, Jean-Jacques, *Le chanvre* 20
running *amuck*, idiom 158–9
rush (*Juncus* species) 49, 53
Russia *38*, 68, *70*, 85, 126, 141
Russian hemp, international commerce
    in 62, 66, 68–70, 72, 78–81, *83*,
    85–6, 125

St Helena 102
Sahel region 108, *109*
São Tome 107
sativa (folk species) 23–5, 47, 89
sativa (genetic species), definition
    20–22, 28–30
Scythia 51–2, 56
Senegal 109
Serbia 65, *65*, 125
sex 104, *114*, 153, 158
shamanism 35
Shiva, Hindu deity *45*, 46, *171*, *172*
shives 123
ship's riggings *70*, 84–5, *84*
Siberia 29, 31, 35, 40, 49, 51
Sierra Leone 96, 102–4, 153
Silvestre de Sacy, Antoine 153, 159
sisal (*Agave rígida*) 18, 67, 83
smoking pipes
    African water pipes 95, *95*, 100,
    127–130, *129*, *130*
    bong 128–9, *133*
    cachimbo as racial stereotype 162
    'cachimbo', etymology 131–2
    dry pipes 130–34, *130*, *132*, *135*
    earth pipes 131, 186
    Eurasian smoke inhalation devices
    46, 51, 128
    hookah as Orientalist motif *131*, 149,
    150, 154
    improvised water pipes *97*, 130
    invention in sub-Saharan Africa 46,
    94–5, 127
    Native American tobacco pipes i
    on slave ships 99
    Persian water pipe (or hookah)
    128–9, *131*
    possible invention in Southeast Asia
    128

soma/haoma 43
South Africa
    anti-drug policies 115, 164
    colonial psychiatry in 158
    drug production 142–4
    drug use in *95*, 96, *96*, 103–4, 193
    hemp in 75, 181
    slaves and other labourers in
    101–2
South Carolina 109
South Sudan 93
Southeast Asia, region *37*, 38, 47, 97,
    105–6, 127–9, 142, 158
Soviet Union 85, *86*, 88
Spain
    drug use in 114–15, 134
    hemp in Spanish colonies 66–8, *68*,
    75
    hemp production 54, 65–6
    low importance of hemp 65
    reliance on imported hemp 56, 65,
    70
spinning *52*, 76, *76*
Sri Lanka 95, 148, 163
Stanley, Henry Morton 156
string *124*
Surgeon General, U.S. 158
Swaziland 143
Sweden 49, 69
Switzerland 53

Taoism 35, 146
Tarim Basin 34–6, 42–3, 139
Tasmania 185
taxonomy 10–12, 19–21, 25–6, 154,
    183–4
Tennessee 80
Texas 109, *141*
textiles
    canvas 53–4, 124
    denim 124
    linen *73*, *74*, 124
    'Negro cloth' 190
    ramie 32, 37, 85
    sackcloth 67, 74, 85, 79, 85, 165–6,
    189–90
    sailcloth 32, 53–4, 65–6, 79

silks 37, 52, 85
woollens 52–3, 78, 124, 189
THC
  botany 27–8, 46
  chemistry 12, 21, 41, 181
  pharmacology 46, 89, 127
  quantities in *Cannabis* products 110,
    144, 176
Thrace 50–53
Tibet 38, 41, 43
Tien Shan mountains 29
tincture 127, 138
tobacco
  meaning marijuana 99–101, 186
  meaning *Nicotiana* species 72, 81, 95,
    99, 131, 159–60
Togo 103, 107
Trinidad 102
Tunisia 103, 139
Turkey 53, 62, 88
Turkmenistan *41*, 42, 86, 125
twine 30, 53, 79, 81–83, 124,
    166, *166*

Ukraine 49
United Kingdom
  anti-drug policies 115, 164
  arrival of drug *Cannabis* 148–9
  death by hanging 147–8
  domestic hemp production 65, 71,
    74–5
  hemp in prisons and poorhouses *164*,
    165
  inducements for hemp production
    71–2
  place names 70
  reliance on imported hemp 56, 69–72
  Roman Britannia 53
  trade policies 71–3
United States
  arrival of *Cannabis* 67–8, 107–8
  bong in 128–9
  Cannabis eradication efforts 31, 110,
    111, 118
  death by hanging *147*
  Declaration of Independence
    124

domestic drug production 109,
    116–18, 141–2
domestic hemp production 72–5,
    78–83, *83*, 86–88, 122–3, 141, *163*, 182
drug commerce in 118, 138, 140–42,
    169–70, 175
drug control policies 26, 140–41,
    141, 158–9, 164, 166–8, *168*, 176, 183
Drug Enforcement Administration
    111, 134, *168*, 176
drug use in 118, 127, 138, 143, 171,
    173–5, 185
first U.S. flag 189
Food and Drug Administration 181,
    188
hemp in prisons 165–6, *166*, 192
place names 70–71
slavery in 101, 164–5
U.S. Army 74, 104, 109, 114–16, 158,
    169–70
use of term *marihuana* 155
War on Drugs in 169–71, 175
Uruguay 133, 169

Venice *54*, 57, 61–5, *62*
Victoria, queen of Great Britain 185–6,
    187
Vietnam conflict 115
Virginia 72, 109, 165

War on Drugs 111, 116, 169–70, 175
Washington, U.S. state 118, 140
Washington, George 79, 182, 185, *185*
waste fibre 37, 76, 123
weaver's broom (*Spartium junceum*) 49
weaving 32, *37*, *73*, *178*
weediness of *Cannabis* 31, 41, 73, 78, 100,
    110–11, 114, 164, 193
West Africa, region 103, 162
wild *dagga* (*Leonotis leonurus*) 95, 104
Wisconsin 83, 88, *166*, *188*
women 76

Yemen 128
Yugoslavia 88

Zoroastrianism 43–5